Amelia's Story

by

D.G. Torrens

(The Child First and Foremost)

Copyright 2014 D. G. Torrens

License notes: This book is for your personal enjoyment only. This book may not be re-sold or given away to other people. If you Would like to share this book with another person, please purchase an additional Copy for each person you share it with, if your reading this book and did not Purchase it, or it was not purchased for your use only, then you should Return to Amazon.com and purchase your own copy. Thank you for respecting the hard work of this author.

ISBN-13: 978-1499646788
ISBN-10: 149964678X

Cover Design by H F Pixel & Ares Jun

Acknowledgements

A special mention goes to my beautiful daughter, Lilliah, the light of my life, my princess. I love you more than words can ever say.

To my family, for your continuous support and your undeniable love. You are all amazing. I love you deeply.

To my Grandma and Grandad, my life is now complete. Thank you. I love you both from the bottom of my heart. Our time together is precious to me.

To Blanche Hunt, who has been a guiding star in my life, for making a difference, and taking a chance on me, for caring, and for being a kind and genuine friend to this very day.

To HF Pixel and Ares Jun, two amazing book designers. For designing the perfect cover between you and one that conveys my story perfectly.

To Peter Woods, actor and friend, who has been in some great films such as, "Land Girls" and "Prime Suspect." He took on the mammoth task of completing the first edit on my manuscript. Thank you so very much for affording me the time from your very busy life.

Finally, to all of my readers, for reading my story and for your amazing compassion and wonderful messages... You are truly wonderful. Thank you.

If my story makes a positive difference to just one person, then it has achieved its aim.

For my beautiful daughter, it is for you that I have written this book. To help you understand your mother's life and answer any questions you might have. You are my inspiration, my heart, and my life. I love you princess.

Table of Contents

Prologue

The Beginning

Llandewii

Colton Hall

The Arrival of Susie

Broughton Estate

Highfield House Children's Home

Breeton House (1st Visit)

Broughton Estate (Back Home)

Breeton House Children's Home

Maidstone Children's Home

Bryn Tyn

A Dangerous Encounter

Near Death

A Surprise Christmas

The Great Escape

Westbrook Hall

The Norwegians

Westbrook Hall (Football Event)

Broken Trust

Prologue

A Hard Decision

The Reunion

Modeling

Trying to be a Teenager

A Road Less Travelled

One Step Forward Two Steps Back

The Call That Changed My Life

Moving to Birmingham

Drifting Apart

My Complete Breakdown

Starting Over Once Again

Adrian

New York

Brussels

Shocking Revelations

Blanche

Josie

Finally, My Own Home

Re-visiting Old Ghosts

The Breakup

The Affair

My Soldier

My Husband

Pregnant

The Death of a Special Friend

The Birth of Lilliah

Discovering My Family

Becoming a Writer: My Destiny

Bonus photographs

Baby Amelia

Prologue

Where do I start princess? One day you will turn around and ask me why I have never spoken about my childhood and that my sweetheart is when I shall hand you this book. Once you have read the words from cover to cover, you will have the answer to your question.

For some, a childhood can be a very scary part of their life and for me it was. I learned that when your life and destiny is in the hands of the devil himself (or in my case the devil herself) there is only one safe place of escape and retreat – your mind.

While reading this book you will be taken on a journey of a young woman, you will not know or recognise. That woman is me sweetheart, your Mama. You may cry and feel the pain and struggle of a young woman, but in turn, you will wonder at her strength and will to carry on. I never knew how I would tell you my life story, it is not a straightforward chapter from my life – there are many diversions, which is why I decided writing this book for you was the best way for both of us.

First, my princess let me talk about you and what I wanted for you. My hopes and dreams…

At the time of writing this, you are only two years and eight months old. With the energy of a hundred children and confidence of so many more! You are extremely intelligent and never fail to surprise me. I wonder at your creative skills and learning capabilities, which many have said exceed your years. This is probably why you are not in the least bit interested in sleeping at any time - your brain is far too busy! Only when your body has said enough is enough are you forced to sleep!

Driven by my own childhood, I had to be sure you wanted for nothing. You were to feel so loved, safe, and secure that you would grow up to be a loving, independent, beautiful woman, without insecurities and doubts. I hope you can honestly say that you never knew fear, rejection, or pain. The most important thing for me is that you always feel happiness when looking back on your own childhood. All those memories will cement the fact that you were, and always will be, loved unconditionally.

A few things I want you to remember and take with you through your own life: five things you can never recover: A stone once thrown: A word after it is said: An occasion once missed: Time when it has passed: A person after they have passed on. Do not go through your life with regrets darling - make the most of every single moment.

Princess, you have brought me so much more love than I ever dreamed of and more than I ever believed possible. You are my inspiration and my whole world. I love you x

Now to end this prologue with a favourite phrase of mine by an unknown Author; **life is not measured by the breaths we take, but by the moments that take our breath away.**

Amelia's Story - The Beginning

I was thrust onto this planet with great force on a cold December morning, following a thirty-hour labour suffered by my mother Heidi Sue Thomas. This was the day my tragic childhood began. My birth was not to be the great family celebration it should have been. Alas, quite the opposite. My mother was a young 20-year-old woman, a rebel for her own cause! She met her first love (my father) Christopher Jason Gillingham in a conservative club in Manchester during the summer of 1968, while my father was on a two week leave from the R.A.F. They fell in love and within three months were officially engaged.

My mother was born Heidi Sue Thomas 1947 in Denton, Manchester. She was born without emotion and did not feel for the needs of others, only for herself, she was incapable of feeling; it was not something that came naturally to her. She could not identify with the word sympathy at all.

I was to find out much later in life (during my 30's) some very truthful hurts about my mother; she was admitted to a psychiatric ward in her late teens, she was an uncontrollable destructive force, full of hate for everyone. She poisoned everything good that encountered her, a true destroyer of good. She never felt remorse for her actions and was a human being that could not be reasoned with at all. So to me not really human at all. If diagnosed in this day and age, she would more than likely have been diagnosed a sociopath for sure.

However, this was the 1960's and it was a completely different world back then, with a completely different set of rules, shame was something no family wanted to suffer least of all my Grandma and Grandad Thomas (my mother's parents). They were such proud people, churchgoers every Sunday. Grandad Thomas was a scout leader and a factory foreman, my Grandmother a housewife and full-time mother. Therefore, they did what many families did in that period to cover up the shame - dealt with it quietly, so as not to draw attention upon themselves from the rest of their community.

They were the first family in their street to own a car (Morris Minor I believe). To own one car was a luxury in those days, unlike today where there are multiple cars per family. The streets were so much quieter; children could play safely on the road, that's how rare it was to see a car. My Grandparents bought their first house for £2,500 – a large sum in those days. My mother was an extremely attractive woman with dark sultry looks and deep brown eyes, and she knew it to, and used this to her advantage to get what she wanted and get away with anything she needed to.

My mother had a normal childhood and was brought up by fairly strict parents; they were a typical nuclear family. My mother had a brother called Geoffrey and they were ten years apart in age. They were dressed, fed, and cared for well. Mother had a good education and went to grammar school. She would receive a good clip round the ear if she were out of line by her father, which was also pretty normal back then.

At the time of their meeting, my mother and father were both 19-years-old, but the law at the time stated that any couple wishing to marry without parental consent had to be 21-years-old. My father's parents were against the marriage as they thought Heidi was not good enough for their son, rumours had spilled out into the village with regards to her promiscuous antics and general behaviour.

Her parents could no longer control their own daughter, so Grandad Thomas would knock her from one end of the kitchen to the other, and still she would smile back, finding it all hilarious. He did not beat her often; however, when she was totally out of control he would hit her about the house. They reached the point of sheer frustration with my mother and eventually were happy to relinquish all responsibility and pass her on to Christopher, my father.

However, Christopher's parents had knowledge of Heidi's previous stint in the psychiatric ward due to some investigations carried out when their own concerns about Heidi were raised. Grandma and Grandad George, Christopher's parents, paid a visit to the local doctors and behind closed doors, they asked my mother's physician for some insight into what was wrong with her.

They stated that their son was about to marry Heidi and that they knew something was not right, the public outbursts, uncontrollable temper, unreasonable behaviour, and unwarranted hate. The physician of course, was not at liberty to discuss patient information, however, he advised Christopher's parents to tell their son that when it gets difficult then he should just run the other way and don't look back. Of course, this is not a response that would be given today - this was a small community village - where everyone knew each other and they were all friends. Family situations were handled so very differently back then.

Christopher's parents refused marital consent, so a long engagement ensued, during which time holes started to appear in their relationship, and arguments became a daily occurrence. My mother's public outbursts became an embarrassment and my father could not control when these would occur, as they were not goaded in anyway whatsoever.

They could be walking down a street and for no apparent reason, mother would start screaming and shouting, occasionally even lashing out. Father was no longer keen to marry Heidi and called off the engagement, but had no idea that she was with child (me). However, mother knew what it was she wanted and just how to ensure she had her wish, my father's hand in marriage.

Mother made the trip from Hull to Beverly to request a meeting with the base padre Rev. Hemmingway, at R.A.F. Leaconsfield, to announce the pregnancy and explain how she had felt that father had jilted her. What happened following this meeting could not be comprehended in 2011, the church, armed forces, and mother all came together to collude in what was to be a forced marriage.

This meeting took place without my father's knowledge and up to this point; he had no idea that my mother was pregnant.

Very soon following this meeting, my father was called to HQ for an urgent meeting with his CO. He was puzzled, anxious, and wondered what could be so serious that warranted an urgent meeting at base. On his arrival, my father was directed to the general office and ordered to wait outside until he was called. As he stood waiting by the door, my father began to feel more and more anxious.

Suddenly, the office door opened and he was called in by his CO. Father straightened his uniform and walked in. What he was to see before him, made him freeze with nerves - Rev. Hemmingway and Heidi. He wondered what could have been so important that required him and mother to be present, and a little part of him knew that it was mother who had instigated this situation, but why, he had no idea.

Father was informed in no uncertain terms that mother was pregnant with his child. At that exact moment, he felt their eyes piercing through him as Heidi stood there with tears rolling down her face, the perfect picture of a wronged woman, as the padre patted her on the back with a consoling hand. His CO and Rev. Hemmingway continued to stare towards my father coldly, whose facial expression by now read like a book, a scared 20-year-old man, caught in a trap.

Father was offered a few choices as his misdemeanors were laid out before him: he was going to be charged on several accounts of contravening camp standing orders; for being away from his station without permission, for not assisting with chores: and so the list of fantasy petty charges continued to spill out before him.

Last but not least, the Rev. Hemmingway then went on to mention that deserting his fiancée while pregnant was not good for anyone.

The CO went on to explain the choices my father had:

1: Choose to ignore your responsibilities - then you will face all charges as mentioned earlier.

2: If you do the right thing by proceeding to marry Heidi and accept your responsibilities, then no such charges will be brought against you.

Entrapment worked. As a young 20-year-old man, passionate about his career in the R.A.F, did the only thing he could do and agreed to marry mother. Following his decision all charges were dropped. Hard to believe such a thing could happen, but back then this was common and not unheard of at all. Reluctantly, both sets of parents signed the relevant documents to allow them to marry.

My mother and father had a very small wedding, and they were married by none other than the RT Rev. Hemmingway and only attended by a small number of people. Everyone knew this was not the pairing of those two souls who had once wanted to be together, so the whole affair was kept minimal.

Forced smiles were placed on faces for the group photos and everyone moved on to the small reception that took place in a pub over-looking the square. They went on a two-week honeymoon to Scotland, where they spent some time in a cosy cottage over-looking the sea. My father soon had to return to base with his new assignment in the cable bay, where he worked as a wireman, to make up wire looms for aircraft modification.

Mother was growing daily, and so were her unpredictable moods (more so than usual), which father put down to pregnancy hormones. This went on until the night I was born, a cold wintry night on the 14th December. No sooner was I in this world, than father headed off to the local pub for a few drinks. Mother remained in hospital for a further couple of days.

Within a short period of time, mother and father were given an R.A.F. house on base as a permanent residence, which was a palace compared to the bed-sit they were originally residing. It was a spacious three-bedroom house, fitted with everything they would need and this is where all three of us stayed until my brother, Jake, was born 18 months later. My father was training to be an Aircraft Engineer, which served him in good stead much later on in his career as he went on to secure a position working directly for the Sultan of Brunei, as Chief Engineer for his many private planes.

However, my mother was getting itchy feet, and she started going out more and more to social clubs with her friend, while my father was away on assignments. On one such occasion she met a man called Robert Thomas, with whom she began an affair. When my father was posted away, she would use this time to build her relationship with Robert. One day after being away with the R.A.F. for a few weeks, my father returned home earlier than expected to find my mother and Robert naked in bed. I do not know where Jake and I were at this time, but thankfully not anywhere in the vicinity. Father flew into a violent rage and beat the living daylights out of Robert and then turned on my mother and gave her a beating also.

He was arrested but not formerly charged with assault. This was to finalise the end of a doomed relationship. Luckily, for my father, this was not to affect his career as a promising young Aircraft Engineer. He was not at all interested in Jake and me, or what might happen to us, as long as he was as far away from Heidi as possible.

Father had never had the time or the piece of mind to form a bond with his two children, so missing us was not a worry for him. Our father could not have been happier for his eventual escape to his new life; this was what he had been dreaming about. He never looked back, not once.

As for my mother, her affair was to change all our lives forever. Mother moved in with Robert almost immediately, things were once again tough and we were all living in a cramped little bed-sit, with virtually no money and a bad tempered mother. Robert and mother eventually married and Robert decided he wanted to adopt us with a little help in the decision from our mother. The adoption took place a couple of years later. This was met with no resistance at all from my father, who was more than happy to sign the relevant documents and hand over complete responsibility, so he could continue the rest of his life. He felt he had no bond with Jake or me and did not want to fight for his right as a father, something he made abundantly clear, much to the disgust of his parents who tried everything to persuade him not to sign the papers. My Grandparents had pleaded with my father not to sign his rights away. Grandma George was on her knees, crying and pleading to our father, but it was to no avail. This was to be the end of my father's presence in our lives for over three decades.

This was something I have since discovered broke my Grandma's heart, she never really forgave my father for doing what he did. There was a bridge leading into the village where my Grandparents lived, and they both lived in hope that one day, when we were old enough, Jake and I would walk over it together to see them once again.

My Grandparents said their goodbyes knowing my mother would never allow them to visit their Grandchildren ever again. She had lied to everyone and led my father's family to believe she and Robert were immigrating to Switzerland with both Jake and me, a terrible deceit by anyone's standards. To keep children away from their Grandparents is unthinkable, they were good people who often took care of us and had a lot of love to give, as if we were their own children. Jake and I were their first Grandchildren and stayed with Grandma and Grandad George for over a month during a period when mother and father were trying to reconcile their differences. The bond our Grandparents had with Jake and me was very strong.

Llandewii

My mother and Robert left shortly after their affair was discovered. They moved to a tiny village in North Wales and rented an old terraced house from the Welsh Council, which backed on to a cornfield with just a farmer's dirt track separating the house from the field. Our new home was cold as there was no central heating, only an old coal fire in the centre of the small living room, by the side of which was a bucket of coal. I remember the coal man used to knock on the door every Friday selling coal to everyone in our street.

We had moved there in the depths of winter, the snow would reach up to our knees; we could not open the back gate for the snow blocking the path, which was only occasionally used by the farmer and his family. At nighttime, we would have three or four blankets wrapped around our freezing bodies to keep us warm, as quilts were an invention for the future.

I remember screaming one night at my first sight of a rat crawling along the wall in my bedroom. I jumped on the bed screaming, our stepfather ran upstairs and took care of it.

Jake and I were very young and our memory banks were just approaching the age of storing memories for the future. Jake was very cold this one particular day and he was crying non-stop which was annoying our mother immensely. She would shout at the top of her voice, "Shut up for God's sake, or I will put you outside until you stop." Of course, Jake cried harder then, so our mother took off his clothes in temper and put him in just a pair of shorts and a t-shirt. She opened the door, pushed him outside, and told him he would have to remain there until he stops whining.

The snow was at least two-feet deep, I could barely see him. By this time, I was crying very quietly so not to arouse my mother to the fact. I kept looking outside to see if Jake was all right, he was crouched down in the corner of the garden sobbing quietly. A long while later she opened the door and let him in, she gave him back his clothes and told him to be quiet, "I don't want to hear another word from you today Jake or you will be straight back outside do you hear?" She asked him in that tone that made me feel like someone was running their nails down a blackboard. Jake and I never said another word that day; we sat behind the sofa playing quietly, so as not to disturb our mother while she was watching her programme and smoking away like a chimney.

We would receive a powerful slap most days now just for looking at our mother in the wrong way, we only had to slightly raise our voice when she was watching television and we would receive a barrage of verbal abuse, followed by an almighty slap around the head.

Times were very tough and we had no money at all. Jake and I were given a regular chore, each day we had to go out into the farmer's fields and collect the old swedes that were thrown out for the sheep to eat. We would be given an old basket to fill up. If we were lucky the farmer sometimes threw out old cabbages too, this would make for a much tastier stew that night. We would sneak around the field and one of us would be on look out, while the other would pick up the old vegetables and if we saw a glimpse of the farmer, we would run as fast as we could back home!

On our return, our mother would sort the bad from the bad, and cut out the remaining edible bits to throw in the pot, to make a vegetable stew with a few old potatoes and some fresh garden peas, which were also taken from a garden down the road. Life was hard and money was virtually non-existent. We had to make do with whatever was available, socks were darned, old clothes would be recycled to make something else and holes in our trousers would be patched up. There were many a time when we would spend nights by candlelight because our electricity had been cut off, or we were told to hide behind the sofa when the door knocked as it was always someone chasing our mother for money. There was no money for the bus to school, so we had to make a two-mile walk everyday and this was not easy when the harsh winter was upon us, but we did it everyday and actually enjoyed the trip to school. We both knew that as soon as we reached our destination, there would be warmth as well as a hot dinner later that day.

Not forgetting the two glasses of milk we received at break times. Worth walking the two-miles each and every day as far as we were concerned! It gave us a much-needed break from the cold damp house and vegetable stew.

Wales proved to be far too isolated for our mother and it was not long before we were on the move again. We all moved to a very poor council estate in Shropshire and Robert managed to secure a job packing shelves in a nearby supermarket. I remember that mother put up the net curtains taken from the old house to re-use in the new one. Every Friday on his return home from the supermarket, Robert was always armed with large bags of sweets for us all. This was the highlight of our week; we used to wait by the front door watching for him coming up the front path. Our stepfather always looked tired and weary, he worked longs hours for very little money and then once his shift was over, he would walk the three-mile journey home.

This never satisfied our mother, he tried very hard to please her all the time to keep her wrath at bay. Her temper had become a lot worse and it was becoming even more frequent now. She would lash out and attack Jake and me. There were times when our stepfather would stand between mother and myself when she was about to attack me, simply because I was the one nearest to her.

My mother had no intention of working; she relied far too much on her looks to get her what she wanted, only this time her looks landed her with a poor man, who now had a job that paid the absolute minimal.

As best as I can remember our stepfather tried his best to please her, but it was never good enough. The lack of cash was starting to agitate my mother more and more as each day went on. She could not cope with the situation, despite Robert's best attempts, and was gradually getting angrier and more unpredictable by the day. She would often scream at Robert because she saw him as a let down, "You're useless, get a real job, like a real man, I don't know what I saw in you," were her favourite phrases.

He knew not to respond and just to let it go for all our sakes. She was not a woman who could be reasoned with, and reacting to her would only feed her anger; this meant we were all victims of her wrath. As she hit lower depths, mother was now locking our bedroom doors on a nightly basis from the outside with huge industrial bolts. She placed potties in our rooms, which would not be emptied until the following morning, regardless of the number of times we may have used them during the night. She removed the light bulbs from our rooms and even nailed down the window, to stop us from alerting the neighbour's to what was going on behind closed doors. At this point I was around seven-year's-old and Jake one-year younger, we were both petrified of our mother. I remember to this day she only had to move and I would flinch. The frightening thing was she seemed to enjoy scaring us, the more frightened we were, the more amused she became and the worse she would be. We learned never to look her directly in the eye when she was at her worst, as this would only encourage a beating or two.

Jake and I have spoken in depth about our childhood and have never understood our mother - we tried to make sense of it all – reasons and excuses for her behaviour, but there is no reason or excuse for locking your seven-year-old child in a room, with no lighting and the windows bolted down. I have learned over time that sometimes we human beings look for reason where there is none, only pure evil.

Unknown to me (as we were far too young) my mother was already on the Social Services watch list for neglect of my brother and me. We soon started being sent to our rooms after our evening meal and were not allowed out until the following morning, the doors would be locked to ensure we did not venture out. This was quite normal to me at this time; mother would lock us in our rooms, then get ready, and go out for the evening to the local pub, leaving us home all alone. I have discovered through my research, that mother would put sleeping pills into our drinks to ensure that once we were out, we stayed that way for a long time.

When we rose from our sleeps the following morning, our doors would already be unlocked if she had been out drinking the night before – this would be her last job of the night as she knew full well that it would be a late start for her. However, if she had not been out the night before, we would have to wait until she decided to unlock our bedroom doors.

We both hated being locked in our rooms at night; we could not understand why she had taken to doing this. Jake and I were petrified of the dark and she knew this about us, and still she locked us in our rooms nightly and would not allow us the simple request of a light on.

On the mornings that our doors were unlocked following her drunken spree, we would tiptoe down the stairs mindful not to wake our mother. As always, we would help ourselves to breakfast trying not to leave a mess in our wake. We would be so quiet you could hear a pin drop. Jake and I would get dressed and quietly let ourselves out of the front door, leaving the back door on its latch so we could get back in.

This one particular day I had dressed myself in a very pretty blue skirt; I loved it and wanted to show my friend across the square. However, when my mother woke up and saw me playing in this skirt, she flew outside in her dressing gown, hurling expletives at me. I was ordered to get back inside the house and take off the skirt. She told me I was only allowed to wear it when she said I could and then gave me such a hard slap across the face that I ran upstairs crying. I had no idea I was not allowed to wear the skirt, it was kept with all my other clothes so why could I not wear it? Maybe it was just another reason for her to vent whilst feeling hung over from the night before.

Mother had soon begun to fall out with all her neighbours, there were frequent arguments, and we would be strictly forbidden from playing with the children, whose parents she had fallen out with. Of course, we children would just meet up around the corner, out of sight of our argumentative parents.

Jake and I were very careful not to be seen as we would receive an almighty slap right there and then in front of our friends. There was an underpass where we used to meet and play two-ball up against the walls, this was a favourite game of mine and I was really good at it, this was because I spent more time outside of the house than inside.

Our mother shared all her troubles and woes with us, the falling out with her neighbour's, or the last person she had assaulted in the street for daring to stand up to her. Even though we did not understand these troubles, we would just nod in agreement not daring to ask questions. She was always in the right of course, and everybody else was always at fault. These were things you should not discuss with your children, let alone involve them in the arguments.

Jake and I both feared our mother immensely, we sometimes felt as though we were walking on quicksand most of the time and it was very hard not to sink. We were quite often blamed for her bad luck and many problems. Over time, my fear of the dark developed deeper and so did Jake's. I would often cry out in the night for my mother in fear, as it was so pitch black in my bedroom and I was unable to put the light on, of course, my cries were ignored, always. Instead, she would seize this opportunity to make frightening shadows at the top of my door, where there was a small window she would create echo-like noises to increase the effect, knowing I was already in a state of fear. Mother appeared to enjoy the fact that her children were scared and scared because of her. I cried myself to sleep many a night, all the time my mother finding it highly amusing. She would target me some days for total humiliation and then turn on my brother. One such day my brother being only six-years-old, was tied to a chair in the kitchen, then mother sealed his mouth with brown carpet tape and he was carried upstairs with the chair he was tied to and left alone in his bedroom unable to move. She screamed at him, "You bad, bad, boy," all I could hear downstairs were Jake's muffled cries. My mother looked to me then and said, "One word and you're next." I sat at the top of the stairs for three-to-four hours trying to comfort Jake, talking to him through the door, while our mother paid a brief visit to a friend's house leaving us alone again.

On her return, she finally went upstairs and untied Jake; she ripped the tape off his mouth then gave him a hug and told him to be a good boy. When he went downstairs mother decided it would be hilarious to put Jake in a frilly dress. She then tied pigtails in his hair and pushed him outside the front of the house where the other children were playing football. He cried and pleaded with mother to let him in, however, he was met with her twisted screams of laughter. It was a long time later that she got bored of this latest humiliation technique and finally let him in. We were both petrified of our mother as she could turn on the flip of a coin - this would be so unexpected and often took us by surprise. Yes, even after all this time, the speed in which her mood changed still had that element of surprise from time to time.

My mother was drinking heavily by this time, she had also developed a liking for barbiturates, swallowing them daily like they were sweets, this did not help our situation one bit, as our home life was becoming more and more unpredictable. I used to kneel by my bed most nights and pray to God to make all this go away, to make our mother happy so that we could be happy and we no longer needed to fear her. (My prayers were never answered.) As a child, I would think that perhaps God was just too busy.

The relationship between our stepfather and mother was becoming more and more volatile. Our stepfather could no longer cope with my mother's temper and unpredictable moods. When she was like this, Jake and I could not do right, we only had to look at her the wrong way and she would order Robert to pull down our trousers and give us the belt. He was far too afraid to refuse her; this was a heavy buckled belt, wide and made of leather, it had studs in-bedded through the centre. I was always the first and remember the belt to this day. I would often try to fight him off, pleading with him not to strike, but this fell on deaf ears, as he was far more afraid of mother's wrath than he was of the injuries he may cause us. Mother would stand by the door watching while we received at least ten lashings of the belt. Then, when she thought we had received enough and could take no more, she would order our stepfather to stop.

I knew there would be no use crying, she never soothed our cries and actually seemed to enjoy the tears. The imprints left on our bodies from the buckled belt would remain as a reminder for days.

We would then be made to go to our room until she decided we had learned our lesson, then and only then would she unlock the door. At this time in my life, I was confused and feared my mother but desperately needed to please her. I needed her to be happy with me, and wanted her to love me.

I did everything I could around the house, vacuuming, washing up, and looking after my little brother so she could watch her movies quietly. I would keep him entertained in the garden for hours.

However, it was never enough, and every day she picked out something I was doing wrong and suddenly, without any warning, I would receive an almighty slap or even a punch across the face. Jake and I were losing concentration at school, as unknown to us our bodies were harbouring small amounts of sleeping pills on a regular basis and this was affecting us more and more each day.

I did not know what it was like to live without fear, or to wake up in the morning with my mother in the kitchen getting breakfast ready. I woke up each morning to closed curtains, mother still in bed drunk from the night before (nursing a bad headache).

On days like these, Jake and I awoke to our bedroom doors unlocked and can only assume she thought to unlock them in advance of her drunken spree, while we were already asleep. We had to get our own breakfast every day (ready brek and cornflakes were a favourite, I recall!) During the winter, we would favour porridge, but there was no microwave back then so we would have to make do with cold milk if mother was unable to get out of bed. I could not reach for the cupboards - they were far too high - so I would stand on a chair and climb onto the kitchen worktop. After feeding and dressing ourselves, we would go outside the front of the house and play with the other children. More often than not, it would be near one o'clock in the afternoon before our mother surfaced and always in a bad mood, shouting and screaming because we had left a mess in the kitchen. After she had berated us to the point of bringing us to tears, mother would then throw us out of the house and shout further abuse at us and in front of the other children.

We would not be allowed back into the house until after dark, however, this suited both Jake and me.

During the hot summer days, we would play with the older children from our square and often all head down to the wide river, with over-hanging trees. The other kids had been going down to the river long before Jake and me. They had made a makeshift swing out of an old tyre and a bit of rope, (we thought this was the best thing ever!) We spent whole days hanging onto the swing and would jump off into the deep river below without any fear at all. Those days away from our mother were good days and earned a place in my memory bank for the future, which was pretty empty. We also spent many summer days scrumping in an old orchard attached to an old ruin near Shepton School. The orchard was well stocked with damson, pear, apple, and plum trees, and many blackberry bushes too. We would be armed with old Carrefour plastic bags - lots of them - and all would eventually be filled with fruit until they were bursting, forgetting we would have to carry them all the way home!

Jake and I would climb to the top of the trees teasing each other and seeing who could climb the fastest. There were many times when we would slip and fall, but this did not stop us, we would get straight back up on to our feet and within seconds, we would be at the top of the tree again. In the grounds of the old ruin there was a sundial several hundred years old, I remember this so well, because I was transfixed by it as a child, thinking it was beautiful. Just outside the front of the old ruin was a small lake, which we used to skim stones into. We would hold competitions to see who could skim the furthest.

I believe this old ruin has now been made into a luxury hotel. However, back then, this beautiful old building with large overgrown gardens was our place, Jake and Amelia's secret place, faraway from the clutches of our torturous mother. At the end of the day, we would carry our bulging bags all the way home in the hope of pleasing our mother. On these occasions, even for just a little while, she would smile accept the fruit and start baking apple pies, blackberry pies, and plum pies. They were delicious, our mother was a great cook and produced great wholesome food, and when she was on form she could be quite pleasant during her more peaceful periods, but it never lasted. Not ever.

I thank God for our secret place, our very own secret garden, somewhere we could retreat to when things got really bad, this was the only place where we were truly happy. To us, this place was our "Garden of Eden," with all the beautiful fruit trees and birds, it almost looked untouched by the modern world. This truly wondrous place was ours, Jake and Amelia's, and it always would be.

One day when we were sent home from school, (I was seven and Jake was six) the Headmaster urgently called our mother in following complaints by our form teachers that we were both drunk and had fallen asleep at our desks during class. One of the teachers raised the concern when they could not rouse us from our sleep and could smell alcohol on our breath. The school reported our mother to the Social Services to cover their backs as this was normal protocol. Jake and I had gotten hold of our mother's alcohol earlier that morning, not realising what it was at all.

The bottles had been left in the bottom kitchen cupboard; we came across them while we were making our breakfast and had drunk some before school thinking it was pop, but we had not drank very much at all, as the taste to us was pungent.

However, it had not mixed too well with the sleeping pills our mother had slipped into our hot milk the night before. As you can imagine, she never took us to the doctor's or rushed us to A&E because she knew she would be in serious trouble if they found these in our systems once they had pumped our stomachs. Instead, she managed again to keep the Social Workers at bay with a very convincing story and apologising for not putting the alcohol out of our reach. Claiming the only reason it was there was due to a party she had been to recently and had forgot to store the drink in a safe place on her return from the party.

Jake and I were feeling groggy most mornings now when we awakened up, of course at this time we had no idea why we always felt like this in a morning. Our lives had become quite unbearable by now and we spent all our time trying to keep out of our mother's way. In fact, we had turned it into an art form fit for MI5.

Colton Hall

Things were slightly better for a while following the incident with our school. Mother was less unpredictable and made a small effort but this was for her own gain more than for Jake and me. She knew she was on very thin ground once again and needed to keep the authorities at bay; our temporary reprieve was not out of guilt for her terrible actions, but purely for selfish reasons, not wanting to be found out once again for the un-fit mother she truly was.

We were told by our mother that we would soon be having a new brother or sister, and that she needed all the help that we could give her especially from me. She told me that she would be relying on me heavily in future to help with more chores around the house and look after the children.

Our mother was still smoking and drinking heavily throughout her pregnancy, yet again, the further her pregnancy advanced the more bad tempered she got. A couple of months before Jenny was born we were told that we would have to go into care for a while as she needed some space.

Shortly after this, she voluntarily placed both Jake and me into care. Again, she could not cope with the responsibility of Jake and me while she was expecting her third child. We were sent to Colton Hall Children's Nursery Home in Shropshire. I remember it very well. I cried believing she was unable to cope because we were naughty children. She carried on drinking all through her pregnancy with her third child, eating very little and smoking in a manner that made you wonder if cigarettes were going to become extinct soon. Unfortunately, Jenny was born physically disabled and with cerebral palsy.

Jake and I spent all of the Christmas holidays in Colton Hall with no visitors. I remember Christmas day we woke up in strange somber surroundings, as I looked around, I could see we were in a dormitory with at least ten other children, who were already awake and huddled together laughing at us. Then one child pointed to our beds and Jake shouted, "Look Amelia your bed." I looked down at my bed and the bottom half was soiled. Jake's was just the same too. We climbed out of our beds and just sat on the floor close to each other until a member of staff came into the dormitory.

We were to discover a little later that all new kids got this treatment on their arrival at Colton Hall. That same morning we noticed that there was a plastic see through bag at the end of our beds, this contained fruit and a few little pleasures such as a coloring book and a bar of chocolate. All the other children were hurriedly searching through their bags to see what Father Christmas had brought for them.

Some of the more fortunate children were blessed with visits from their parents on this special day and some were not so fortunate. I remember that during our time at Colton Hall, I felt lonely and I wanted to go home. I did not understand why we were there, where was our mother and why had she not stopped by to see us over Christmas? To a seven-year-old child this was a very emotional thing to deal with; to even try and make sense of it all was a sheer impossibility. I just know I felt that Jake and I were to blame for everything; we really believed that everything was our fault because we had been naughty. We did not take well to Colton Hall and spent most of our time crying or sitting together and not saying much to anyone from one day to the next.

Eventually, we were allowed home and greeted with smiles and pleasantries, our mother made an effort for a while with promises that everything was going to be much better from now on and that we all have to stick together. However, this was not to last for very long before mother fell foul to her usual and cruel ways.

Soon after our half-sister was born, it became apparent that the rest of the world was to blame for Jenny's disabilities. Mother was struggling to cope with Jenny as she was born disabled and one leg was a little shorter than the other was, so hospital visits and the frequent journeys were becoming too much for her to bear.

Jenny was unable to walk by herself for a very long time. Jenny was beautiful despite her obvious disability, she was always smiling and laughing, in fact, she was so unaware of her surroundings, it's fair to say she was the happiest of us all and thank God for that small mercy. Jake and I loved her instantly, Jenny had a shock of beautiful yellow hair and bright blue eyes, her smile reached from one end of her face to the other, she was a true blessing for Jake and me. I loved her with all of my being and was amazed with this tiny new addition to our family. Jenny was a good few months old when we arrived home.

Totally out of the blue, a short while later, Jenny, Jake and me were urgently whisked away without any warning and with just a few clothes to cover us for the next few days. We had been told that our mother and father had been taken ill and needed to recuperate for a while. We had been left at a neighbour's house the day before but our parents never returned home. Everyone was anxious but they were trying so hard not to worry us.

As the events unfolded, I discovered that mother and Robert had both taken a suicide pact and overdosed together. They were eventually found by concerned neighbour's who had climbed over the back gate and let themselves into the house. They immediately called an ambulance, and then they called the Social Services. Jake and I were both devastated, we had very little knowledge of what was going on; only that it was very serious. Of course, we both knew where this was going to lead again. We were sure that we would be placed in yet another children's home. Once again, we were left fearing our immediate future, the familiar feeling of instability, insecurity, and fear was what we felt at that moment in time.

We were all sent to Colton Hall again, while our mother and father were being investigated by Social Services and the health services for their stability as parents. We at least were familiar with the surroundings of Colton Hall. We knew one or two of the children who were permanent residents until they reached a certain age and then they would be moved on to another home. So settling in the second time was far easier on us all than it was the first time. We were spared the usual ritual of our beds being soiled, which was a relief to both Jake and me. The staff did all they could to make us feel welcome and I remember that our breakfast sitting was the very first time I had tasted honey. I was encouraged to try some with my porridge and it was delicious! I have loved it ever since. I will never forget that first taste in my mouth, a beautiful mixture of honey and oats! As the days passed by, we were all settling into a routine. We were quite happy and had adapted well to our temporary surroundings, I loved the fact that we had a set breakfast time each day.

In the morning when the alarm rang out like a billowing horn, we would all jump out of bed and get washed before we were all escorted

to the small dining hall where there was a feast fit for a king set out before us; this was something we most definitely were not used to at all. The tables were laid with plain plastic cloths and small-sized cutlery, the table was adorned with mini-sized boxes of cereal for us to choose from, there was warm toast delicately cut into triangles in a neat little toast rack, and the option to have warm porridge was there if we preferred.

I never wanted to leave the table, I wanted to eat everything set out before me, and most mornings I did! After breakfast, we were all led into the nursery area, which also doubled into a play area for the five-to-seven-year-olds. Activities would be arranged to keep us amused until lunchtime arrived. Once again, we would be greeted with a delicious feast of meat and potatoes and a side dish of peas, simple wholesome food. I loved it and the regular routine was so good for us all.

We thought about our parents less and less mainly due to the regular stability Colton Hall had provided us. While at Colton Hall, a problem that I developed in the form of bed-wetting had stopped after a while; I no longer woke up in the middle of the night soaking wet and crying out. Jake's confidence had also increased - normally he was exceptionally shy – however, he had become more outgoing and was joining in with the other children more often these days, rather than sitting alone in the corner. Jenny was just happy no matter what thankfully, she was far too young to know what was going on; she was also taken very good care of at Colton.

Unfortunately, our current welcomed stable lives were about to be disrupted once more. Our mother and stepfather had now recovered from their overdose and had been discharged by the psychiatric consultant, who deemed them fit once more to be capable parents. The Social Services department had an urgent meeting following receipt of the health service's psychiatric reports on them both. They were no longer a danger to themselves or their children. All governing bodies were convinced and in complete agreement that their children could now be returned home once more.

Sounds surreal but this was the 1970's and things were dealt with far differently then than they are today. We were assigned a Social Worker who looked in on us all from time to time. I recall her visits very clearly. On the morning of her visit mother would actually be up and out of bed, cooking breakfast and laying the table. We would all be kitted out in our Sunday best, and because mother was happy, we children were happy (and she knew then that all would be well).

The Social Worker would arrive on time, as always, mother would greet her at the door presenting the perfect family image. The house would be spotless as were us children, and we would all be playing happily together, the perfect family picture. Mother always prepped us before the Social Worker arrived, warning us that if we were naughty while she was there that we would all be taken away, and we would never be allowed home again. This would put the fear of God into us and was enough to ensure we were on our best behaviour. Our mother always led us to believe that Social Workers were interfering busybodies who had no business calling on her all the time.

On the surface, we looked like most families and the Social Worker would be happy. She would be armed with her black clipboard, all the while writing away as she was talking to our mother ticking her boxes and satisfying herself that all was well. She would finish her tea and then leave until her next visit. As soon as she left, mother would almost immediately revert to type. We were instantly ordered to get changed out of our Sunday best and put our old playing clothes back on; the shouting and stressing would start soon after. We would all be ordered to go outside the front of the house to play so she could have peace and quiet. Translated, this usually meant she needed a drink or three. Eventually, when we were allowed back into the house we could tell our mother was different, she would slur her words and stumble around the house.

The arguments had become more frequent, more frightening, mother became terribly erratic, she would fly into an uncontrollable rage more often than not, and her target was nearly always me. She would lash out at me with anything she held in her hands at that moment in time, a rolling pin, a saucepan, even a dog chain. She would turn into a mad woman, sometimes calling me all the ugly names she could muster from within herself and with the front door wide open for all to hear and then I would be thrown outside. Tears would fall down my face in bucket loads; I would barely be able to breathe through my crying, I would feel humiliated and embarrassed and pray the ground would just open up and swallow me. This would always be justified one way or another, and if she felt a shadow of guilt, she would punish me for making her feel bad.

I was to blame for her miserable life as far as she was concerned and I was reminded of this on an almost daily basis. She would screech at me, "It's your fault your real father left us, you were too demanding and you were a naughty child." I was two-years-old when he left, how could any of this be my fault? The more she blamed me the more I believed her. She would shout out, "He hated you Amelia, he tried to drown you in the bath when you were two-years-old." I would cry back, "You're lying, you're lying, stop it." Again, I would feel the force of her hand clip around my cheekbones;

the sting would be felt for hours later. I spent the whole of my life believing my father tried to kill me by drowning.

She would drink more and more on days like these, we would be sent to our rooms with a cup of warm milk or chocolate (laced with small amounts of sleeping pills) to ensure we would not wake up during the night. Again, our doors would be bolted tight and each of our bedrooms would have a potty in the corner should we wake up and be in need of the toilet. Jake, being a little younger than me, around six at the time, had taken to rocking himself to sleep, as he too was frightened of the dark, it was his only way of coping.

Then our mother would put on her makeup, get dressed, and leave us home all alone while she went out for the evening. I hated it when she came back drunk in the middle of the night. She would deliberately start banging on my door calling me names and shouting at me that I was nothing and never would be. I was petrified of her when she was like this as she became so unpredictable. I loved her and disliked her. She was my mother so I know I had to love her, however, I could not make sense of how she made me feel and why. I was feeling so bad about myself every single day, but I felt it was deserved for some reason, because my mother told me it was. Jake and I took solace in the fact that we had each other. We were very close and looked out for each other all the time. When things got really crazy we knew if we tried to treat our mother like a princess - offer to do the housework, played very quietly, or even kept Jenny amused for her - then we would get a reprieve for a very short while from her temper, which was worth its weight in gold. We were learning how to detect one of our mother's episodes, and sometimes this helped us escape a lashing or two, as we would stay out of her way or practically behave like her slave. It was exhausting most of the time, I could barely concentrate at school, there was always so much going on at home it was impossible to focus.

I did enjoy school and discovered very early on that I had a knack for reading and writing and soon enough they became passions of mine and they were the two things I loved to do most. The amount of schooling we missed because we would be pulled out for one reason or another and placed into care was colossal. However, the time I was at school I threw myself into my lessons in a way the other kids did not. This was a deliberate act on my part because I never knew when I would be taken away again, and I wanted to make the most of it as much as I could. Life had been very unkind to Jake and me up to this point and I did not see it getting any better in the foreseeable future either.

Each day became more and more of a struggle, so much so, that we were too scared to go into the kitchen if our mother was cooking and in a bad mood, as she would slice the carrots like they were being slaughtered. Knowing how unpredictable she was we were never entirely sure whether or not she would one day use the kitchen knife on us. So this was a cleverly thought out move on our part, we always stayed clear of the kitchen when she was cooking.

The Arrival of Susie

Mother was to announce her fourth pregnancy to us all. I just felt fear and dread run cold through my veins; to me this meant more work, more beatings and more responsibilities. I was only just eight-years-old and already carrying the burden of an adult. The weight that was put on my young shoulders was far too much to bear at times. I knew once this baby was born that life was going to get a whole lot worse for us all. Money was sparse and again during her fourth pregnancy we were placed into care, but this time it was foster care not Colton Hall.

They were not bad foster parents, but not particularly nice either as they were quite strict and slightly removed from the job in hand. However, I guess they have to be really, as to get attached would make it too hard for them to foster, knowing they will have to say goodbye eventually. It was so hard being shifted from one place to the next, you would think that it would be something we would have got used to, but that was not the case.

We longed for the lives that other children had with some stability, love, and attention. Jake and I used to talk about how amazing it would be to have a normal life, just like the very children we were staying with at our temporary foster parents.

The children's rooms were incredible; they had so many toys, the bed sets matched their curtains, and they had their own writing desks upon which to complete their homework. The bedrooms were like fantasy rooms to Jake and me; we had never seen anything like them before in our whole lives. At first, Jake and I thought the foster parents were wealthy, but it turns out they were just a very hard working couple who saved and provided well for their family - but to Jake and me they were millionaires!

We were to remain with our new foster parents until the new baby was born and our mother was into a routine. Jake and I could still not quite warm to our foster parents, part of the reason was that the two children they had were treated very differently to us in the most obvious ways. Although we were not mistreated, it was obvious that we did not belong there, and for that reason did not want to be there.

When we were eventually returned home, it was to a new half-sister, Susie. I could not believe how miniature our half-sister was; she had a shock of black hair, and the tiniest fingers I had ever seen. My time was immediately taken up fetching and carrying for my mother, which I did not mind in the slightest, as it kept mother busy enough for a while and took the onus off Jake and me. My daily job was basically taking care of Jake and Jenny most of the time. Jenny had a large blue and white striped buggy, which I used to place her in and take her for a walk around the rough council estate, partially because

I wanted to be away from mother but also because mother had some peace and quiet, allowing her time to be focused on Susie. Social Workers were a frequent presence once again, popping in and out at every opportunity, checking on our welfare, and imparting their advice to mother.

By this time, we were now all calling Robert dad, and he was still the fearful man I remember, too afraid of mother, always doing what she told him, no matter how impossible the task. This was making him quite obviously depressed and he was no longer happy, there was rarely a smile from him, and it became noticeably clear to Jake and me that he was suddenly away from home often. We began to see less and less of him and when he was around, he seemed to develop a little backbone. Perhaps being away from mother more often was changing him. They were in each other's company a lot less, which meant she did not have that complete hold over him anymore. When Robert was around, it was just pure carnage, the rows became more two-sided as time went on and when tempers flared, they reached new heights.

Their fights became quite frightening at times, pots and pans would be thrown at each other, our mother's temper knew no bounds, and I am sure this is one woman that would be capable of raising the blood pressure of a monk. It was not unusual for windows to get smashed during their rows, which would then be boarded up for a few weeks with thick brown carpet tape, until the council came to replace them. As usual, mother knew how to get what she wanted and a few dramatic stories later, the glass was always replaced free of charge.

One day when we arrived home from school we walked into mayhem - there was arguing and screaming - our stepfather was packing his bags and preparing to leave. Mother was in such a rage we could see the hatred seeping out of her eyes, so Jake and I grabbed our two sisters and hid in the corner of the living room, as far out of sight as we could possibly get. We were all crying and sobbing uncontrollably, fearful of what our mother was going to do next and which one of us would take the punishment for the latest row. Sadly, Jake and I were very aware that when she was like this, just about anything could happen and there was nothing anyone could do about it. Jenny and Susie were shaking in our arms as they continued to cry hysterically.

We were eventually sent to our rooms where we were told to remain, so we all sat close together huddled tightly listening to what was our life's soundtrack coming from below, banging, screaming, swearing, smashing. I was sure this could be heard all the way to the end of the street. Then all went quiet. Sometime later mother came up stairs crying and hugging us all, telling us that our dad had left. She left no detail out during her explicit explanation, which totally shocked Jake and me.

We did not believe her at first, knowing that if ever there was a woman fit for amateur dramatics, it was Heidi Sue Thomas. However, on this particular occasion she was right. Our stepfather left to begin a new chapter in his life, something that shocked us all, not helped by mother's descriptive way of informing us Robert had left her to be with another man.

Mother had found Robert in bed with another man, and he admitted to being gay without hesitation when asked. During the row that took place before his departure, Robert could be heard telling mother how intolerable she had become and advised her to seek treatment for her temper. Mother was heard shouting expletives into the street for all to hear as usual, while Robert walked away. As much as he had begun to argue back with mother, Robert had the dignity to keep this indoors and did not cave into mother's attempt to make him vent in public. I respected him for this, as I was at an age where I was aware of other people's attitudes towards our family, by which time I had begun to feel embarrassed about it.

The neighbour's were not favourable towards our family in the least and I was now noticing the strange looks we received from them, along with the pointing and staring. Some of the local children were told to keep their distance from us by their parents, due to our foul-mouthed mother, something any respectful parent would do.

My relationship with mother became more volatile as I started sticking up for Jake, Robert's departure had changed me a little and I knew that there was no longer an adult around to defend us.

I was now the oldest sane member of this household. It started to become very apparent to me that the way we were being treated was not the norm at all.

I started asking myself many questions: Why us? Why our mother? Were we so bad, was it so terrible having us around? I had no idea why I could do nothing right in my mother's eyes.

I felt sad most of the time, as did Jake; life was just too hard. Although I still feared mother, I told myself that I needed to stick up for Jake when she hit him for no reason, or called him terrible names to humiliate him. Robert leaving mother continued to have a downward effect on her and the atmosphere became tenser in the house. Mother was drinking far more than ever before and she could now tolerate us even less. We were often left outside all day, regardless of weather conditions, only to be allowed back into the house from teatime onwards. We were guaranteed a barrage of abuse when it was time to go in and would once again be made to feel worthless. Another guarantee was an empty bottle of vodka somewhere in the house that mother had devoured.

    I remember that one morning mother got up early and informed me I was having my hair cut - and I assumed this meant a trim - but mother had other ideas. I had lovely long dark hair and was very proud of those locks. We went to see a friend of mother's and she was told to give me a feather cut, it was short, layered and horrible. I hated it. This was done purely out of spite and not because I needed a haircut. I spent the rest of that day in tears, looking at myself in the mirror my lovely girly locks had gone and to me; I now looked like a boy. Mother smiled and giggled her way through the day, obviously finding it all very amusing. Unsurprisingly, all the other kids in our square laughed at me, pointing and staring, it was just humiliating. A friend of mine told me that I still looked pretty, but I know I didn't. To top it all off, I knew that I would have to face school on Monday morning and no doubt the pointing and laughing would start again. For the next few days, I prayed that my hair would grow back quickly, but that was obviously not going to happen. Monday soon came around and I think building myself up for such a terrible time made the day a little easier - I managed to get through that Monday morning just about, and the other children had moved on from their insults by the afternoon.

Back at home, we soon started to notice the arrival of a man in an R.A.F uniform; he was a very handsome and well-dressed man, always turning up at our house armed with bags of sweets and lots of chocolate. We were told to call him Uncle Steven and this was fine with us, as he was very pleasant. More to the point, so was our mother when he was around. For Jake and me, mother being so happy was like being in heaven; we were temporarily relieved from our miserable lives. Uncle Steven would take us all into the car park to see his green Ford Cortina; we were not used to seeing cars on our estate, at least not new ones with all the tyres on!

We were allowed to sit up front and beep the horn, for that moment in time we were the envy of all the other kids on the estate. I had never felt like that, as a child, for all eyes to be on Jake and me in envy, has to be one of my proudest memories. Uncle Steven became a frequent visitor and we all thought he was great. He introduced us to chocolate spread on toast - Mmm I loved it! He always came armed with a stack of chocolate spread, which Jake and I thought was the best thing ever, the chocolate jar would be almost clean by the time we had finished and most of it would be all over our faces! Uncle Steven was on leave for a couple of days and he was staying the night with us. This was the only time we really liked our mother, when he was around. He seemed to bring the best out in her for a reason we did not know and he genuinely seemed to like us kids too, which was a plus point. We all felt so proud when he walked up to our house on a visit, the neighbour's curtains would be twitching at the sight of this tall handsome man in his R.A.F. uniform.

    Uncle Steven always gave our mother money to pay any outstanding bills and a bit extra so she could stock up on cigarettes and vodka. He was very generous and I thought he was a gift from God. For a while, we felt like we were a normal family whenever he was around. Our mother was lovely to us and happy in his presence. We all laughed and joked together; mother would send us out to play for a while during his visit telling us she needed some private time with Uncle Steven. Of course, we were happy to oblige and would run outside, sit next to the green Ford Cortina and eating our sweets happily! We would watch over his car protecting it against the thieves, which were rife on the estate. When his visit ended mother would be in a great mood for a while. She even attempted to get up early in the morning and helped us all to get ready for school and occasionally did my hair in my favourite princess style, by now my hair had grown a fair bit, I loved my hair like that. As time went on, we had totally forgotten that Uncle Steven was not our real uncle. We had accepted him into the family whole-heartedly and wished every time that he did not have to leave. We were fascinated with his stories of the Air Force and all his worldly travels to Singapore and the like; he was fast becoming our hero. Jake wanted to grow up to be just like him. He talked endlessly of joining the Air Force when he grew up. For a while, things at home were quite calm and mother's temper did not surface very often; she had her moments but they had lessened.

Uncle Steven seemed to have a calming affect on her, which was for now at least, transforming our lives - a calmer life for us all.

Uncle Steven's next visit was a month later. We were all dressed in our Sunday best and extremely happy and excited as he had promised presents for us all! I watched for his car at my bedroom window, which over-looked the road at the back of the house; I dreamt of him being our new father as we all thought he was perfect. Jake and I talked at length when mother was not around about how lovely it would be to live a normal life and to have a proper family, our mother would be happy and so we would all be happy. Oh how we prayed this would be. I squealed with delight when I saw his green Cortina speeding up the road. As far as Jake and I were concerned this was like a Rolls Royce to us.

I ran downstairs shouting, "He's here everyone, he's here." Mother was excited too, she smiled, asking us all to calm down and to give him time to get through the door before we all jumped on him! It seemed like forever since we had last seen him.

As soon as the door opened, (mother had supplied him with a key of his own), we jumped all over him, he looked so smart in his uniform and hat and we were all so proud. Mother told us all to go and sit down while she took him into the kitchen for a chat. She always ensured this was the first thing she did when he arrived. All the red-letter bills were displayed in a line on the kitchen counter in order of importance of which he would go through, writing out cheques for each and every one. Once that was out of the way, mother unleashed us on him and we would all sit down listening to his stories while mother cooked a roast dinner.

I had noticed a significant shift in their relationship. Things were definitely getting more serious. Jake and I were taking bets on how long it would be before he was a permanent member of the family. Oh, how we prayed, hoped and talked at length about it. Were we lucky enough to have such a wonderful thing happen to us, would he propose to our mother? Oh how we hoped so with all our heart. We imagined a life with happy parents, holidays to Uncle Steven's cottage in Oxford. Were we really lucky enough to be granted with such a wish? We prayed hard and often that we would be.

Uncle Steven felt like our last chance at a happy life, Jake and I had pinned all our hopes on this happening.

We of course played our part when he stayed with us; we would take his coat, pass him his slippers, fetch him water, we would ensure that both mother and Uncle Steven had all the private time they needed and Jake and I would take care of Jenny and Susie. It was almost as if our mother had had a personality transplant; for the most part, we hardly recognised her, as she was so nice to us when he was around.

Broughton Estate

It was not long before mother announced we were being re-housed to a four-bedroom house on another rough estate some three miles away. At first, Jake and I were saddened at the news as it seemed to us we were always on the move. We never stayed in one place for very long, just as we had made new friends and become used to our new schools, we were uprooted yet again. Eventually, we came round to the idea, knowing it was going to happen anyway and soon mustered up enough positive energy to embrace the move.

For several days mother seemed in good spirits while we were all busy packing up ready to move into our new home, her jolly mood was infectious. Along with the regular visits from Uncle Steven, life was definitely on the up.

The day of the big move the removal men packed all the boxes and furniture into the lorry, mother made sure she had unscrewed all the light bulbs and took down all the netting and carpets were taken up to be refitted into our new home.

...den plants were uprooted, as these were mother's pride

On arrival at our new home, the excitement was evident; mother assured us this was going to be a fresh start for all of us. We basked in this glorious news and were rushing around the new house all placing claim to our chosen bedroom. Jake and I had the smallest of the three rooms available, Jenny and Susie had to share a room so they had the largest one. Mother had the master bedroom. I caught her adding those large bolts to each of our rooms, watching her while she was doing this, my stomach feeling queasy at the very thought of it. I was hoping with this fresh start that mother would do away with the locks and bolts on our bedroom doors. For the first time ever I questioned the bolts and asked her why? I was met with a cold reply, a reply that was a harsh reminder that our real mother was still hovering around; "To stop you from leaving your bedrooms of course," she replied coldly.

I knew then that our unpredictable bad tempered mother had not gone away, that she would again resurface before long; there was a look in her eye that made my blood run cold. I was no longer feeling so positive, no longer feeling that this was a fresh start. I knew all too well that our unpredictable mother would still make our lives unbearable. We would still be locked in our rooms with no lights most of the time, that we would still have to spend all day at weekends outside no matter what the weather, because she could not cope with us all in the house when school was out.

The house was a basic four-bedroom council house sandwiched in a row of three on Broughton Estate.

We had a new house, a new school, a new life. Once again, we had to make a new friend, which was not a hard task on this estate as it was full of kids of a similar age - and everyone was living in poverty of one form or another. Uncle Steven was a regular visitor at our new house and helped mother out a lot on his visits, fixing this and that around the house and making sure mother had enough money.

Then one day, mother gathered us all around the table in the dining room and announced she was getting married to Uncle Steven. We were all delighted, and our screams could be heard all the way down the street. On his next visit he was armed with gifts for us all, mother was telling us how we were all going to live together – music to our ears. Uncle Steven had a son from a previous marriage, who was older than I was at 13-years-old. We had not met him yet, as he had not been very well for some time, but we had seen a photo of him. We knew he was not well, however, we had no idea what the problem was or how serious his condition was. Uncle Steven did not speak of him much.

He was always talking of the future and making elaborate promises. I was promised a flat when I reached 18-years-old and Jake was promised a top of the range motorbike! These were dreams beyond our wildest imagination; we had never in our life been this happy. However, it was not to last. Uncle Steven left us all on that visit full of hope and promise for the future, but it soon transpired that we were never to see him again. It was to be a week later when we were to enroll for the first time into our new school, Broughton Middle School. We settled in well and took an immediate liking to this new school. Most of the children who attended were from poor families, who also lived on our new estate, so we did not stand out at all. In fact, we blended in very well and made many friends. I loved school and it was my favourite place to be; sometimes it felt like a sanctuary from our home life.

I was in the year above Jake but we always met up at break times, and after school, I would wait for Jake outside the school gates so we could walk home together. We had a dog called Sooty – I cannot remember how or when we took her into our home – but I always remember how she met us at the school gates every day. Sooty loved us and was so loyal, we took her everywhere with us. As we went through the gates Sooty was jumping all over us wagging her tail. Jake and I would smother her with kisses, as we were just as pleased to see her.

On our arrival home from school one day, we walked into the house and were greeted by our mother who stood in the hallway crying aloud. There was a neighbour consoling her. When she saw me, she came at me like a crazed woman giving me the biggest almighty slap around the face. She began using her fists and was punching me hard in the face, holding a letter in her hand waving it at me screaming, "This is all your fault, you stupid bitch," screamed mother. I had no idea what she was talking about and no idea what I had done, but apparently I had done something.

No matter what went wrong in mother's life, she always blamed me. There were times when she would scream at me, "I wish you were never born, I never really wanted you at all, and you're just like your father." I started to realise that I was a permanent reminder for her every day of Christopher, that she was taking her hate for him out on me.

Mother had something new to blame me for with Steven's departure; she laid into me with both fists as I curled up into a ball. The neighbour, along with Jake, used all their strength to pull her off me. I ran upstairs and hid in my room with my head buried in my pillow sobbing my heart out. She never apologised for that or explained how in the world it was my fault. What we did discover is that the letter from Uncle Steven revealed he was to break off the engagement, as his son had passed away and he just could not go through with the wedding, for reasons I do not know to this day. As the days passed by, our mother became more and more volatile and more dependant on the drink. She never picked us up from school, she never walked us to school, and she was never up before midday unless there was a visit from the Social Worker. Then she would make the usual effort to hide the truth about how we were really living. She had reverted to her old awful self.

At almost nine-years-old, I felt totally responsible for Jake, Jenny, and Susie. I did as much as someone my age could do to amuse them and keep them out of our mother's way, but there was always a reason for her to slap me or to strike me with the dog chain if it was at hand; the dog chain was my least favourite as this hurt the most. School was a safe place, a friendly place, the only place where we could be our true selves. I never walked home from school without Jake, not ever. We used to tease each other on the walk home and prolonged it as much as possible, as there was nothing to hurry home for. Sometimes we would play knock-and-run all the way home, sometimes being chased by the annoyed occupants! We loved that game, all the kids on the estate played knock-and-run. One day when we arrived home there was no answer so we walked around to the back gate and climbed over, letting ourselves in through the unlocked back door and walked into the house. We found our mother passed out on the sofa surrounded by empty bottles. My immediate thought was that mother was dead. Both Jake and I filled with fear, not knowing what to do at first. I gently touched her face hoping this would rouse her, and after a few attempts, she opened her eyes.

"Amelia what time is it?" she asked.

"Four o'clock mum," I replied nervously.

"Don't lie to me you bitch, why are you not at school?" Then she reached up and grabbed my hair, pulling me down close to her face, "Don't lie to me I said," then she slapped me hard across the face.

"Mum we have been to school, I promise it's nearly teatime, Jenny is due to be dropped off anytime soon."

Mother sat up from the sofa, her hair stuck to the side of her face, yelling at me to get out and take Jake with me.

Jake and I ran upstairs to change out of our school uniforms and then went outside to wait for Jenny's special school van to drop her off. The side of my face was bright red and stinging. I wiped the tears from my face and looked at Jake, he just smiled at me and said, "Don't let her get to you Amelia, she's not worth it." In front of our house was a fantastic steep hill, along each side of the hill were houses dotted about. We took our old makeshift skateboards to the top and lay down flat with our arms stretched out like a bird, and then we would race down to the bottom. All the kids used to line up and take turns flying down this hill on their skateboards; it was great fun and kept us busy for hours upon hours. However, this day we had to keep a watchful eye out for Jenny to return home. She was almost three-years-old and attended a special nursery school for the physically disabled. As the van approached, I ran towards it to collect Jenny. The driver asked where my mother was. I told him she was unwell and having a lie down. I said goodbye and then carried Jenny into the house.

Mother was in the kitchen cursing to herself – she told us all to go and watch television quietly while she was preparing dinner; there was no sign of the bottles on the floor or the overflowing ashtray that greeted us when we came home from school earlier. We all sat down for our dinner in relative silence. The table, which was simply laid out with knives and forks, looked sparse and uninviting. There was a large plate in the middle of the table full of buttered bread and salt and pepper pots on either side.

We ate in silence and were then ordered to bed soon after. Mother had made it abundantly clear that if she heard one sound from any of us then she would not be held responsible for her actions.

This is how life continued for a while. When weekends arrived, Jake and I spent all our time outside. We would take our old battered bikes on adventures for miles armed with a puncture kit and jam sandwiches which we had made for ourselves that morning. We would cycle to our favourite place - the old ruin with the sumptuous orchard! Oh, how I loved this place - it was so magical and full of life. One day we walked around the old ruin looking for a way in. The windows were all boarded up with corrugated iron, but we were so curious to see inside because we had dreamt up all kinds of theories as to whom once lived there and what had happened to them and why it was left to wrack and ruin. As we came to the large window at the bottom right of the building, we saw a way in; it looked like someone had tried before us. How dare they I thought, this was our place, Jake and Amelia's.

We pulled back the bent iron sheet just enough so we could squeeze through. I climbed in first - after all, I was the oldest, then Jake followed. It was very dark and dank inside. We stuck close by one another as we set about on our adventure inside the old ruin. We were awestruck at the sheer enormity of the place. As we made our way towards the stairs, I turned around to look at Jake.

"I'm ok, carry on," he said confidently. The stairs were very unsafe; parts of which were missing, there was no banister and lots of missing steps, and we very carefully climbed the stairs mindful not to fall into the empty holes that were once steps.

As we reached the top there was a rustling sound coming from a room on the far left. I'm sure our hearts stopped for just a second. We were frozen to the spot, and then all of a sudden and without warning, a very scruffy dirty man with scraggly hair appeared in front of us. We jumped out of our skins screaming and ran all the way downstairs and back outside into the orchard.

From that day forth we never attempted to go inside the ruin; however, we did make many more visits to the orchard. The old man who was living in the ruin was homeless, nameless, he never bothered us, and we never bothered him again.

Highfield House Children's Home

Things became so bad at home following my mother's drunken spree; it was as if she had forgotten that she had any children at all. Scenes like this became the norm with the days that followed. One Sunday we were all sitting down to lunch and mother was in a very bad mood. We were all sat down very quietly not daring to speak. Mother came into the room and sat down. I was sitting opposite her, not feeling very hungry and so not wanting my dinner. Mother went ballistic and called me an ungrateful bitch, then without warning, she stood up, reached across the table and gave me the most almighty slap around the face, knocking my dinner all over me during the process. It was so unexpected it took me by complete surprise and almost knocked me off my chair.

I then shouted, "I hate you," and she hit me again. Therefore, I ran out of the back door, through the garden and leaped over the fence. I ran down the hill towards the main road and sat on the grass bank crying. Before I knew what was happening, my mother came running around the corner towards me, calling me all the names under the sun. She then grabbed me by my hair and dragged me all the way up the hill back home, all the while shouting and screaming. Everyone was looking out of their windows, children stopped playing and they were pointing at us; it was humiliating to say the least.

As soon as we were back inside the house she threw me into my bedroom and bolted the door screaming, "You will stay in there until tomorrow you defiant bitch." I was so upset I started banging on the door begging her to let me out, but I was met with her sharp nasty tongue. I was not allowed out of my room until the following day. The shouting, screaming, and arguments became an all too frequent event in our lives once more.

Unsurprisingly, this started to raise the neighbour's suspicions and after I received yet another beating and was thrown out of the house again the neighbour's made an anonymous phone call to the Social Services. I was subsequently removed from my mother's care and I was taken very swiftly to Highfield House Children's Home for my own safety. Mother had started taking all her troubles out on me – being the oldest, I was the one who faced her wrath more and more. However, she was very clever at convincing the powers that be that I was the one at fault. Back then there was a motto I often heard - *children should be seen and not heard.* Unlike today, there was nowhere a child could turn to in situations like this, no help lines or charities that we were aware of set up to help children in distressed situations.

I arrived during the middle of the night, tired and upset. From the moment I entered the old dark building situated at the top of the hill I despised it. There was a cold feeling to the place. I did not receive a very warm welcome from the moment I entered the building, not from the staff, not from the children, not from anyone. I was shown to my bedroom and left to go to bed, but before the staff member left, she said, "One step out of line young lady and you will know about it."

I did not belong there. I will never forget that night as long as I live. I felt like I was being punished for my mother's failings; it seemed no matter what I did, life was getting worse by the day. I cried like a baby all night, my pillow was sodden with my tears. Right there, right then, I would have given anything to be at the old ruin with Jake, climbing trees, and scrumping fruit.

I awakened to a loud shrill like noise at 7:30 a.m. and jumped with fright as a woman walked into the room. She greeted me with a nonchalant hello and told me to get washed and down to breakfast by 8:00 a.m. sharp, no later. She pointed in the direction of the washrooms and left me to it. I was petrified and felt like the staff had taken an immediate dislike to me and I just knew I was in for a hard time. I hated it there; I started crying for my mother but my cries went unheard. It does not matter how a child is treated by their parents, they will still love them, even when they fear them. I needed her to come and get me; I was scared and alone at this time. Jake was not with me. I had been placed into care by myself, alone, without my brother and sisters. Confusion and fear was setting in fast, feelings I was all too familiar with. At that moment in time I would rather have faced my mother's wrath than remain there. At least I knew what was to be expected and could be with my siblings, watching out for them.

I did not go down to breakfast; I didn't know where the dining hall was or which way to go as the building was huge. I had also wet the bed and was afraid to leave the sheets where they were in fear of being punished. Eventually, a female member of staff came to collect me. She was harsh and to the point. I was escorted to a communal area and advised, "You have missed breakfast now; lunch will be at one o'clock" I was also advised to stay within the confines of the communal area until lunchtime.

I was not allowed to go outside, I was not allowed to leave the communal area, the door was locked and you could only leave the room with a member of staff by your side. It felt like I was in prison. There were only a few children residing at Highfield House during my time there, it was lonely, the staff made no effort to make you feel at home - or even at ease - I was just another passing statistic to deal with. There was very little to do on a daily basis; the communal room had a few chairs and sofas scattered about, a television in the corner, which displayed a very poor snowy picture and a very old pool table that had been donated to the home, and that was it. They just did not have the resources; this was a temporary place for children to stay while decisions regarding their future were being made by the powers that be. A child in this place could not possibly feel more alone in the world, it was cold and unfeeling.

After about a month into my stay at Highfield House, I had a visit from my Social Worker and was advised that I was going to be transferred to Breeton House children's home the following day. A rush of relief swept through me. I was told it was a pleasant place and it was run like a large family home. My Social Worker convinced me this was the best decision for me. The Social Worker informed me that mother had made it quite clear she no longer wanted me home. This obviously brought tears to my eyes and pain in my heart. I cried asking why? What about my bother and sisters? I had never felt so rejected in my life; the feeling of despair that was deep within me was taking root.

Breeton House (IST Visit)

The following day my Social Worker arrived and signed the relevant release papers, urging me to collect my belongings as we had quite a journey in front of us.

The long journey to Breeton House was a very quiet one; I was deep in thought, staring out of the window at the passing farms and mass rape fields laid out on the countryside, like blankets of gold, a truly beautiful sight. These fields glowed like a bulb, so yellow and so bright. I wondered what was waiting for me at the end of my journey, would I like it? Would the other children be nice to me? Would the staff talk to me? I would soon find out.

My young head was a buzz with questions and full with anxiety. Yet another move to somewhere unknown; you never got used to it no matter how many times you were shuffled around from one place to the next. I never felt settled and never felt secure in my life, there was no routine as such, however, this was how it would be and I had to accept it. My schooling was greatly affected by all the moves in my life. I was never in one place long enough for the school to make a real difference, and with all the troubles in my home life I was constantly distracted, or too worn out emotionally to take to my studies, although I tried with all my being.

After a long and thoughtful journey, we arrived at Breeton House. The first thing I noticed was the enormous solid old oak door with a large round iron knocker that stood before us at the entrance. It was unlike anything I had ever seen before, I had no idea doors could be so huge. It was rather intimidating to say the least. The large impressive building was extremely old and built in the Victorian era. A very friendly man who turned out to be the head of the house greeted us, his name was Gary Cotterage and he had a face full of hair in the form of a very large beard. I liked him immediately, he seemed kind and gentle, and he made me feel less nervous. Gary made it his job to put me at ease straight away; I was asked if I needed a drink before I was escorted to his office to receive the rules of Breeton House. I jumped at the chance of a glass of warm milk accompanied with two malt biscuits; there was an old woman with a white overcoat on standing over a large old cream stove situated in the centre of the kitchen.

She had a cigarette hanging from her mouth with a long stem of ash which looked like it was about to fall into the pot! Gary informed me that she was Dotty the cook. I liked her immediately too and she gave me a wink and a smile before continuing to cook. I was taken to the office and asked to sit down while he read out the rules of the house to me.

The rules are as follows:

1.) You will receive £1.10 pence pocket money each week to spend on what ever you like at the local shop accompanied by a member of staff.

2.) You must keep your room tidy and make your bed each morning.

3.) Each child must take their turn to serve dinner once it has been prepared by cook.

4.) Each child must take their turn to wash up/put away.

5.) You are not allowed outside of the grounds without the supervision of a valid member of staff.

6.) You can make one phone call per week.

7.) You will attend a school outside of the premises.

8.) Breakfast at 7:30 A.M. lunch at 12.30 P.M. dinner at 5:00 P.M. and finally supper at 8:00 P.M. – followed by bed at 8.30 P.M.

9.) If you run away, you will be brought back straight away and all privileges such as pocket money suspended, you will have your shoes and socks taken away only to be returned when you attend school.

All things considered this sounded just fine to me; all I kept thinking about was the £1.10 pence pocket money that I would receive each Saturday morning. This was an immense amount of money to me, not to mention I had never received pocket money before, in fact, I had never had my own money at all. I was asked if I had any questions – shaking my head to indicate I did not. Gary then took me into the main area to meet the other children.

Unfortunately, there was one girl I took an instant dislike to her name was Glenda. She was huge, the size of a bear, she looked at me with evil eyes and pulled faces at me. She was much older than I was – about 13-years-old at least – to a nine-year-old Glenda was definitely a towering figure. I knew from that day forward she was not going to make my life an easy one at all. The days that followed proved my original feelings regards Glenda were to be correct: she was, in simple terms, a bully and I was her new target much to the delight of the other children as they were given a reprieve.

I spent most of my time dodging her fist. I was always running to one member of staff or another but they did not do anything, in fact, I think one or two of them were frightened of her. It was Glenda that had made life difficult in this home and I was pushed to the point that it was time to run away. I waited until all the staff were asleep and sat patiently waiting for the night watchmen to do their rounds. Then I just got dressed and sneaked out of the downstairs toilet window. I ran until I could run no more, having no idea what time it was, just that it was very late. I chose my direction and followed the lights towards the town.

It wasn't long before a police car pulled up along side me and told me to get in. Boy was I in trouble. They returned me to Breeton House and I was berated on my arrival, with the staff taking a new attitude towards me. They decided to teach me a lesson and put me in a room with the very girl who was bullying me. I tried to explain why I had run away, but it was to no avail. They were not interested and I was told to conform or I would make life very difficult for myself.

All my privileges were revoked: so no pocket money, no day trips on Saturdays and no shoes or socks. No one ever listened, they asked you why you ran away, so you try to explain your reasons to them, and then you were punished for telling tales. This did not make sense to me at all. I was to learn very quickly that it was best to keep things to yourself; a child in care was not easily believed. It was very hard to prove your case when you were met with so much resistance from the very people who were there to protect you.

For the next few days, I just kept my head down in the grave hope I went unnoticed by everyone. I guess this was my reality, I had to get used to a whole new set of rules known nowhere other than the care-system. I was now just a number to be counted every morning and counted in every evening - this was similar to assembly to ensure all children were present and correct and no one was missing.

Breeton House was not so bad as far as children's homes were concerned. This place could have been a lot worse; it was just one or two of its occupants that made life for me quite difficult at times. Nevertheless, the longer I was there the more confident I became and the more friends and allies I made. I started to learn how to stand up for myself, Glenda got bored of me and soon moved on to her next poor victim. I was to find out later that most of the other younger girls had been through the same ordeal with her and the staff just turned a blind eye.

I was now sharing a dormitory with four other girls with whom I had become friends, we were always running around Breeton House playing hide and seek. Then, one day I passed Glenda on the stairs, she started calling me horrible names, so I shouted back, "Fatty!" and then ran for my life. She chased me all around the house until she caught up with me on the winding stone staircase. She wasted no time in grabbing me by the hair and smashing my head down into the corner of the step, which had metal clips on each corner. I passed out immediately and Glenda ran off scared at what she had done.

The next thing I remember is being lifted into an ambulance. I was in hospital for two days, with five stitches to the top of my right eye in my brow line. My face was swollen and turning black and blue from the severe bruising and I was unable to open my eye for a week. The doctors said if the cut were just a little deeper, I would have been blinded in that eye. My mother was informed and she came to visit me while I was in hospital and the Social Services had agreed to let me go on a home visit for a couple of days to see my siblings, as I had missed them so much. I thought to myself that it was almost worth having lost an eye just to see them again. During my home visit, my mother was quite pleasant. She was sympathetic and said that I would be allowed home soon, all being well. When Jake and I were alone he started crying, holding on to me as if his life depended on it,

"Amelia it's been so hard while you have been away, she takes her bad moods out on me all the time, even Jenny and Susie are getting it now."

I tried to reassure Jake that I would take care of him once I was back home. I could not bear to see him like this; at least if I was home mother was not so hard on him. I hated the thought of going back to Breeton House and leaving him. I hugged him tightly and told him to keep out of her way as much as possible, and do whatever she asks of him. I promised Jake that on my return we would go to the old ruin again for the whole day.

I told my mother how much I missed being at home and how much I missed her too, which was a lie. I just wanted to be close to Jake so I could take care of him.

On my return to Breeton House, I was determined more than ever to have my case reviewed regards going home. I needed to be there for my siblings - they needed me more than ever now. I went to see the head of the house, Gary; he was more than happy to give me some private time to hear me out. I asked him when could I go home as my mother wants me back, she has changed, she is happier now. Gary advised me that sending me home was something they were considering and they will come back to me once they have spoken to my Social Worker. Gary also advised me that the police and my Social Worker wanted to talk to me about my accident, that this was normal practice for their records. I was interrogated by the staff and police as to whom had done this to me, I just said I had fallen down the stairs as the thought of more problems at my door frightened me after Glenda's attack. The police had to be called in, as any injury to a child has to be reported and investigated. On my return to Breeton House, the staff made a point of telling me how worried Glenda was about me and that she had been asking after me almost by the hour. Of course, I knew why, and a short while later when I was alone in my room Glenda came in to see me. She asked if I had told anyone. I said no, and she said she was really sorry and had never meant to hurt me like that, she just lost control. She begged me never to tell and I promised to abide by her wish as long as she left us all alone going forward, as we had had enough of her.

Glenda changed after that and the bullying stopped she could not do enough for me and she actually became quite pleasant to be around. All the other kids were a lot happier too, so it seemed my beating was not in vain!

I spent 12 months in Breeton House, during which time I was attending a local all girl's school called Mount Pleasant School for Girls. This was a great school and I was doing well, above what was considered average for my age in English and Math's. The teachers went on to say I could excel in these areas and do well in future exams. However, regular visits to Breeton House from my mother had started to disrupt my behaviour again.

She would arrive stinking of alcohol, swearing and screaming at me in front of everyone. This was just too much for me to bear and was not helping my case for going home at all. I felt as if she was doing it on purpose so I would not be allowed home. It was always like this when I was doing well at something too; it was like she could not bear for me to be doing well at anything. She was the only person on this planet capable of stealing my confidence with a few lashings of her tongue; her life's mission seemed to be directed at making mine as miserable as possible. Why couldn't she just be proud of me, put her arms around me and say I love you? Why did everything have to be about her? It was so little to ask and so easy to give.

The decision was made to reduce her weekly visits to twice monthly and this suited me fine. I missed my siblings so much it hurt tremendously, and I still needed to get home no matter how much I did not want to live with her. All I wanted was for her to love me and be proud of me it was very little to ask, I thought. I started truanting from school shortly after and my subjects were noticeably suffering. I could not bear to be the only child in the school that did not go home to a family at the end of each school day. All the parents would be gathered outside the school gates, arms wide open to greet their angels, and I was greeted by a member of staff checking their watch as they were coming to the end of their shift.

Despite having friends at the home, something was always missing and I still felt like my life was a lonely and futile existence.

I loved my school, but hated the fact that it was a constant reminder of what I did not have and made me long for it even more. I felt so different from all the other girls at my school, and all the other girls treated me as if I was different, not in a bad way, just different. My life had been steeped in drama ever since I could remember; a normal, quiet life was all I wanted.

One particular day on my arrival from school, I saw an ambulance outside the main entrance of Breeton House. I watched as the medics hurriedly lifted a stretcher into the back, quickly closing the doors, but not before a female member of staff climbed in the back. All the other kids were talking about Cindy; she was probably the most mixed up child in the whole place (and there were many). She had taken a razor blade to her wrists and had obviously been very serious about killing herself.

The staff found her in the bathroom on the floor with blood everywhere. Cindy was only 13-years-old. I felt a chill run through me after hearing the sad details of Cindy's past. She was unhappy and hated being alive, she spoke often of death. Her history involved sexual abuse by her stepfather, and beatings by her mother, to her at 13-years-old life was not worth living. We heard later that evening that Cindy was stable and on suicide watch for the next 48 hours. Following that incident, Cindy was never returned to Breeton House instead she was sent to a psychiatric hospital for evaluation.

The following day there was a new female arrival at Breeton House called Angela, she was 11-years-old, very pretty with beautiful raven hair and deep blues eyes.

She would not look directly at anyone or barely lift her head up to speak. I discovered several days later, she was pregnant.

"Pregnant," I said.

"How can this be possible?" I asked.

The member of staff watching over her advised the rest of the children to give her lots of space as she was in a delicate way. This in itself was enough to raise the curiosity of all 30 children residing at Breeton House. Her father had systematically abused her for years and I remember the chilling shock I felt about her pregnancy – I did not think children could get pregnant.

Almost as soon as she arrived, she was gone again, just like that. This sort of thing happened a lot, but I just could not stop thinking about Angela for a long time. The haunted look in her eyes; she was like a frightened child, too scared to move. All I kept thinking about was how could that happen. It horrified me and scared me. Sadly, stories like this were all too common place in children's homes.

There was soon to be a case review, which was held every six months for each child in care. My case review was next on the list and I prayed so hard most nights running up to my review for approval to be sent home. I could not bear to think what Jake was going through. These meetings were held to determine your future going forward. They never asked me how I was doing, or how I was getting on, are they treating you well at Breeton House? They just weren't interested in what I had to say.

At the case review meeting, there would be my headmaster, from Mount Pleasant Girl's School, my 2N form teacher, my Social Worker, Gary the head of Breeton House and a member of staff. I dreaded these case reviews, as this was where everybody got to talk about you and your life - except you. Did it not occur to these people that having a little input from the child they were discussing would make life so much easier for all concerned, as everyone would understand the child so much more, then maybe, just maybe, the child would be better placed going forward. This would have been far too logical for them and don't forget that I was living in times where the child should be seen and not heard. After my case review, I was called to the office. Gary asked me to take a seat and he proceeded to tell me that it had been decided that I was to return home for a trial period only.

This was a huge shock and despite praying for this decision, I was not sure how I felt. I felt excited at the prospect of being with my brother Jake and my sisters Jenny and Susie once again, but a part of me felt dread - yes, I longed to be with my family more than anything in the world. However, I had not missed the complexity of daily life with my mother.

All those emotions must have poured out through my face as Gary looked at me very confused and said, "I thought you would be happy Amelia."

"I am," was my response not quite telling the truth. I then asked myself why did I say that and why didn't I just share my fears with him? More importantly, why didn't I ask him whether mother wanted me home, was this at her request or was it the sole decision of the case review panel? This was very important, as this would determine how life would be for me once I had been released into my mother's care for the umpteenth time. I wanted to share with him the real reason for my wanting to go home so desperately, but I just couldn't, in fear that I would scupper this opportunity put before me.

Broughton Estate (Back Home)

I was back at home once again. My Social Worker walked me up the path to the front door, I'm sure my heart skipped a beat when the doorbell rang. As the door opened Jake ran up to me with arms open wide and with a big smile on his face. He was delighted at seeing me and mother seemed quite pleased too, but I sensed an atmosphere between us and I'm sure my pleasant greeting from her was for the benefit of my Social Worker. Mother asked the Social Worker to come in and made her a cup of tea. They chatted for a little while then my Social Worker left.

The days that followed included the occasional visit from our stepfather Robert. I even remember he and his boyfriend taking us all on a week's holiday to Rhyl in North Wales, a good holiday too - the only one I ever remember going on whilst in my mother's care. Mother did not come with us, she enjoyed a week off, but little did we know she was lining up hubby number three already. I already knew she had a boyfriend. Jake had told me previously, "Amelia mother's got a new boyfriend, I don't like him very much because he's a bit moody!" I told him not to worry, it probably would not last as mother had many boyfriends who came and went.

Kieran was a violent alcoholic, an unemployed man, doing the odd bit of labouring on the side when he was sober. My mother was very smitten with him and hung on his every word. We children always took a back seat when she had a man in her life. Kieran and mother were a bad combination as they were both alcoholics and they both encouraged each other to drink. They would get so drunk, that some days our mother would forget to unlock our bedroom doors in the morning; I would be banging on the wall to get her attention and rouse her from a deep sleep. She would then stagger to my bedroom door, unlock it, and tell me to let the others out and go downstairs. "Do not make a sound," she would say.

All four of us would sit in the front room watching the "Saturday morning picture show," followed by, "Champion the wonder horse," and then there would be a Saturday morning movie, usually a "Norman Wisdom" one set in black and white. Everyone only had three channels back then, BBC1, BBC2, and ATV - not very many people had colour TVs on the estate, as this was reserved for the better off. Jake and I would make breakfast for us all and we would all sit together with our bowls of ready brek or cornflakes, still in our nightclothes watching TV. We were very careful not to make a sound, and kept the TV on very low, so as not to disturb our mother and her new boyfriend. They would surface around lunchtime, with bad headaches and bad moods. Mother would start her day shouting at Jake and me for making a mess in the kitchen and not putting the cereal boxes away, and then we would be told to get dressed and go outside to play and leave them in peace. Jake and I would take our younger sisters out for a walk. We would take a pushchair each and take them to the big dip, this was a great place that all the kids used to go to play at weekends, and we loved it. The big dip was a large green with a great big hole in the middle, the council had made steps down the side of the dip and at the bottom, there were slides and swings, lots of trees and bushes, and this was a huge playing area for the local children. However, when we had Jenny and Susie with us, it proved a challenge to get them down to the bottom with the push chairs especially with Jenny, as we had to be so careful and mindful of her disability; her capabilities were not as ours were. Jenny loved being taken out for walks by Jake and me there were nearly always tears when we had to return home.

We spent as much time as possible outside of the house as being at home was akin to being in a war zone. Mother and Kieran were always fighting, only this time mother had a boyfriend who gave as good as he got. They would beat each other all around the house without a care in the world for us children, who would be cowering in a corner wherever we could, observing the violence before us.

One particular occasion they had an almighty fall out following a drinking session that Kieran had been on alone. He had spent all his wages and had nothing left for food. Our mother was livid and she jumped on him and started punching him in the head with her fists. Kieran immediately responded and we were all screaming in fear. Kieran smashed a glass over our mother's head and she fell to the ground, he then ran out of the house. Mother called the police and told them she wanted Kieran formally charged. The police very quickly picked him up and kept him in a cell over night.

The following day, once he was released, he made his way straight home. Mother would not let him in and so he started banging on the doors, shouting and screaming to be let in.

Mother locked us all in the living room, Kieran had got into the back garden and he pressed his face against the living room window, shouting that we were all going to die. We all started crying louder. I was calling for our mother and Kieran screamed, "She can't help you, I'm going to set fire to the house, there's no way out for any of you now." He started a small fire. Mother had escaped to a neighbour's house to use their phone to call the police and it was not long before the police arrived and arrested Kieran once again. I truly believed we were all going to die that day.

He was again charged, but for reasons unknown to me, mother dropped the charges with promises from Kieran that he would change and would no longer drink. It was as if they could not function without each other, they seemed to enjoy all the drama they caused around them on a daily basis. Mother tried to convince us that he was a changed man and that he wanted to be a proper father to us all, that he was going to get a new job and all would be well.

Jake and I said nothing - there was nothing we could say but go along with her wishes. We knew it was not true, nothing would change, it never did, and things continued to get worse, this was our abyss. It was soon to be announced that they were to marry. Mother was trying hard to encourage us to call Kieran "dad" but this did not sit well with me at all, I did not want to call him dad. He was a very strange man with dark hair, big sideburns, and a temper that could match the devil himself.

He was still drinking and although the fights were less frequent, they still fought and when they did, it was monumental. Kieran was weary of me. He was not in the least bit happy that I refused to call him dad. I had no intentions of doing so, he was not worthy of the name dad as far as I was concerned. Mother was on a short-term high as she had found someone to relieve her of some of her daily duties. If she needed to get away or needed a break, we would be left in his care. He was not very good with us and often slapped us around or gave us the belt. This very soon formed part of our every day life.

Mother would often humiliate Kieran and goad him on purpose in public like a mad woman and he always retaliated with a beating. He would snap in an instant. They were two peas in a pod, she would also give as good as she got and throw pots and pans at him, yelling, screaming, and swearing all the while shouting at us to stand back. She never did this out of our earshot. They sometimes attacked each other with kitchen knives causing minor injuries to one another.

She always involved us and there were many times when we were caught up in the crossfire.

I remember one particular time Jenny ended up in hospital for a few days and we were again, thrust into Social Services care. By this time, my mother was on a watch list as a person of great concern with the Social Services. The sad thing was that my mother could not be reasoned with at all; she was beyond reason, if anyone tried to point out where she was going wrong or even dared to advise her on parental issues, she would fly into a maniacal rage beyond anyone's belief.

She had lashed out at Social Workers in the past and even the police; no one was above her attacks. It really had to be seen to be believed. I am sure she would have frightened the devil himself. As the oldest of four children, I was the one that faced her wrath often and even if she thought I looked at her the wrong way, she would jump on me and start hitting me like a maniac. The word eggshells just did not cover the ground I had to walk on daily.

Whilst sleeping one night, we were woken by screaming coming from downstairs. Jenny and Susie were crying in their rooms, I sneaked out of my room and crawled round to Jake's room; he was awake and banging his head on the pillow in an attempt to block out the screams. I told Jake to come to my room; I gathered Jenny and Susie also.

Mother and Kieran were having the battle of all battles - he was drunk beyond belief and punching our mother rather repeatedly. Jake and I went downstairs screaming at him to stop. Mother was swearing back at him goading him further, but finally Kieran's temper took a step further and he picked up the heavy yellow telephone and smashed it over our mother's head. Jake ran towards him to stop him but Kieran just threw him to the side, we were all crying by now and Kieran ran out of the house.

As he left, the neighbour's came in. They immediately rang an ambulance for our mother when they spotted her lying on the floor with blood gushing from her head. Then they phoned the police. Mother's head was covered in blood; it was everywhere and she was rushed to hospital. Marge, a kind neighbour, took all four of us kids in; she was so lovely and made us all hot milk. We all slept on makeshift beds on the floor that night.

The following day mother was released from hospital and came home. We were all very concerned and did everything we could to make her feel comfortable. The police came round to take her statement, soon after Kieran was arrested and sent to Shrewsbury Remand Centre. I can safely say that we were not at all upset to see the last of him.

Over the next week, things were relatively calm and mother was recovering well. She informed us that she would have to go out for the whole day soon and stated that when we came home from school, we were to go to Marge's house until she returned. When we returned home from school on the said day, Marge made us all a delicious dinner, a beautiful hearty stew and we all sat down quietly, savouring every last bit of the meal. When we had all finished our meal we sat down to watch, "Alastair and Crystal Tips" on television. It was getting rather late and our mother had not returned as expected. I noticed Marge and her husband were getting anxious and constantly looking up at the clock on the wall. It was after dark when a knock came at the door. We all jumped up thinking it was our mother, but standing tall at the door were two police officers.

Marge beckoned for them to enter; we were ushered into the dining room. We waited and waited until the door opened and the two police officers came into the room. They told us that our mother was not coming home that evening, as she had been detained at Shrewsbury Remand Centre. They went on to explain that there was a Social Worker on the way and that we were going to have to spend some time at Breeton House again.

Later on that same evening, the Social Worker arrived and took us on the long journey to Breeton House. We all snuggled together in the back of the car wondering what had happened to our mother this time. We later discovered that she had made her way to Shrewsbury Remand Centre, on the pretence she was visiting her husband Kieran, in the hope of reconciliation. She waited for him to be escorted to the visitor's room, then on sight of him, immediately pulled a kitchen carving knife out of her clothing and lunged for him stabbing him in the arm. She was herself remanded in custody to await trial.

This was the beginning of a new road for Jake, Jenny, Susie and me, as following these events, a section 11 order was placed on all four of us until the age of 16-years-old. We were now permanently wards of the state and placed on the "at risk register" She was deemed an unfit mother not capable of taking care of her children.

Breeton House Children's Home

Breeton House was a small children's home on the outskirts of Shrewsbury Town and this was my second stay at the home, but my first time here with all of my siblings. We arrived late in the middle of the night; the staff members were pleasant enough – they had prepared supper for us, which we ate gratefully while standing around a large oak table in the large kitchen, drinking hot milk. Dotty the cook was still there from the last time I stayed. A care worker named Gill gave us some nightclothes to change into. I did not remember Gill from my first stay so assumed she was a new member of staff; she had a kind smile and a gentle persona. Gill then led us to our rooms, and said everyone else was asleep so urged us to be quiet so as not to wake anyone.

I remember that night as if it was yesterday; I was so scared of being put into a room with four other girls (who were fast asleep) I had a little bed in a corner of the room, which I ran to and buried myself beneath the sheets, crying myself to sleep. When I awakened the next morning, I was too scared to leave my bed as I had soaked it during the night. I was ten-years-old and ashamed of my bed-wetting and also scared that the other girls would taunt me, so I waited until they went down for breakfast. Then I took the sheets off my bed and put them in the laundry basket outside the dorm.

I took a bath, got myself dressed, then made my way to the nursery area to see Jenny and Susie who were having their hair brushed by a member of the nursery staff. They were smiling and seemed undeterred by their new surroundings. I on the other hand was much older and very aware why we were there, but for how long I had no idea. I waited with Susie and Jenny until they were ready to go down to the dining hall for breakfast, as I did not want to go down alone.

On entering the large oak doors to the dining hall, I was greeted with a large room full of small tables, which seated up to five children. Nearly all the tables were full except one reserved for us. I had never been so nervous; there were children of all different ages and race ranging from 3-to-15-years-old. I remember thinking to myself, why are all these children here. Where are their parents? There were so many more here than the last time I stayed.

The room was full of chatter and laughter and a few children started to ask my name. I did not recognise any children from my previous visit; I imagine they had all moved on to other homes, foster parents, or even back home in some cases. Some of the children were very curious at our late night arrival the evening before; I just smiled at them and came over all shy. However, I was starting to sense a friendlier atmosphere, which was a welcome surprise. I was feeling a little less nervous now I sat down to breakfast and had cornflakes with tea and toast.

A young girl called Leanne Tabbot took it upon herself to befriend me and show me the ropes! I liked her, she was a tomboy but as strange as it may sound, I could not help but notice she had very big breasts for someone so young. In fact, she looked like a boy with boobs! Leanne was funny and well known for running away on a regular basis. There was another girl called Sonia Story who was very skinny and very shy. Jake and Sonia became very close friends; she was known very well for telling lies and when she wasn't telling lies, she could be found telling tales! These are the two girls I remember the most as we shared a dormitory, but most of all we shared what few clothes we had and even our troubles and thoughts. As children do, we all fell out on a regular basis but we soon made up again, all smiles, and plotting how we would get into the pantry to sneak a packet of crisps once the kitchen was closed for the day!

Breeton House was not as bad as children's homes go. We had three meals a day, we were washed and clothed and had activities arranged for us at weekends to keep us entertained. The staff were quite pleasant and they did what they could to make Breeton feel more like a home rather than a state residence. They worked on a shift basis and we each had our favourites, of course!

Schooling was outside of the grounds, unlike many homes where the schooling took place within the perimeters of the compound. I was again, placed at Mount Pleasant School for Girls the other side of Shrewsbury Town. I used to walk to school under the supervision of a member of staff (in case I ran away!) My escort would deliver me to the gates and pick me up at the gates.

Mount Pleasant School for Girls was a decent school by all accounts; I did well and developed my English enormously while there. However, I was the only pupil in my school that came from a children's home and they all knew it. This was not pleasant as I felt like an outcast surrounded by perfectly turned out girls. They looked immaculate from my standpoint; they were dropped off by their parents and greeted by them at the end of the school day, much like before. I was not and that hurt a lot, making me feel like I did not belong. I tried very hard but started feeling rebellious, as not knowing where your true home is can be quite bad enough without being surrounded by children with what I classed as picture perfect lives. I wanted to be noticed and for someone to care about me – what every child is entitled to, a normal family.

Jake was enrolled into A. Fleming School for Boys; he liked his new school and was happy there. Our lives had become all about routine, something we were not accustomed to at all, but welcomed with ease. We had to be up at 7:00 a.m. breakfast at 7:30 a.m. lunch would be 12.30 p.m. and dinner at 5:00 p.m. Every single day the routine never changed, they had two cooks that were employed to come in and prepare the meals each day, but the clearing of the tables and the washing up after we had all eaten, was done by the children.

Oh my goodness, I remember so well the endless piles of plates that would be stacked high, ready to be washed. Each child was put on a rota and we all took turns two at a time, one child would wash up and another would dry and put away! I hated it, as this particular chore seemed never ending. However, we all had to take our turn.

Breeton House was a huge Victorian construction. From the outside, it looked most impressive, and the entrance boasted a large wooden oak door with a giant black iron knocker on the front. I remember staring up at it in wonder the first time I saw it; I had asked myself what could be waiting for me on the other side. As the large door creaked open, I found myself stood in the atrium of sorts. There was a large curved staircase leading off one way and there were double doors leading to the enormous living area. I looked to my right and there was a smaller single door leading to the sparse games room and library, the room had a very old pool table and lots of donated books, of which I read many.

I spent a lot of time curled up in a corner reading the many books and on one such occasion, I came across a biography about the life of Marilyn Monroe (aka Norma Jean). It was all in black and white with beautiful pictures of this sad woman I had never heard of. I read the book from cover to cover and was fascinated with this woman because she had spent her childhood in foster homes and had a bad childhood herself. I developed the utmost respect for her, wondering how she had done so well for herself, she had nothing, and yet in the end the whole world knew her name, this to me was truly inspiring.

From that day forth I made a promise to myself that I too would not become a statistic, that I would make something of myself no matter what. I just had to get through my childhood, then, my destiny would be in my own hands, no one else's. My goals were set. I never told anyone. I kept them to myself, as I did not want to hear that I would amount to nothing. I had heard that all my life.

I carried on reading my way through more biographies and I would lose myself in Enid Blyton's adventures! I fell in love with reading and soon I would read just about anything available, "Ann Frank's Diary," and so on. This was to be my saviour for many hard years that followed.

My existence was a futile one at times. I questioned life a lot and I questioned the finality and peace of death even more. No child should go through their childhood with such thoughts. However, sadly, many do and this will always be so. I questioned God so much. I believed in him, but at the same time, I wondered at a God that could stand by and do nothing when there was so much sadness and pain in the world. I was ten-years-old and just could not make sense of it at all.

During my second time at Breeton House, I found it easier to settle in as I had all my siblings with me, which was enough security for all of us for the time being - the thought of us being separated just did not bear thinking about. Unfortunately, we were about to learn that our fate would soon be just that.

Jenny and Susie were in the nursery this one day; they had been dressed in pretty clothes as if they were going somewhere. I asked Gill, a female member of staff, "Are Jenny and Susie going somewhere today?" Gill replied, "No Amelia, they just have some visitors today, a very nice lady and gentleman." My heart sank, as I knew instantly that the translation of this meant they were going to be fostered. All the young children in Breeton House were never there for very long, they were often given long-term foster parents. We had seen a few of the children leave Breeton House this way. I always found it hard saying goodbye to children we had become fond of and close to, knowing that once they were gone, we would never see them again. I could not believe we had not been prepared for this - after all, Jake and I were their siblings, we were family; did they think we would not notice? Of course, we noticed we were not blind, however we were children and our opinions and thoughts did not count for much during these harsh times.

Later that morning I waited in the large atrium and sat on an old reproduction monk seat; I wanted to see what was going on. I had also rallied Jake. We were so scared because we knew once we were separated we would never see each other again. This was a very frequent occurrence within the care-system for siblings; they would often be split up from one another and that would be that.

The large oak doors opened. I was craning my neck to get a good view of the prospective foster parents; they seemed nice enough, quite normal really and all smiles. They were shown into the nursery where Jenny and Susie were playing together happily; where they remained for at least an hour. Once they had emerged from the nursery, I noticed the big smiles and hand shakes with the head of Breeton House, Gary. He showed them out of the door and made his way to the office.

Straight away Jake and I ran over to him, "Gary, please tell us what is going on. Are they going to take Jenny and Susie home?" I asked.

"Amelia please come in and sit down, you too Jake," urged Gary. He proceeded to tell us that Mr. and Mrs. Bolton were soon to be Jenny and Susie's new foster parents. I had suspected as much, but hearing it aloud just broke my heart; we just could not take it all in.

Gary went on to explain that Jenny and Susie were amongst the youngest residents at Breeton House and now that they were permanent wards-of-the-state until they reached 16-years-old, the best route for them was to be fostered into a caring family home, to give them a fighting chance at a normal life.

Jenny and Susie seemed to take to the Bolton's, who visited them regularly for a while; this was standard procedure so they could all get used to each other before the big move. They often brought with them little gifts, which were gratefully received by the girls.

They never acknowledged Jake or me; it was as if we did not exist. I tried to throw a smile their way whenever I caught their eye, but they just looked away. Very odd behaviour, I thought. Why couldn't they be kind enough to take us all? None of it made sense to me no matter how much it was explained to me. Jake and I hatched a plan; we would not stand by and allow these people to separate us all forever. We were going to do something about it.

Jake was 10-years-old and I was 11-years-old by now and we had decided to fight for what we believed – that the four of us should not be separated. Jake and I hatched a plan and packed a bag – all we needed now was the darkness of the night. We had arranged to meet outside at the end of the driveway, after lights were out. I crept quietly down the long winding staircase so not to be heard. I found my way into the games room, left through the window, and ran as fast as I could to the end of the driveway, hiding behind some evergreen bushes to await Jake's arrival. I was so anxious and kept willing Jake to come running down the drive. I was getting worried now and I was beginning to wonder if he had been caught. It seemed like I was waiting forever. Then I saw him, Jake running as fast as his little legs would carry him! We hugged each other tightly and smiled at each other very proudly as we had made our great escape. Destination was to be Head of Social Services in the centre of town. We knew the way, as we had been there several times over the years for one reason or another, however, this time we were going for a cause, this was Amelia and Jake's cause.

We were going to beg the Social Services not to separate us - that they can't do that as we all belonged together. We knew all too well that once we were separated we would never see each other ever again. That was the norm, and we had heard so many similar stories, we just did not want to be one of those stories.

We started the long walk to Sears's Hall. It was dark but thankfully dry and not too cold. We both had our pajamas, slippers, and dressing gowns on, as there was no time to change into proper clothes. We got many funny looks from strangers along the way; one or two concerned people stopped and asked if we were okay. We just kept our heads down determined to make it to our destination. If we saw a police car en route, we would just duck behind a tree or hedge.

Finally, Sears Hall was in sight of us and we picked up our pace, linking arms. We reached the car park and stopped to look around. There seemed to be many entrances; the building was lit up but it was clear that it was all locked up. We were both excited, the adrenalin was coursing through our veins, we held onto each other very tight while deciding which way to go. We made our way to what looked like the main entrance, pausing before pressing the buzzer to our right. We waited, and then a voice came through, "Hello how can I help you?"

the voice asked. "My name is Amelia and I want to see the boss urgently," I replied.

We waited for a moment but there was no reply from the man in the box. I tried pressing the buzzer again but still no reply. Then Jake said, "Look Amelia someone's coming." Jake was right; there was a tall man in a uniform walking towards us along the corridor from inside the building.

He unlocked the door and said, "My, oh my, you are very young to be out on your own at this time of night, and in your pajamas too." I proceeded to tell him our plight and he was gracious enough not to interrupt me. On completion of my story, he beckoned us in and took us up to his office. He assured me that the boss would hear our story; however, he was unavailable at present. The man turned out to be the Security Guard for Sears Hall and he was very polite and very understanding. He called Breeton House to let them know we were there safe and sound and he called our Social Worker too. While we waited to be picked up, the Security Guard bought us a bag of chips wrapped up in newspaper, they were delicious! He told us funny stories about the old Sears building and made us laugh.

It was not long before we had to face the reality of what we had done. We were taken back to Breeton House, and our Social Worker Sarah Golding explained to us that it would be impossible for all four us to stay together, as they were not able to find foster parents willing to take all four of us on. However, it was decided that this was the best chance Jenny and Susie were going to get.

We were told that it was very hard to place older children in permanent foster care as prospective foster parents were looking for younger children. Jake and I broke down in tears. We were too young to understand why someone would want to separate us, we could not bear the pain we were feeling and we knew we would never see them again. I tried to convince my Social Worker that we would be really well behaved and the foster parents would not even know we were there most of the time.

I went on to say how good I was at hoovering and cleaning and that I would be a great help to them. My Social Worker just smiled and said, "Oh Amelia you are too young to understand right now, but one day you will see that this really has been the best decision made for Jenny and Susie." Right there, right then, I knew our battle to stay together was lost - that much was easy enough to understand.

It would only be a short while later that we had to say our goodbyes to Jenny and Susie, our hearts were broken; we all hugged and cried and then hugged some more. Jake and I watched through the games room window as Jenny and Susie were taken to the car with their belongings. I had never felt such despair, such hopelessness, in my entire life. I feared I may never be the same again, and my fears were too right.

We were not allowed any contact with Jenny and Susie. In the weeks that followed. We asked and we begged but it was decided in the best interest of Jenny and Susie to restrict all contact as this may unsettle them. It just would not register with me. I could not understand the reasoning behind the decision to not allow even a phone call.

Jake and I became angry, which led to an even more rebellious personality. We had started running away from Breeton House on a regular basis by now and lost all faith in the very adults who were taking care of us. Every time we ran away, we were always caught, brought straight back, and subsequently stripped of all privileges. None of that mattered any more as far as we were concerned - we had been stripped of our family so had nothing left to lose.

As stripping our privileges was not acting as a deterrent, it was decided that every time we absconded from Breeton in the future, the privileges of the other children would be taken away as well. This was a very clever decision on their part, as for a while this did make us think twice about running way. We felt like no one understood why we were behaving so badly - we would refuse to do our chores, we would make our way onto the high roof top and throw stones off the building; we just wanted to be understood, we needed to be heard. Jake and I refused to go to school and were soon suspended, as we would just walk out of the premises as soon as we had registered our name at assembly. We would then walk into the city centre. When lunchtime came round and the hunger kicked in, we would swipe some apples outside the front of the grocer's shop, running down the street as fast as we could as not to get caught.

Our rebellious and misunderstood behaviour became of great concern to the Social Workers and the staff at Breeton House. It was decided an urgent meeting was required to discuss our fate going forward. Unknown to us at that time they were planning on separating Jake and me also.

Over the days that followed, we were on lock-down; not allowed to go outside at all, not allowed to eat with the other children, not even allowed to speak to each other as they had decided to keep Jake and me separated. No one seemed to understand how much we were hurting, no one sat down and asked us if we were okay or how were we feeling about the whole situation, or how we were feeling about the separation from our siblings.

It did not seem to occur to anybody that all we wanted was to speak to our sisters; to have a little contact was better than nothing at all.

It felt like we had been punished our whole lives for reasons we did not understand. We began to feel like Jenny and Susie had been wiped off the face of the earth, never to be seen or heard from again. Our feelings were over-looked, they were not important, there was just nothingness and we were left with an empty space. How did everybody expect us to react if not sad, angry, and rebellious? I more so than Jake had lost faith in everyone, no longer trusting the very people that were taking care of us. I saw adults as separate beings to myself, beings that I needed to be wary of at all times and never to be trusted.

It was not long before a decision was made on separating Jake and me – and it was a final one, so no matter what we said or how we promised to change, nothing was going to change the situation. I was to be transferred to yet another unknown place. This felt like a final blow direct into our hearts very core. Jake was inconsolable when the news about my transfer was announced. He just could not take it in and broke down. His personality changed dramatically and he became a shadow of his former self for a while. Soon after the news was announced, I was leaving Breeton Hall for the final time.

On the day of my transfer, Sarah, my Social Worker, arrived to pick me up. I said goodbye to my friends and then finally hugged Jake as tight as I could. We were both sobbing so hard we could barely breathe; we literally had to be prised apart. I was escorted to the car and was heading to Maidstone Children's Home in Shropshire.

I cried all the way and asked Sarah if I would be able to stay in contact with Jake. She said, "I am sure something could be arranged." I knew she was just appeasing me and that I would never see Jake again, at least not until I reached adulthood. The very thought broke my heart into a million pieces. I just could not imagine my life without Jake in it; we had been through everything together, we kept each other going when things got really tough and we understood each other. How would Jake manage without me? As far as I was concerned I had been stripped of the last important thing in my life, what did I care what happened to me now? I just wanted to die; I no longer wanted to live any more. Life was far too painful there was no joy in living.

__Maidstone Children's Home__

I had not long turned 12-years-old when I arrived at Maidstone Children's Home. This was a small unit within the grounds of the main Maidstone complex, the purpose of which was to determine the best place to send me in the near future, depending on their observation of me.

If they thought you could cope with being sent far away to a large children's home, which would house at least one hundred children at any one time, then that is where they would send you, as this was best for them financially. If they thought that you were not able to deal with such a placement then you would remain at the Maidstone Children's Home and be transferred to their main unit. However, places were very limited and not often available, so on occasion they had no choice but to send you wherever there was a placement available. Large institutions were rife in the 70s and 80s. These children's homes were dotted all over the country and they were full of faceless children, who as far as the rest of the world were concerned, were under the radar and did not exist.

I was to remain at Maidstone Children's Home for three months, and I was not sent to school during this period of time while I was being assessed. I was to remain in the confines of the unit; a member of staff had to be present at all times except when you went to the bathroom.

It was at Maidstone Children's Home when my first period arrived I woke up one morning crying, there was blood everywhere and I had no idea what had happened to me. I thought I was seriously ill I started screaming.

A member of staff came running up the stairs calling, "Amelia what is it, are you okay?" I pulled back my bedclothes and cried. Tracy, her name was, looked at me with the most genuine smile displayed upon her face. She held my hand and went on to explain exactly what had happened to me. My body had made the transition from child to woman over night while I was sleeping. I had never been educated on such things before so the arrival of this was a total shock and most unexpected. Tracy went and fetched me the necessary toiletries needed on such an important day. She went on to say that, I may not feel myself for a few days and that I may have tummy cramps. I did not like this transition into womanhood one little bit; it was rather painful to say the least and most inconvenient.

There was not much to do at Maidstone, which gave me ample time to think about Jake, Jenny, and Susie. I was filled with sadness from head to toe. I asked if I could make a phone call to Breeton House to speak to Jake, but my request was denied, I was informed it was in both our interests.

I refused to speak to anyone for two days following this denial and could not understand how a simple and understandable request could be denied. What could be the harm in allowing me to speak to my brother Jake? I later found out Jake had made similar requests and was also denied them. Just hearing his voice would have made me feel so much better, maybe given me the lift that I needed to make it easier to deal with the coming days ahead.

I was given a literacy test while I was there and scored above average for my age, coming out at age 14-years rather than the 12-years that I was. I was also tested on my mathematic skills and again scored above average, which I felt rather proud of. They were very surprised at this considering my upbringing and poor schooling. They were openly amazed at my reading and writing skills and said as much, which was really good to hear; as hearing positive things about myself was not something I was accustomed to.

My mother was always telling me I was no good, I would never amount to anything. When you hear those words often enough you start to believe them. I was asked many questions, what would I like to do when I grow up? What were my dreams and desires? My answer was always the same; I just want to survive my childhood. Following my final assessment at the Maidstone Children's Home, they said they had found a place for me in a boarding school next to a farm. The school worked closely with the farm and they thought this would be a good move for my education rather than losing me in the system and placing me in just another children's home somewhere in the country.

I had passed the necessary tests to warrant a placement in such a great school. I liked this idea. I was informed that the boarding school was an all girl's school; the cost would be met by Social Services as they thought I was a perfect candidate and had a lot of potential. This was the first time in my life anyone had taken the trouble to see me, I mean really see me, someone actually cared about what happened to me and was trying to do their best by me. Things were looking up and I was excited about leaving the care-system once and for all. I could not wait to start my new school, although they could not fix a date until my mother had signed the forms agreeing to all this.

Even though I was a ward-of-the-state, the Social Services still needed my mother's permission on many decisions made in my life. It was explained to her that this would be good for me, that I could go far in life with the relevant support; these words alone were enough for my mother to refuse her signature. "I don't want Amelia growing up thinking she is better than me," were my mother's exact words. She never signed the relevant documents and so my placement was given to another very lucky girl.

I cried for days. Why would she not sign the forms? Why did she hate me so much? Why was she there with a stopper at every stage in my life? More importantly, why was she allowed to be? I was a ward-of-the-state so could they do nothing? It seemed as though my mother had made it her life's mission to ensure that any good thing that came my way to improve my life was hers to take away. The very thought of improvement in my life angered her. I was so devastated at the very thought of remaining in a children's home until I was 16.

I knew I would be lost in the system like hundreds before me, I knew my mother had taken away the one and only chance I had of a normal life. She must have felt so much hatred and resentment towards me to keep doing these things.

Bryn Tyn

This meant my fate was sealed and I was to be transferred to North Wales, Bryn Tyn Children's Home. I cried like I had never cried before. Yet again on the move to goodness knows where, this time, miles away from Shropshire. I was taken out shopping to buy some new clothes to take with me to Bryn Tyn; each child in care was allocated so much money for clothing allowance per year. I had just spent mine; it was nice to have new clothes and go to a proper shop to buy them, and I was like a kid in a candy store. I bought two new skirts, two new tops, a pair of jeans, and a pair of shoes, which would have to last me the next 12 months.

Before I was transferred to Bryn Tyn, my mother had requested a home visit as she told them it would be a long time before she saw me again.

I felt nervous about this and was not happy at all; however, I reluctantly agreed, as I wanted to ask her why she had denied me the chance to go to boarding school. I was dropped off at home for one day to be picked up around teatime. My mother seemed really pleased to see me. She was all smiles and hugs, which was very unlike her. She said we were going on a picnic to Thomas Moor Lake as she said she wanted to spend one last day with me before I was sent to Bryn Tyn. I believed her and thought maybe she was feeling sorry for denying the state's request to send me to boarding school. Little did I know she had ulterior motives for wanting to see me?

When we reached the park, it was full of families having picnics with their children. There were very small boats gliding up and down the lake, the sun was shining, it was a lovely day. I was wearing my new clothes and sporting a new haircut, well a trim really. After about an hour my mother stood up unexpectedly and started to scream her usual insults.

"You slut, you're a dirty slut," she screamed at the top of her voice. Everyone was looking at us. I shouted back at her, "What are you talking about and why are you saying those things? Mum please stop this."

I did not know this was all a set up by her to aid a complaint she had made against Kieran her husband. She slapped me across the face so hard and then just walked off and left me. I had no idea what had just happened. I was sobbing so hard. I called Maidstone Children's Home and asked to be picked up from the park as my mother had just walked off and left me.

On my return to the children's home, Tracy sat me down and then asked me what had happened. I told her everything. I asked her what I had done wrong. Tracy said, "You have done nothing wrong Amelia, don't ever think that all of this is your fault." That was the first time anyone had ever said that to me. I did not hear any more from my mother for a few days until one morning, the day before I was about to be transferred to Bryn Tyn, I was called into the manager's office. Sitting there already was my Social Worker and a police officer.

I looked around and asked, "What's happened, is it my brother and sisters? What's happened to them?" They told me to sit down and the Social Worker started talking first, she said my mother had made a complaint to the police regards her husband Kieran.

I said, "What does that have to do with me?" The Social Worker went on to explain that my mother had made claims that Kieran had sexually abused me. This came like a bolt of lightning straight through me. I tried to convince them that she was wrong, nothing like that had happened to me, I would certainly know if it had. However, they said they still needed to go through with an internal examination. That same day I had to go through the awful experience of my first internal. It was painful and humiliating and I cried the whole time. There was a member of staff present throughout the whole process, as well as my Social Worker. Following the examination they concluded that I had not been sexually abused recently, like mother had claimed. My mother's probation officer paid her a visit and asked her about these claims.

My mother said no such thing had happened and she retracted her story. She was just angry with her husband and wanted to get back at him. I could not believe she made me suffer like that just to score a point in their endless battles. I was humiliated beyond belief and she was the reason once again. I was made to feel so small and worthless; I had never felt so ashamed in my whole life. It wasn't enough for her that she had removed any chance I had at a normal life; she wanted to take my innocence away too. She knew what I would have to go through following her complaint and that I would have to suffer the humiliation of a thorough internal examination at just 12-years-old.

I will never forget that long journey up the A5 from Shropshire to Wales. I was more frightened than I had ever been. I had heard terrible stories about Bryn Tyn. It was set in the middle of nowhere; it was a three-mile walk to the nearest shop. Bryn Tyn was set in acres and acres of land surrounded by woodland. It was owned by a man called John Allen, who also owned four other children's homes; three of them were scattered around North Wales too and the fourth one was situated near Shifnal in Shropshire. Nothing but fields could be seen for miles. It was apparently strict beyond belief and housed up to a hundred children at any one time. In short, I could not have been sent to a worse place. Schooling took place on the premises in portakabins and we were taught by teachers who each worked part-time, giving their own time up for free. Bryn Tyn was a law unto itself and abided by the laws set by John Allen, the owner of the Bryn Tyn community.

As we were getting nearer to the children's home there was a large blue and white sign indicating a turning on the left to Bryn Tyn. After we had taken that left, there was a dusty track that led to the exceptionally long driveway, leading finally to Bryn Tyn Hall. Nothing could be seen at all, just acres and acres of vast countryside.

It looked huge, unlike anywhere I had ever been before and I was petrified. It looked so intimidating; the sheer size of the place took my breath away. It was just as people had described to me and it was set in acres of its own land. Nothing could be seen for miles, and my first thought was how on earth does a person escape from here? I was filled with dread and like so many times before on approaching a new home, the tears just fell from my eyes.

My Social Worker parked her car in the staff car park, and we both got out and walked to the reception area. We were asked to sit down while someone sent for the head of Brixton House. I was nervously looking around; I could see a group of boys playing football, and there were a couple of Jamaican girls peering through the window taking a curious peek at the new arrival. As Mr. Walsh entered the room, he said a brief hello and then addressed my Social Worker. They had been expecting me he said, "I believe you will be here until you're 16-years-old, so the best thing I would do if I was you Amelia would be to just try and make the best of the place. It's not so bad once you get used it."

There were three sections to Bryn Tyn Hall: Brixton House, Lindasfarne Unit, and Ainsley Unit. I was placed in Brixton House, the largest of all the units; this was where all newbie's were sent to start with.

Lindasfarne was the young boys unit, and Ainsley House was for the older children who had earned a scheme called "trust" once you earned your "trust" you earned the right to have your own room in Ainsley unit. That would be a long time away for me.

I was placed in a dormitory with six other girls. We were not allowed to keep our clothes in our bedrooms; we were assigned a locker where our clothes were kept in the main house. This locker room was run by two women and if we ever needed a pair of knickers or socks, etc, then we had to go to the locker room and sign them out under the supervision of the locker staff. This was something I was not used to at all; it puzzled me and I just could not get my head around it at all. We were never allowed to leave the grounds; it was an incredibly large place, bigger than anything I had ever seen.

There were children from all walks of life, children from Brixton in London, Moss Side in Manchester. The children were all admitted for many different reasons and there were many children in care for their own safety just like me. However, there were children who were sent to Bryn Tyn for arson, grievous bodily harm, the use of a weapon with intent, burglary, breaking and entering - the list goes on.

I was scared to death, there were some frightening characters that I dared not look at directly for fear of reprisal. I was in the wrong place; this was a mistake and I did not belong there. This was my gift from my mother. I decided as soon as it was physically possible I would make my escape. I thought to myself if I just kept my head down for a while, they would not watch me so closely if they thought I had settled in well. Then maybe once their guard was down, I could make a break for it.

The days that followed were not easy, it is never easy being a new person wherever you are, but being a newbie in a children's home was hard. For a while, you became everyone's target. You would be tested beyond belief, picked on, bullied; the few personal belongings that you treasured were stolen. It was very hard.

No matter how much you tried to keep your head down there were always those people who just won't let you be. There were too many bullies vying for top dog position; I was just one of their prey along with many others. I learned very early on that to survive there I needed to get strong, I needed to stand my ground, or I was going to get swallowed up. Four more years I had to wait before my destiny would be in my own hands, no one else's. I told myself that so often, it was that very thought that kept me going.

The first week was hard at Bryn Tyn. I was lonely, I was a newbie and I had no friends. I was stuck in the middle of nowhere, which may as well have been another planet and worst of all my siblings had been torn from my life, just like that, with no thought or care as to how it would affect all our lives in the future. Jenny and Susie I could just about comprehend. Yes, they were right, it was far better that they were fostered than have to bear the fate that Jake and I did, but to sever all contact between us still upset me. No, I will never comprehend that decision at all; it was beyond any normal reasoning as far as I could see. Then there was Jake - not only had we been separated but our contact had been severed also. We had no information on each other's whereabouts, and we were not given contact details of any kind. For goodness sake, we were family, brother and sister, lost like so many in the care-system, they had taken our fundamental right away, our right to be brother and sister and our right to contact one another. I could not bear to think about it. This was for the best, or at least that's what the powers that be had told me on a regular basis. "It will only unsettle the pair of you." We were told when we each requested a phone call.

Just one little phone call was all I wanted, to speak to Jake, to ask him if he was okay, if he was coping, what was it like where he was placed? I just wanted to know such basic things, but this was denied. I just could not fathom a system that wanted to separate siblings like that, not to even allow them contact of any kind. What had we done so wrong to deserve this? I asked myself that question every single day.

It was while I was in Bryn Tyn that my Grandmother passed away from rheumatoid arthritis. I was called into the office and given the terrible news. This came as such a shock and one I really was not expecting. After I had composed myself, my first question was could I attend my Grandma's funeral. My question had already been anticipated and my request was denied as they thought this could be unsettling for me. Again, I was denied something so precious. I started feeling as if life was not worth living, thoughts of suicide entered my mind – I just did not see the point any more. The big fight just to survive and retain some basic human rights, was just proving too much to cope with.

This made Bryn Tyn even harder to bear at times because I had never felt so alone in my life, and there was no one around me that cared much for how I was feeling either. I realised very early on that I needed to look after number one now and make it through each day. I decided to rise above my sadness. It was not too long before I started making a couple of friends. I gained the trust of two girls and they gained my trust in return.

I was assigned a key worker called Paul. This was a member of staff who was assigned to look after my emotional needs. If I had any problems or concerns then I would report to Paul. Each member of staff had a group of children that they were responsible for. Paul was great I thought, but he was not very popular with the other kids - he was nicknamed "Beef" as he was built like a house and very strong. Mary and Sue, my new best friends, were also unhappy at Bryn Tyn – there were too many bullies making daily life more difficult for everyone, which nobody needed on top of being rejected by their own family and constantly let down by the system.

A Dangerous Encounter

Mary, Sue, and I hatched an escape plan. We each had to sneak some food from cooks' kitchen, hide it under our beds, pack our bags in advance of the great run and make sure we had warm clothes. It had been snowing outside and it was now turning to slush. This was Wales and the winters were harsh and very cold.

Each evening there were two night watchmen who did their rounds every other hour, so it was imperative that we made our move straight after they had checked our dorms. We gathered our bags, wrapped ourselves up in layers and layers of clothing, which we had carefully slipped out of the clothing room when the staff were too busy chatting, and one by one we sneaked out of our rooms, mindful not to make any noise at all. Once we were out of the building, we had to then make it outside of the vast grounds. There were night-lights on everywhere, so we had to duck underneath these to make our way across the fields, through the woods, across the stream and finally over a rather high fence. We were on our way; we knew once the night watchmen set about on their second rounds the alarm would be raised, if they were clever enough to realise that our beds were stuffed with pillows!

The weather was bitter. We all had socks on our hands to act as gloves and a warm barrier against the bitter cold; we had no idea that the forecast for that night was a severe snow blizzard. At first, it was our adrenalin that kept us moving, the sheer excitement of our great escape into the big wide world. For a while, we decided to follow the line of the river so we were out of sight of the traffic over the bank, as the last thing we needed was to be caught.

We were heading to Manchester to my Granddad's home in Denton; Mary also had family in Manchester so it seemed like the best option for all of us. On arrival, we would reach our destination and state our case, after which we were confident all would be well.

After several hours of trudging through wet marshland along the river, we were cold and our feet were sodden. We all agreed after much discussion to make our way up to the main road, as this would allow us to increase our speed. Once on the road towards Chester, we started thumbing for a lift – looking back now, I cannot believe we did this but then again, as three young children riding high on an adrenalin rush, maybe I can! I remember we decided to flag down a lift as there were three of us, so what could possibly happen? Well it appeared more than we had bargained for.

It was about an hour later when we realised how very tired and weary we had become and just at that point, a red car pulled over. A scruffy man with long hair wound down the passenger window and asked us where we were heading. The three of us were so pleased that someone had stopped and we told him our intended destination. His response was, "Well what are you waiting for hop in."

We squealed in delight at this good fortune, looked at each other, and all agreed to get in the car. We were thrilled at the prospect of sitting in a warm car, our hands and feet felt like they were going to drop off.

Mary and Sue hopped into the back straight away leaving me to climb in the front, which I was not happy about one bit; however, I really did not have a choice. As I was putting my seat belt on the stranger looked at me very oddly, and with that, a cold chill ran down my spine. Something just did not feel right. I had the urge to just get out of the car and run, every instinct I had was urging me to just run; but I didn't.

The car pulled off and we all sat silently in the car, "Okay ladies, who are you running away from?" asked the strange man.

Mary and Sue let it all out and told him we had just run away from a children's home. I sat there very quietly.

He said, "Oh dear, well I won't tell anyone, and you are safe with me."

He leant over me and pushed down the lock, that's when I noticed a large stanley knife next to the gear stick. The obvious question echoed in my mind, why would he have a knife in the front of his car? He noticed that I was looking at the stanley knife and must have read the concern on my face, "Don't worry I only keep it there just in case," the strange man said before he started laughing.

The alarm bells were ringing all round now. Mary, Sue, and I knew we had to act fast or we were going to be in big trouble. I looked around at them both in the back of the car and just looked at their doors indicating to them, we need to make a run for it. They just nodded and understood what I was trying to communicate.

I looked at the man and said, "Would you mind if I just went to the toilet? I'm bursting; I promise I will be quick."

He was not too happy at having to stop the car and said it was not a good idea. I pleaded with him, trying not to show any concern at all, just smiling and maintaining an unconcerned look on my face. Eventually, he agreed to stop the car and let me out. He reached across, unlocked the passenger door, and told me to hurry up. The minute I was out of the car Mary and Sue piled out of the back seats almost falling over themselves to get away. We ran like we had never run before; we jumped over some evergreen bushes into a farmer's field and lay down on the ground. The red car circled the road surrounding the field several times, and just when we thought it was safe to get up, the car returned and stopped. He got out of the car shouting in our direction.

car shouting in our direction. We were petrified and we all got up and started running towards the farm, the man got back in his car and before we knew it, all we could see of him were his taillights in the far distance. As we approached the old farmhouse, the security lights came on and the front door to the house opened. A man and woman stood there. We ran up to them wet and exhausted telling them that a man

117

was after us, pleading for them to help us. The farm owners were lovely; they took us in, sat us all down by the fire and kindly listened to our story. They then called the police and while we were waiting, the lovely couple made us all hot chocolate and warm buttered toast - it was delicious!

We were so scared that we abandoned all thoughts of running away for now. We told the farmers that we had run away from the children's home several miles away. They knew which home we were talking about - apparently it was well known in North Wales. The farmers called Bryn Tyn to let them know we were there and that the police were on their way following an incident. We had at last started to thaw out; my fingers were tingling because of the warmth coming from the open fire.

When the police arrived, we were taken to the station and interviewed at length regarding the man and the red car in the presence of a member of staff. It turned out that there was a nationwide hunt for a man with long hair in a red car fitting the description of the one who had picked us up, following a murder of a young girl only 12-years-old, the same age as me. He was last seen 10 miles up the road near Mould, just before he picked us up. That night it was made very clear that we had had an exceptionally lucky escape. We could not believe it and were just thankful to be alive. The police informed us that they might require further help from us in the future if it turns out that the man in the red car was the same one they were hunting. Someone was definitely watching over us that day, the alternative outcome was not worth thinking about.

This was enough to put any future thoughts of a further escape from our minds.

On our return to Bryn Tyn, we had the telling-off of our lives, and we were stripped of all basic rights. This was the middle of winter and back then, it was common to have sub-zero temperatures with snow up to your knees. We were given our punishment - scrubs - this was the punishment for runaways: you were put in a pair of shorts, a pair of plimsolls without the laces and a t-shirt, that's all you were allowed to wear every day for seven days. You had your meals alone and were not allowed seconds, to me that was the biggest punishment of all!

For a week, we would be shoveling snow from the grounds wearing next to nothing, on a daily basis. They knew you would not try to run away wearing the clothes you had to live in for that week, as it was far too cold; this was a big part of the punishment. Towards the end of our punishment week, I had caught the flu and spent the next five days in bed recovering. Had I learned my lesson? Well yes, for the time being anyway! And all thoughts of running away had been put to the back of my mind.

Once I had recovered from the flu, I kept my head down for a while and decided to make the best of a very bad situation. I started my schooling within the confines of Bryn Tyn, with the determination to do the best I could. The problem was the limited subject options; it was just basic teachings, which I had learned many years before. So instead, I lost myself in books, wrote poems in my journal, which I started when I was just nine-years-old. I decided to try harder at fitting in at Bryn Tyn and do the best possible. I made more friends and for a while, life got a little easier. I was especially close to my key worker Paul who would always listen to me whenever I felt down, picked on, or just needed someone to show that they cared. As more, new hopeless children entered Bryn Tyn during the months that followed, I had established myself as one of the old residents.

There were always fights going on between groups of kids. There were various groups with in Bryn Tyn and some of which did not get on at all. When a fight broke out it was terrifying and someone always got badly hurt. The male members of staff were mostly well-built and tall, probably in place to be able to deal with such situations and eventually get them under control, when it suited them. Some of them liked to watch the fighting for a few minutes before intervening.

Weekends were always quieter at the children's home due to many children going home for authorised breaks to visit their families. The same few people remained at Bryn Tyn every weekend and during all the holidays. I was always one of them, Christmas included. I preferred Bryn Tyn during these times, as it was more fun; there were fewer bullies around and generally, life was so much easier for the few of us that remained behind. We were given special treats like days out in the signature blue and white Bryn Tyn van.

One member of staff called Yvonne was especially lovely. She was quite young herself, only 22-years-old, and worked part-time whilst studying for her degree. Yvonne was kind, gentle, and empathised with most of the children in Bryn Tyn. She was especially kind to me. She used to go through all the clothes she no longer wanted and bring them in for me, they were such beautiful clothes. I remember a canvas pair of skintight trousers and a cream ribbed jumper, as soon as I tried them on, that was it I fell in love with them. Yvonne was so lovely; I really looked forward to her shifts. Sometimes she would take us all for a sauna at the local gym where she was a member in Wrexham we thought this was pure luxury and we were in heaven. Whenever the holidays were upon us, we knew we were in for a treat when Yvonne was on duty. The staff would arrange activities for us like horse riding at a local farm on Sunday mornings. I loved this and was a regular on this activity. They used to take us out for the day to little towns like Llangollen where we would all jump off the bridge in the summer into the river below without a care in the world.

The drop was very high but to reiterate, during moments like this, we did not have a care in the world. I also remember many summer days spent at the Welsh slate pools where the slate mines were situated, the water was deep and so crystal clear. We would spend all day swimming in the slate pools and basking in the summer sun, all the while under constant supervision of course.

Sometimes at weekends, they used to take us out to the woods after dark in the blue and white Bryn Tyn vans and we would play hide and seek. Then we would all climb back into the van and be taken on a journey into the hills while being told ghost stories. There were no lights lining the roads in the hills; they were more like dirt tracks than roads and the only light was that of the headlights lighting up the road ahead. At the time, we thought this was the best thing ever, but now it seems a very strange way to entertain young children, as some were as young as eight-years-old, that said, it did not seem to do us any harm.

The one thing about Bryn Tyn that seemed very unfair, was how the boys were treated better than the girls, they were given great presents, some boys who were particularly favoured had motor cross bikes bought for them by John Allen, the founder of the Bryn Tyn community. Some boys were also chosen to spend weekends at John Allen's great big house, and the rest of us thought this was unfair. It would be many years later before I found out the real reason why they were chosen, and I was very glad that I was not.

Some children would have televisions in their bedrooms and it seemed to the rest of us that they were always receiving one gift or another.

This brought about jealousy amongst the other children, as every one wanted what they had. When the boys were in the field with their bikes, some of us girls would walk up and sit on the sidelines watching in awe. One particular day an older lad came up to me and asked me if I wanted to ride his bike. I jumped at the chance and leapt straight on to the bike full of confidence even though I had never driven anything in my life! I was given some basic instruction, then I was off; the trouble was once I was off I could not stop.

I started screaming, "I can't stop, help me."

Everyone was running after me. I was getting ever closer to the bank at the end of the field; I did the only thing I could do and that was to tilt the bike to the side and tip it over! I was surrounded by everybody fussing over me, asking me if I was fine.

"Of course I am fine, that was the best thrill ever," I replied. Then we all fell about laughing. That was a great day, and there were many great days, but there were many bad ones too.

There was a Jamaican girl called Julia Jones. She was tall, with a musky odor, and was downright horrible to everyone in her sphere. If you looked at her the wrong way she would thump you; if you brushed past her by accident she would thump you; if she was in a bad mood she would thump you - basically she was unpredictable and even the female staff were afraid of her. At 15-years-old, Julia was unusually tall, very strong, and had an almighty bad temper. Julia was going through a phase of humiliating me at every opportunity; in short making my life hell. She would encourage other children to call me names and through fear of her,

they would do just as she wanted. It seemed for a while I could not go anywhere without her in my face. If I complained about her I was met with indifference, they were just not interested. However, if they did pay attention and have a word with her this only fuelled her anger and she made me more of a target. I had had enough, but there was nothing I could do.

Near Death

One day I was walking past Julia and for no reason whatsoever she just laid into me, threatening to break my nose while giving me a good beating. No one did anything to help me. I even complained to my key worker and he just advised me to keep out of her way. How do you keep out of the way of someone like that, and what was the point? It was impossible; when she was bored, Julia would seek me out.

The bad times began to outweigh the good times again – becoming Julia's next target took its toll on me. I felt so low, with nowhere to hide and nowhere to run. The day that Julia laid into me was the day I took an overdose of pills, which I spotted in the staff room when complaining earlier about Julia. I do not recall anything until I woke up in hospital sometime later. Apparently, I had almost succeeded in taking my own life and woke up to be told that I had been unconscious for a while.

My mother had been called to the hospital. Brent Shaughnessy from Bryn Tyn had heard about my overdose and made his way to the hospital to see me, against advice given to him by John Allen himself who had warned Brent to stay away.

Why he was advised against visiting me remains a mystery. He was a kind part-time member of staff at Bryn Tyn, the rest of the time he was a teacher for a school in Chester.

As I lifted my head, unsure for a moment where I was, a nurse said, "Hello, Amelia."

I said hello and asked her what had happened. I was reminded of what I had done; everyone was looking at me and I started sobbing as I started to remember just what I had attempted to do. The nurse proceeded to tell me that I had to be revived during the night and that I was a very lucky girl.

My throat hurt like hell and my tummy was aching. Brent was so concerned; he sat by my side holding my hand asking me why I tried to overdose. I could not speak with anyone at that moment. My mother was standing nearby. She looked at me and smiled, "Well it's great to see you're okay, what was all the drama about?" she hissed.

I did not reply. I just looked away. My mother popped outside for a cigarette, while the doctor gave me the once over, and I was told I could be discharged later that day. When I was left alone for just a moment, I could not stem the flow of tears falling down my face. I was so unhappy and could not believe I was still alive, the feeling I had was of desperation to leave this world.

I was no longer feeling strong enough to cope with a further three years at Bryn Tyn; I could not see my way through any more days let alone years. I felt so hopeless, and now I had to deal with the fallout of what I had done. This was something I had not considered before, as I had not intended on being around. I felt like a trapped bird with broken wings, nowhere to fly, no one to help me. I was imprisoned and lost in the state-care-system. What was worse is that there was still a long way to go.

Following my discharge from hospital, I was immediately returned to Bryn Tyn. I said goodbye to my mother who caught the train back home. I sat quietly in the back of the car staring out of the window without a single thought in my head, just blank, totally blank. On arriving at Bryn Tyn I was escorted to the office and was met by my key worker who had the job of trying to get to the bottom of what I had done and why, but this day I was not one for talking at all. The one person I thought about was Brent and his lovely family. I asked if I could see him to say thank you for coming to see me at the hospital, but my request was denied and I was told that they had dispensed with his services. I was utterly shocked and asked why this was; I was told it was in the interest of Bryn Tyn. This made no sense to me whatsoever. Brent was one of the nicer members of staff as he actually cared about the children. I had even spent the previous Christmas with him and his family, and it was a lovely traditional Christmas with turkey, presents, and the Wizard of Oz on the television. I remember Brent and his wife bought me a beautiful make up set in a beautiful red and gold box, it was full of lipstick, blushers, eye shadows, and mascara;

this was the best present I had had for many years. They treated me like a member of the family and I was very happy that Christmas. So why was he no longer working at Bryn Tyn? This I never did find out and it always remains a mystery.

The days following my discharge from the hospital were particularly difficult ones; I had been placed on suicide watch for a while. I had lost weight and was very sad. It was approaching Christmas time again and I had turned 13-years-old, a big age for a child entering the beginnings of their teenage years. Birthdays in care went by unnoticed for the most part; no big party, no presents, or balloons, and most certainly, no cake, you were lucky if you got a card from someone. I was to stay at Bryn Tyn for the Christmas holidays again.

A Surprise Christmas

Just a couple of days before Christmas I was called into the staff room and told to sit down. Paul, my key worker, asked whether, if possible, I would like to spend Christmas day with mother and Jake. Wow, the feeling I had when he uttered those words was one that I had not felt for some time. I had tears in my eyes and so many emotions built up inside me within seconds of him uttering Jake's name. I was not expecting that at all I was trying to take in the question that had been put before me.

"Would Jake really be there?" I asked him. And he assured me that Jake would indeed be there.

Of course, I jumped at the chance – it had been nearly two years since Jake had last been within sight. It was reiterated to me that the visit would be just the one day and I had to return to Bryn Tyn that same night – truth be told, I did not care if it was only one hour, as long as I was going to see Jake again.

On Christmas morning, I was up at seven o'clock dressed and ready to go! My key worker Paul was to drive me home that morning in the signature blue and white Bryn Tyn van. The journey would take approximately 1.15 hours. I can't remember the last time I had felt this level of happiness. Paul told me that it had been decided following my overdose that going home for the day and seeing Jake would be good for me. I could not agree more. I could not believe I was going to see Jake again. I wondered how he was coping, what was the children's home he was in like? Had he made friends? Were they bullying him? I had so many questions buzzing around inside my head I thought it might explode there and then!

On arrival at mother's house, I was both nervous and excited, as I did not know what sort of reception I was going to receive. However, as it turned out my mother greeted me well and we all went inside. I immediately looked around for Jake, "Mum where's Jake?" I asked. "Jake could not be here today Amelia," she replied.

My whole insides felt like they were sinking. I was devastated.

"But why?" I begged.

"It was decided at the last minute it would be in both your interests." There were those words again, "in our interest" I was tired of hearing those words over the years, and what did they know about our interest? Paul sat down and mother rallied round like the perfect mother, making tea, then unexpectedly, she invited Paul to stay for dinner, it would be just the three of us. I thought this was a bit strange but went along with it anyway. The day was to be not as bad as I had thought it might be. We had a traditional Christmas dinner, mother had a few presents under the tree for me, and there were also some presents under the tree for Jake too. My mother made an effort that day. She was pleasant and jovial. Paul and my mother got on extremely well and I noticed a spark between them, which made me feel uncomfortable.

I asked mother about Kieran, and she told me they were separated now and that she had not seen him for a few weeks. She was making another one of her fresh starts. The day passed by smoothly without a bad word said between us, partly due to the fact that my mother was preoccupied with Paul; I was not in the least bit happy at this turn of events. I just hoped they were being friendly what with it being Christmas day. I buried myself in a book for most of the afternoon.

When it was time to go I said goodbye to my mother and climbed into the van. Paul stood for a while talking to my mother then followed me into the van. On the way back he was very chatty, asking me questions about my mother. It was clear to me she had charmed him. Following that day a brief affair developed between my mother and Paul, which was not good news as he had been good to me since my arrival at Bryn Tyn and was not someone who deserved to be drawn into mother's world of deceit. As usual, their time together was not to be everlasting and when mother did not get her way, it turned rather nasty and once again, I was used as a weapon in her quest to get him into trouble.

Following the end of their brief affair, which Paul had ended due to wanting to save his marriage, my mother decided she did not want him to be my key worker anymore.

Therefore, she embarked on a cruel mission set to almost ruin his career. She made a complaint to the head of Bryn Tyn Hall insisting that he be removed as my key worker due to inappropriate statements apparently made by Paul to my mother, insinuating that he had an interest in me other than that of a key worker.

She could not just walk away and accept that it was all over, she had to make my life harder and more difficult in the process. Paul was due to go off on long-term leave anyway for a heart bypass in the near future, so they said that was why I was assigned a new key worker going forward. I was devastated, as I really liked Paul and he had been my key worker for nearly two years.

I was assigned a female key worker. Paul was off work for a long time - nearly six months - and on his return, he was very different towards me. This brief affair between my mother and Paul did not make things any easier for me in care at all; the other members of staff were aware of this too and they had all stuck by Paul. Thankfully, mother's claims were not taken seriously, nevertheless this had affected my friendship with Paul. Why did her mistakes have to affect me so much? This was always the case, why did she always use me as a battering ram for everything? This was something I had come to expect when things did not work out for her. I was quiet for a long while and spent a lot of time in my room, writing poetry. I found solace in writing; I could put all my feelings down in a way that made sense to me. I loved writing so much and this was to be my way of escaping going forward. One thing I had promised myself, I will never be like my mother. I will never turn out like her and decided then that when I was in charge of my own destiny I would make something of my life.

I will not become a statistic. These thoughts started to lift me out of myself slowly and I spent a lot of time reading and writing poems in my journal as a way to escape my miserable existence.

Once again, I started working hard to earn something called "Trust" an initiative set up by the staff for the best-behaved and most helpful children. This would mean more pocket money and more privileges going forward. I desperately wanted to be moved to the Ainsley unit within Bryn Tyn; I would then have my own room and would no longer have to share a dormitory with lots of others. I would finally have the privacy I had begun to crave so much.

Eventually, I earned the "Trust" award and was very delighted. This meant I was able to walk outside of the grounds unattended to the shop in Llay village once a week if I wanted to. I was also moved to the Ainsley unit and given my own room. Earning the "Trust" also meant on Saturdays, when we were taken into Wrexham Town in the blue and white van to spend our pocket money, which we had earned from doing chores, I was able to wander around the shops with a friend without a member of staff for an hour or two.

Mary and Sue thought this was fantastic; for a couple of hours a week we felt like any normal teenager shopping around town. We would buy things to make our rooms look pretty - posters or plaques; we liked to buy make up from the chemist or pop into the local café and have a cup of tea.

I was 13 going on 14, and I was very interested in all things girly, clothes, makeup, and I had developed a liking for shoes! I used to observe what all the other teenagers my age were wearing on a Saturday and longed to be able to dress like them, and look like them, as to me they were all perfect. We had very few clothes in care that were kept in a small locker room, and they had to last a very long time. We were bought one pair of shoes per year and had a very small clothing allowance for the necessities. Thankfully, I had a few more than the others due to the hand-me-downs given to me by Yvonne, but there was nothing like picking your own clothes from a shop rail.

Theft was rife in care, if you had anything worth stealing it would be taken; none of us had too many belongings really. This was something we were all used to and all had in common. Once or twice a year a hairdresser was hired to come onto the premises and cut all our hair, we were allowed to choose our own haircut. Mine was always a classic bob; I liked my bob not to mention it was very easy to manage.

Some of the wilder children would have punk hairstyles and use their pocket money to buy crazy colored hair dye, like bright pink or orange! Many of the children smoked too and this was also allowed once you hit 14-years-of-age. At this age you were officially allowed to smoke but you had to buy your own cigarettes out of the pocket money you earned from your chores each week.

I had a regular job cleaning the large games hall every night after it was closed for the day at 8:00 p.m. I would have to sweep the floor, take out the rubbish, and make sure it was tidy, oh and ensure the Space Invader machines were turned off! I did this from Monday to Friday and earned myself £5.00 per week; that was a huge amount of money to me and I could do an awful lot with it too.

For a while, things were calm. I was more settled and more accepting of my fate. One day seemingly merged into the next for a while.

Then before I knew it my 14th birthday was upon me, another year another tick, just two more years to go then I am out of here, to where? Remains a mystery. This was a thought I often had during the time I was a ward-of-the-state I knew I had to remain in their care until the age of 16. My mother was not allowed to have any of her children home before the ages of 18, when they were adults, and then it would be up to us what we wanted to do. This was not an issue with me, as I knew I would never go home; I could not imagine a worse fate. I had dreams of going to night school, passing all my exams, and having a career. I never wanted to be poor again. I wanted to travel the world; one particular place at the top of my list was the Valley of the Kings. I did not want my adult life to be steeped in poverty or misery. Securing my own home was at the top of my list. It became so important, as I wanted a place that I could call home, a place that was all mine, no one else's. I wanted to make something of myself; I wanted to see the world outside of the grey walls I was living in.

I wanted to fly on a huge plane, and see the world from high up in the sky – I had so many dreams, and my heart would skip a beat just thinking about them. I had just two more years to go, what would happen then was anyone's guess. Yet again, my birthday slipped by unnoticed. I did not receive a card from my mother. My Social Worker had advised me that she was back with Kieran and her life was full of arguments, fights, and injunctions yet again. Christmas was a week away and I was to spend the whole of Christmas at Bryn Tyn. This year I was not too bothered, as I had made many good friends who were also in the same boat. The Bryn Tyn staff did their best to make

Christmas day a bit more special for the few of us that remained behind. Cook had produced a great feast for lunch, we were all given a present, and we spent the afternoon watching videos of our choice - all in all it could have been a lot worse.

Life in Ainsley unit was easier and more independent. We were given more of a free rein; even relationships between the teenagers were not discouraged, and there were a few. They used to take off down the field together for some private time and anything else they could get away with. The Bryn Tyn fields were huge and if a couple wanted some privacy it wasn't hard to find in the vast grounds.

I was not interested in a boyfriend at all, although I had become rather close to one particular boy, Robbie, who was older than me. Very tall and very good looking, he always watched out for me and sought me out wherever I was. We used to play fight all the time, but he never tried to take it any further and cross that line, despite making it clear that he really liked me.

I remember one day I was ill with a bad cold and stayed in bed all day. Robbie sneaked into the kitchen and made me chocolate spread sandwiches while the cook was on her break, and all day he popped in and out to check if I was okay. We were very close but never in a sexual way, although if I had given him any sign of being interested, I was sure he would have jumped at the opportunity!

There were often fights between the boys over the girls. If one boy liked a girl and another started flirting with them all hell would break loose, and a fight would take place. This was very common; the girls would stand back and watch while the staff on duty at the time would do their best to break up the fights.

The school was on the premises and consisted of 10 portakabins all clustered together at the back of the games room. From Monday to Friday, we were all called for assembly at 9:00 a.m., which took place in the games room. Our names would be called out from a register and then we would each make our way to our designated classroom. Lessons were very easy and the tasks set out before us were quite simple, I thought. Our lessons consisted of basic teachings, which would have been better suited for primary aged children; they were not challenging enough at all. However, at least it was better than nothing. All children left without any qualifications whatsoever; Bryn Tyn just did not have the means to cater for examinations or the preparation for them. All the teachers were part-time, some offered their time voluntarily, some were hired from local schools in the area to work part-time as and when they could.

Many of the tougher kids from Brixton were very disruptive in class and made it very hard for any of us to read or write - the teachers could not control them at all and in most cases feared them. They would throw objects of any kind at anyone attempting to learn something. You just had to keep those children happy or they could make life very uncomfortable for you after school. After all, it wasn't like we all went our separate ways to our nice families and nice homes after school; we all lived together 24 hours a day. If someone wanted to make your day a tough one, there was not always enough staff on duty to run to or to help you. The best way to get through your days was to not stand out in any way, shape, or form. If you were smelly, you would be bullied; if you looked different, you would be bullied;

if you were a grass and you were found out, then your life would be a very tough one. If you were well behaved, you would be picked on; occasionally, there would be the odd riot for one reason or another and if you did not join in you would know about it. All in all you could never do right for wrong by someone's eyes. If you were to do right by one person, then this act would annoy another. You had to be pretty quick and very clever to survive your time in care and come out the other end intact.

One day we were all informed of a new arrival. A girl called Josie, a similar age to me was being sent from another children's home far away. Josie arrived much later in the day. She was tall and feisty and as I learned over time, she was hilarious. I took to her immediately. We soon became good friends and were to become inseparable in the days that followed. Josie was the confident one out of the two of us, and a force to be reckoned with.

She was great and life became a lot more eventful once she had arrived. Josie was a breath of fresh air and I really liked her, she made me laugh all the time. Josie and I were always getting up to mischief after lights were out and the remaining members of staff who were on night duty were settled in the staff room, writing their daily reports. This is when we would sneak out of our bedrooms and make our way to the kitchen at the end of the long wide corridor. This required some skill on our part as the kitchen was always locked; however, we had mastered the art of picking the old locks inside the building, all that was needed was a hair clip and we were home dry! One of us would keep lookout while the other picked the lock. Once we were in the kitchen we would make ourselves a midnight feast to be proud of, quite often the other children would sneak into the kitchen to join us. We always had a two-hour window before it was time for the night watchmen to complete their rounds – these were performed every two hours throughout the night until the morning staff came on duty. During this time, we would all feed our tummies until we were bursting and then we would lock the kitchen up again and make our way to one of the girl's rooms for a chat.

If ever we got caught, which was fairly often we would be punished and put on short term scrubs for a couple of days, with all privileges taken away. Scrubs were not so bad during the summer months. Donned in the custom shorts and t-shirts and lace-less plimsolls, we would sweep all the yards during the day, not be allowed to watch a movie before bed, and we were not allowed to eat with the other children at meal times.

I had become quite familiar with the routine of scrubs, as I often ran away and was always caught. I would be brought straight back and, of course placed on scrubs.

Josie and I were always running away from Bryn Tyn and on one occasion, we managed to make our way to Liverpool to Josie's Aunt's house, but we were soon to be returned to Bryn Tyn. Our punishment this time was one whole month on kitchen duty; however, we had other plans. Within a week we had runaway again; this time to Shropshire to my mother's in the hope that she would listen to my request to see Jake again. We hitched a lift from a passing lorry driver who was kind enough to drop us off in Shropshire and share his sandwiches along the way.

Once we reached my mother's house we were greeted with a very shocked mother who fed us then called the children's home to inform them we had arrived at her house.

A couple of hours later, we were picked up by a member of staff who made it quite clear we were in big trouble. Josie and I sat in the back of the van on the way back whispering to each other about our fate on our return. Josie and I were kindred spirits - we got each other, we totally understood each other, we thought alike and had the same sense of humour. She made my days happier because she was so funny and we were always getting up to something! We always looked out for one another and had each other's back all the time.

We finally reached Bryn Tyn and were escorted straight into the office for another reprimand. As usual, we were stripped of our privileges, which by now were not many due to the number of times we had runaway!

We were to be put on scrubs for two weeks, no pocket money and meals were to be taken separate from everyone else, no trips into town at the weekend, and no possibility of earning extra money either. All in all, we were just scrubbing the floors for the next two weeks in a pair of shorts and t-shirt. Once we completed our punishment, we were back on normal privileges, except "trust" we would not have this privilege for a very long time. We stayed put for a while and tried to blend into the background. I often wondered how I would be living my life if I had been born into a normal loving family. I wondered about the family holidays, the Christmas get-togethers, the family gatherings, all the things I still longed for, but knew this was never to be.

This was all I knew, life within the confines of the care-system. After a while you become institutionalised, although you dream of a life outside in the world, you also become to fear it, you start to feel differently, you feel as if everybody can tell just by looking at you that you are from a children's home. You worry about their immediate judgment of you. Most people just assume you must have done something wrong, or they keep a safe distance from you. The truth is that most children in care homes are there for their own safety, and then sadly abused by the very people that are there to protect them. I had suffered with bouts of depression throughout my time in the care homes.

One day I would just wake up smothered by a choking black cloud, my abyss. I would feel so low that it often brought me to near suicide, I would feel total despair.

I could not understand why it would be such a bad thing at times; after all, living in a world without love for most of your life would inevitably affect anyone eventually. I was a teenager now, 14-years-old, and all I had known was one children's home after another. Some were bad and some not so bad, but these places all had one thing in common; they were all filled to the brim, near bursting in fact, with desperate children all wanting the love and attention from someone. All wanted to be seen and all wanted to be heard. The truth was every child in care has a desperate story to tell, filled with sadness and rejection, abuse and violence. We all wanted to be noticed. when a member of staff talks to you and listens to you for a while or shows a little compassion towards you, it's fair to say you will then shadow that person like a dog trying everything they can to please their master.

And I was no different; I would latch on to a member of staff that showed me any kindness like my life depended on it.

When I was shrouded in depression, I would write poems - lots of them. I was able to communicate very well how I was feeling on paper; this helped me so much during my darkest days. One particular poem I wrote went like this:

When my destiny is in my hands,
I promise to appreciate all of my life.
When my destiny is in my hands,
I promise never to cause any strife.

When my destiny is in my hands,
I promise to love and appreciate my friends.
When my destiny is in my hands,
I promise to be true until the end.

When my destiny is finally in my own hands
the first thing for me is to travel the land.

One particular day, I was in the games room playing table tennis with another boy and in walked my archenemy, Donna. She was bored and decided it would be great fun to pick on me and embarrass me in front of the other children. I decided to walk out and ignore her, which was the only way to deal with her, except this time she followed me.

I ran into Ainsley unit to find safety amongst the staff but I could not see any. I shouted at her to leave me alone but she just ignored me, and started jumping on me, thumping me in the head. I let her do her worst and then ran to my room sobbing, before she left me she warned me not to grass on her or I would receive more of the same.

The Great Escape

I told my new friends Liam and Paul what had happened as they would often fall prey to her bullying ways too, and it was then when they told me they had been planning to escape and run away. They invited me to join them and I jumped at the chance. Liam was from Shropshire like me, so we decided to walk all the way to Shropshire from Bryn Tyn following the river seven and the A5. We waited for a couple of days until it was the weekend as there was always less staff on duty at the weekends, which made it a lot easier to escape. We had all packed our runaway kit, which consisted of crisps, chocolate, a can of pop, some fruit, and our pocket money. This time it was going to be different - we were not going to get caught. We were not going to run to anybody we knew, we were going to survive alone and find somewhere to live once we arrived in Shropshire.

On the Saturday morning after breakfast, we went to collect our weekly pocket money. We told the staff that we were going to play by the stream at the end of the fields by the woods. We went to our rooms, collected our bags, dressed accordingly in preparation for our long journey and then we all met down by the stream. We were all very excited and knew we would be in a lot of trouble if we were caught this time as they had started coming down hard on runaways.

Once we were all present, we just looked at each other and started running, all the while laughing with excitement. We crossed the wide stream, climbed up the bank on the other side, and followed the track through the woods until we reached the main road. We found our way to the river seven and started walking towards Shropshire - we all knew the way, we had all run away many times and then made the return journey by car silently just staring at the signs on the way back. It was a warm summers day and after a few miles we stopped for lunch and sat along the riverside eating our crisps, we then decided it would be great fun to go swimming in the river, so we all stripped down to our underwear and splashed about in the river for the longest time. Eventually we all climbed out again and lay down on the grass to dry off.

After some time we started walking again, we were singing along the way totally oblivious to everything around us including the police car up ahead on the main road, which had pulled over. The two police officers had already climbed out of their car and were heading straight towards us; it was Liam that spotted them,

"*Run for it*," he shouted.

We all looked up, spotted the men in blue, and started running like we had never run before. We soon lost them and slowed down to a walking pace to catch our breath. By this time, we knew it would not be long before nighttime set in so we started looking for somewhere to bed down for the night, after a mile or so we spotted a farm up ahead with quite a few out houses attached. We decided to check it out as this looked to be the perfect place for the night.

As we approached the farm we were very careful not be seen and raise an alarm, we bent down and ran under the window of the farmhouse which appeared to be empty; I peered through the window and could not see anyone. We walked around to the back of the farmhouse and saw that the back door to the kitchen was ajar. We made our way slowly towards the door, looking around all the time in case anyone was coming. We all sneaked into the large country kitchen, it was huge, and there were large pots and pans everywhere. However, what interested us the most was the large uncut loaf on the side and the large plate of cheese – *dinner*, we all thought in unison! We grabbed the bread and cheese and ran out of the back door; we looked around and ran towards one of the three barns situated up ahead. We chose the barn furthest away and with a good view so we could see who was coming at any time from most directions. We all slipped in through the barn door, which consisted mostly of bales of hay, perfect just perfect. We all put our bags down and made ourselves comfortable. The only thing we did not have was water or a drink of any kind. One of us would have to go back to the farmhouse and fetch some water or milk from the fridge.

Liam was the eldest and volunteered, thank goodness, as I was far too scared, and knowing my luck, I would be caught.

Liam made his way back to the farmhouse. He was nearly at the back door when a large pot bellied man came walking around the corner. Liam acted very quickly and ducked down behind the tractor, waiting while the man walked towards the field which kept at the very least 40 sheep.

Paul suddenly spoke in a panic, "*Amelia look over there.*"

A woman was approaching the tractor and Liam had not seen her. "Oh no, what are we going to do now?" I said. Then all of a sudden, Liam rolled under the tractor just in time as the woman walked past and into the farmhouse.

"*Phew that was lucky,*" said Paul.

"*Yes quite,*" I replied, we allowed ourselves to breathe again.

Liam stayed under the tractor for over 30 minutes, until the woman came back out again, and then he ran into the farmhouse kitchen and back out again in quick time, armed with a full bottle of milk and a packet of biscuits. We were very proud of him. We each sat on a bale of hay and ate our sumptuous dinner of bread, cheese, and biscuits, washed down with some fresh cold milk. As dusk crept up on us, we looked around the barn for a safe place to sleep where we would not be seen. We all agreed on climbing the ladder to the floor above and sleeping at the very back under the hay. It was warm and out of sight and that was all we needed.

The following morning we all stood up, and we shook ourselves free of all the hay that was imbedded just about everywhere.

We finished off the remaining bread and cheese from the night before and then set off once more on our journey. Again, we chose to follow the line of the river, as for the most part we were out of sight of the main road. This was now day two of our great escape and we were all feeling very proud of ourselves. We followed the river all day, until we all agreed it was now safe enough to climb up on to the main road and carry on towards Shrewsbury. We had accomplished half of our journey already; it was the weekend and no one would think it strange that a small group of 14-year-olds were walking along the roadside. We took advantage of this and continued on our way.

We were all feeling rather hungry again as the last meal we had eaten was at breakfast. My tummy had been rumbling for over an hour already. Just up ahead we could see a garage, which also sold sweets and crisps. Without any discussion, we upped our pace and headed straight towards the busy garage. We stocked up on crisps, pop, chocolate, and the boys bought 10 John Player special cigarettes, as they were both smokers and had not had a smoke all day. We parked ourselves on a wall, re-fuelling our hungry tummies.

Liam made a suggestion and thought it would be a great idea if we thumbed a lift for the rest of the way. I was not at all keen on the idea and told the boys that I will be walking all the way to Shropshire no matter what, and continued to remind them of the dangers that could befall you if you thumbed a lift. This was enough of a deterrent and it was agreed we would continue to walk the last leg of our journey. As we approached Shrewsbury Town, we were all feeling rather tired and weary so decided that we would stay in the town for the night.

Where we would all sleep was anyone's guess. We started looking around for empty shops and vacant buildings. We must have circled half the town before we happened upon an old derelict building, which sported a great huge DANGER sign all over it. None of us questioned the immediate danger this building could place us in; we just saw this as our only hope for a place to sleep for the night.

We all tugged at the corrugated iron sheets which were nailed tight over the window, and when we had pulled it back far enough for us to fit through, we each carefully climbed through the hole and made our way into the large dank room that greeted us. The room was filthy; there were already a couple of old dirty mattresses lying on the floor nevertheless, we decided to investigate upstairs as it could not possibly be any worse.

As we made our way up the broken steps, we were mindful of treading carefully or we could end up with a broken leg or two. As we neared the top, we could hear a rustling sound coming from the other end of the building. We all stopped dead in our tracks, not knowing whether to carry on or to make a run for it. We stayed like that for a few seconds, then Liam decided he would investigate and told Paul and me to stay put. He quietly made his way up the last couple of steps and then he was out of sight. All we could hear was Liam walking around and the floorboards creaking. Then we could hear talking. Liam shouted down to us to come up that everything was okay. We climbed to the top and made our way to the back of the building Liam was talking to a rather scruffy man, who smelt very bad. The few teeth he owned were either black or cracked, he had on a long dirty grey coat, which was covered in stains and looked like it had never been cleaned.

He had made himself at home on the top floor of the building with an old chair, an old mattress, and some old blankets. He had a few meager belongings in a brown box and that was it, this was his home for now. He went on to explain that he was one of life's wanderers, he liked the open road, and spent his life moving from one place to another, and taking advantage of any opportunity that came his way.

Liam told him our story and that we needed somewhere to stay for the night, that this old building seemed perfect if it was okay with him. The vagrant looked all three of us up and down, then mumbled to himself for a while, and finally agreed we could share the building for the night. I could not sleep that night, I did not feel safe and kept one eye on the vagrant at all times, although I had no real reason to fear him. He was far more interested in the bag of chips he had begged from the chip shop down the road just before it closed.

The following morning we all got up early, straightened ourselves out and then decided to start on our journey once more. We said goodbye to the grumpy vagrant who just mumbled as we made our way down the stairs. When we found our way out of the window and onto the street, we looked at each other and I spoke first, "I'm starving. Liam let's get some breakfast." Liam and Paul agreed and we all pooled our money together and we had the grand total of £7, so we needed to make it last. There was a café across the road and we hurried towards it as our empty stomachs were crying out for food. We all took a seat and waited for the woman to come over. She was very chirpy and waited patiently while we counted out our money and then decided on our order; we all chose a sausage and egg sandwich accompanied by a mug of tea. The woman smiled and took our order, she said, "There's no need to pay until afterwards."

We were to make our way up to the till and pay once we had all finished. Liam suggested we make a run for it, "This would be so easy let's just run." I was not so keen; however, I understood that this would save us at least £3, so that was that, decision made.

After we had finished our breakfast we waited for the woman to go out back into the kitchen, and then we made a run for it. I felt very bad about not paying because the woman was so nice to us, but our need to eat and survive while we were all on the run was tantamount to us getting through each day. We needed to be frugal with what little money we had left and we needed to seize every opportunity that arose. There was nothing worse than being hungry, and I had experienced this feeling on several occasions.

Now our bellies were full to the brim! We knew we would be able to walk for miles quite happily. As we were leaving Shrewsbury Town near the Sears Hall building, we noticed a car slowing down up ahead. It was not a police car so we carried on walking towards it. As we approached it, two men got out. They called out our names and it was then that we realised they were plain-clothed police officers. We just turned on our heels and ran; Paul tripped over and only just escaped the long arm of the law!

We had no idea where we were when we finally stopped. We looked around and could not see any signs, just fields everywhere we looked. It was a very beautiful sight, they were like green and brown blankets covering the earth all laid out in neat squares like a patch work quilt. We all sat down for a while to catch our breath.

"Amelia, do you have any idea where we are?" Liam asked.

"I have no idea Liam, I suggest we pop into that little shop and ask them," I replied.

We headed over to the shop, and I took it up on myself to ask for directions to Shropshire. The woman advised me we were already in Shropshire and asked where specifically we were headed. I told her Iron Bridge. "Ah, that's not too far I'd say about 10 miles from here."

We were all so happy; we had nearly made it to Iron Bridge. I could not believe it, we had walked all the way from North Wales and we were on the home stretch now, this information boosted our moral and we picked up our pace. We bounced along with a kick in our step singing songs along the way. We were on home territory now and it felt good to be in familiar surroundings.

Eventually, after three hours or so, we reached our destination and made our way to the estate we were all too familiar with.

We decided to squat in one of the boarded up council houses (and there were many). We were careful not to be seen by someone who just may recognise us. We went in search of an empty house. After what seemed like an eternity, we found one just beyond the community centre and it was just perfect for now; the important thing for all of us was having somewhere to stay, somewhere we could hide out, somewhere we felt safe. We pulled back one of the boards on the downstairs window and climbed in. Unusually, it was quite clean. There was an old settee sitting in the middle of the living room, the floors still had carpets on them albeit old and a bit musty, but it was more than we had hoped for. There could be any number of reasons why this house was unoccupied? However, that was not our concern. We had a place to stay and that was all that mattered.

We put our bags down and Liam volunteered to fetch us all a bag of chips, which would keep us going until the morning. Then we hatched a plan to wake up with the larks and do a doorstep sweep after the milkman had delivered his goods to all the tenants.

The following morning, Paul and I were up first so we got dressed and slipped out of the window leaving Liam fast asleep. We headed to the row of houses opposite and ran from door-to-door lowering our heads as we sneaked past the kitchen windows. We were loaded with goods on the run back to the house with lots of bread, milk, yogurts, and cheese, just enough food and milk for the next couple of days at least. As far as cash goes, we were left with a grand total of £3, which was enough for another round of chips if we got desperate during the week.

We were all sitting down on the floor in the house talking about our hopes and dreams for the future. Liam was the older one at just 15, whereas Paul and I were 14-years-old. Liam was pretty quiet really. He smiled a lot and did not say too much, he was a thinker. Paul was a comedian and was always joking, and me, well, I was just in a hurry to be an adult, as being a child was far too hard.

I talked about my brother and sisters and how we were all separated several years back. Liam talked about how his father used to beat him badly, and Paul didn't talk about his past at all, only that he could not wait to officially leave Bryn Tyn. We were all in agreement with Paul on that score. We all hated it for the most part; however, strangely enough there were some good times too. Josie and I had a great time getting up to mischief all the time, but when things were bad, they could be intolerable in a place like that.

Unknown to us all while we were all having our heart-to-heart over our sumptuous breakfast, we had been spotted by one of the tenants from over the road, one of the ones we had stolen the bread from. She had watched us climb into the house, then went and called the police. Before we knew it or could act accordingly, there were two police cars outside shouting at us to come out. We could not believe it, after everything we had been through the last couple of days, not to mention the marathon walk we accomplished without thumbing a lift once. We knew we were done for so all climbed out of the window. The police officer was very nice and asked us to get in the car. We told them our names and once they had checked them a red flag came up, and they looked at us saying that there were police all over Shropshire searching for us. Again, we were told how lucky we were as there are a lot of unsavoury people about and we could have landed ourselves in serious trouble. We admitted to taking the bread and milk and explained we only did this because we were hungry and did not have enough money to purchase the goods.

We were taken directly to the local police station, and put in a holding cell until our Social Workers arrived. They gave us dinner and even let the two boys smoke. Because we were listed as runaways, we had to answer a few questions about the last two days: where we had been, had anything happened to us and were we all in good health as far as we knew.

One of the Policemen was kind; he sympathised with us and seemed to understand why we had runaway. He gave us a few pearls of wisdom and said, "You don't have too long left in care now, why don't you just try and keep your heads down and get through it?"

We all looked at him and said nothing. Only someone who was not subjected to our life in care could suggest such a thing. Times just got too hard to bear, we were children, and we felt like we had no one or nothing.

My Social Worker arrived first, then the other two arrived shortly afterwards. It was decided that my Social Worker would drive us all back to Wales. After a briefing at the station, we all left and started the long journey back to Wales. I was really scared now, as I knew we were really in for it on our return, they would be pleasant enough in front of my Social Worker, but once she had left, it would be scrubs for us three once again. None of us spoke a word during the whole journey. My Social Worker put on an old radio station that was cranking out country and western songs, and I don't think any of us heard the songs really. We also knew that we would all be separated on our arrival and that was also part of the punishment - being kept away from your friends. I had that awful sinking feeling again that I had felt so many times before; I dreaded the thought of scrubs and not being able to mix with everyone else. I knew I would have all my privileges stripped once more, but this time I had my bedroom to lose as well. I knew I would probably be put back in a dorm or at the very least a shared room. One thing I did know for sure my "Trust" status would have been removed. That I did deserve to lose, but if only they had listened to me more often then maybe, just maybe, I could have coped better and not runaway so often. You had to be quite tough to survive in care, and I was just not feeling tough enough. I now hated everything that "Trust" represented. This meant we were given a tad more freedom, and I mean a tad. Unlike most teenagers of the same age on the outside, we were hidden away from society under the blanket of the care-system, we were unable to roam freely on a Saturday around town with our friends, we were not allowed outside of the premises unaccompanied by a member of staff. If we had "Trust" status this just allowed us an hour of freedom in the small town of Wrexham on a Saturday morning and not totally out of sight from the member of staff in charge. "Trust" to me felt like something a prisoner earned for good behaviour while doing their time to make life a little easier. Not for children in care who were not at fault for the circumstances their parents placed them in. Trust" was just a permanent reminder that we were not free; we were all just caged birds.

    On my return to Bryn Tyn, I was punished far harder than before. I had my single room taken from me, this I had expected. I was placed in a room with Josie, and this I did not mind at all. In fact, I was so surprised that they actually considered this a good idea because now we were even closer day and night, which meant more mischief! I was yet again on scrubs for the umpteenth time, and it had become such a regular part of my life it no longer bothered me. I worked my punishment and again heeded the advice given to me and kept my head down. I finally came to the conclusion that running away was doing me no good whatsoever. No one listened to my complaints, and no one much cared either. I decided to make the most of a bad situation and finally try to settle down. Over the next couple of months I was well behaved, I took part in weekend activities once more and started doing extra chores to earn some money.

We all had to do daily chores to keep our units clean and this was unpaid, however, you could volunteer to do special chores, which could earn you up to £5.00 per week. More new children were admitted into Bryn Tyn, and older children were released from the care-system once they came of age

Bryn Tyn was part of a community of children's homes, and once a year a sports day was organised between the homes and this would usually take place within the Bryn Tyn grounds as this was the largest of all the homes. This was quite a spectacular event and everyone took part. The local news station was invited to cover the event, this was a big show to the outside world to give the impression that all was well with in these homes. All the children loved sports day, there was so much going on, a pop group was hired to sing for a couple of hours, a lot of local people were invited and some of the kid's parents were also invited. A great day would be had by all and no expense was spared. This would appear in the local paper the next day and mentioned on the local news station. The food was always great on sports day, and we all let our hair down and enjoyed a great feast.

Westbrook Hall

I was approaching my 15th birthday; yet another day that would pass me by unrecognised. I started to wonder a lot about what would happen to me as I only had just over 12 months left in the state-care-system. Where would I go, what would I do? The thought started to scare me. I realised there and then that during all those years spent in care I had actually become institutionalised without realising it. I was beginning to feel what many children had felt before me. I did not know what it was like to just be able to do things without asking permission. I mean we even needed permission to access our clothes from the locker room, or to take a bath. We needed permission for all the things most kids just took for granted, I could not imagine a world where I made all my own decisions.

My birthday came and went much like Christmas that year. It was a very harsh and cold winter and some of the staff was snowed in for a couple of days. This was the middle of winter with snow up to your knees in the middle of North Wales. There were real coal fires situated throughout all the units and plenty of coal stacked high in the bunkers outside. We all wrapped up warm and watched videos chosen for us by the staff until the snow started to melt, and cars could once again come in and out of Bryn Tyn.

By the summer of that year, a case review was held over my future and it was decided that I was to be moved for the last and final time. I was to be sent to Westbrook Hall, one of the homes within the Bryn Tyn community, only this one was situated 50-miles away in Shropshire, about 10-miles from where my mother lived. The reason for this, I was told, was because I originally came from Shropshire and they thought it would be best for me to end my days in care, in familiar surroundings. They would try to help me in the search of gainful employment and try their best to find me a place to live when I turned 16, although, they advised me this was not always possible and they may have to place me in a hostel.

All I could think about was one more year, 12 months and counting, and then my destiny would be in my own hands. The world would again be free to me. I would again be able to walk down the street without having to look over my shoulder, take a simple walk in the park on a lazy Sunday afternoon, go for a meal in a restaurant, to watch the latest film perched in the back row of the cinema; all these things I had never experienced before. This seemed so surreal to me, I would not allow myself to believe it until it happened.

About a month later, I said goodbye to Bryn Tyn and sat in the back of my Social Worker's car for the very last time. On arrival at Westbrook Hall, a very stern man, called Phil, greeted me. He was very tall and very wide, and if I didn't know better I swear he did not like children. He pointed in the direction of the office and started walking. Westbrook was an old stately home bought and converted into a children's home by John Allen, the founder of the Bryn Tyn community. It was a white building in acres and acres of land; the driveway itself was half a mile long.

The children in Westbrook were all a lot older than in Bryn Tyn, the youngest being 13-years-old and the oldest 17-years-old. The average age though was 15 years. I was given the usual rules and regulations and told to make sure I adhered to them. Again, schooling was on the grounds of Westbrook hall, and I was told I had only a few months left to attend school and then I would be found a suitable placement with a local firm so I could support myself on leaving Westbrook. It all seemed so cold and clinical. There was no real preparation for your entry into the big wide world, no great guide or words of wisdom to prepare you for the pitfalls you may come up against.

I did not like Westbrook at all, it was full of egotistical men and that was both the staff and the boys residing there. Many of the boys were hardened to their environment and they had come to believe that life had nothing better to offer them. This was evident to me in their attitude on a daily basis. There were few girls at Westbrook, which made things a bit difficult at times as the place was filled with testosterone.

We were all teenagers and the boys thought about sex a bit too much. They were always trying to grab you here and grope you there. It was hard just trying to stay out of their way, and I made sure I was never far away from a member of staff.

One day a couple of months down the line, I was watching TV in the communal area when a group of boys came in looking suspiciously at me. One of the boys closed the door, while suddenly I was jumped on by another. I was being held down with one hand over my mouth, my arms and legs were pinned tight to the floor, and I could not move. I could feel my eyes filling up as my jeans were torn from me, then my knickers. One boy was lifting my top up as another started climbing on top of me. I tried everything I could to wriggle free but my attempt was in vain. The boy on top of me had unzipped his trousers and was just about to rape me, when the door swung open. All the boys jumped up and scampered away, and I was left on the floor scrambling around for my clothes. The staff member told me to get dressed and advised me to stay in my room; he made me feel like I had committed a cardinal sin. I was later called into the office and given some strong advice. I was told that no good would come of any complaint I made, that he had spoken to each of the boys and this would not happen again. They had apparently been severely reprimanded, and that was supposed to have been enough. The whole incident was treated like a bunch of silly boys who knew no better. Two of the boys were 17-years-old, very big and strong. I was made to feel worthless. I had my clothes torn from my body, was violated, but this was to be brushed under the carpet never to be spoken of again.

It was clear to me that the girls had a harder time at Westbrook than the boys.

I settled in as best as I could and I was to sleep in the cottage with the other girls. It was our private place. We still had to eat in the main dining hall and if we wanted to watch television we also had to head over to the main building, but our sleeping quarters were in the cottage.

My 16th birthday was upon me finally and I could see the light at the end of the tunnel. I felt a lot older than my 16-years suggested. I was more than ready to take on the challenge of a new era coming soon into my life, but I was also scared to death. My birthday was celebrated in the cottage amongst the girls, with a cake they had baked for me and two lovely cards they took the time to create for me. It was probably the best birthday I had ever had. It meant so much to me that they had taken the time to make me cards and make me feel special for that one day, I felt very humbled by their kindness. I was to spend Christmas a week later in the cottage with two other girls who also had nowhere to go.

One of the female members of staff brought us a little Christmas tree for us to put up in the cottage, and we all decided to make each other a Christmas present to put under it so we had something to open on Christmas day. I made memory boxes for each one of them out of old boxes. The other two girls Louise and Sarah made little pouches out of felt to act like purses. On Christmas day we were so excited we could not wait to open our presents, there could have been pure gold wrapped up in that

Christmas paper the way we jumped and screamed with delight we were so happy as we were used to so little.

The Norwegians

Christmas that year left us as quickly as it had approached us.

The New Year had arrived and I had only four months remaining at school. The school classes consisted of the usual portakabins for the basic teachings that we received. Fortunately, for me, I had read every book I could lay my hands on during all the years I had spent in care. Books were donated to almost all children's homes from various charities, local libraries, and just kind people wanting to do their bit and for this, I was eternally grateful. I had a thirst for knowledge I just could not quench at these schools, so found some other way to do so. I watched documentaries on television when everyone else was watching cartoons or movies; I read many books on all the subjects possible; and I wrote my poetry as often as I could. I had managed to drag that journal of poems with me throughout all the children's homes I was placed in.

That journal meant everything to me; it carried in it my darkest moments, my pain, and reminded me of the few good times I had too.

One day I was called into the office and the head of Westbrook Hall was sitting there along with my Social Worker. They asked me to take a seat, as they wanted to talk to me regarding my future.

My Social Worker had a couple of ideas she set out before me. "How would you feel about staying with the Norwegian family that lived not far from your mother before she moved Amelia?"

I sat quietly for a while and took my time to process the information. I remembered and liked the Norwegian family and Mrs. Price was especially kind to me on days when my mother would leave me outside all day when I was younger. She would often invite me into her house for a cup of tea and a slice of homemade Norwegian cake, the most sumptuous taste I had ever experienced.

Mrs. Price was married to an English man and had moved over here many years before. She had two boys named Trond and Segour; I used to play with Trond when I lived on the estate, and we were good friends. Mrs. Price had taken me in a few times when mother was either drunk or detained. She was so kind, and strangely enough, I used to think how lovely it would be if she was my mum. I sat and listened to what they said and thought it would be a great idea and a wonderful chance at some semblance of a normal life, something I had only been able to dream about. I was told that the state-care-order remained so until I turned 18-years-old. This meant that my mother had no rights over me as such and could not request that I go home to live with her. I was also informed that my choices were very limited if I turned down the Norwegian family.

They would have no option but to place me in a hostel – an option I detested, having heard about these hostels, and that was not how I envisaged my life starting once my destiny was in my own hands. Therefore, I jumped at that chance to start a new life with the Norwegians. This was not to happen straight away. It was decided that I would go and stay with them every other weekend starting from the spring just after I officially left school.

I was ecstatic; I could not believe something good was actually happening to me. My Social Worker had told me that, Mrs. Price had often inquired about my well-being during my time in care, as she was very fond of me. And that's why they came up with the idea of approaching her about my coming to live with them. Apparently Mrs. Price was overjoyed and agreed straight way. She had two boys, and had always wanted a girl. Therefore, my immediate future was set. I knew where I would be living, and I felt better knowing that my mother had moved on to yet another council estate a couple of years previous.

Spring sneaked up behind me before I knew it, and I had officially left school, if you can call it that. I had a job lined up for me in a fashion house a few miles away, working from Monday to Friday, 9:00 a.m. to 4:30 p.m. with 30 minutes for lunch. The company was called Kiss Kiss Fashions and owned by a Jamaican businessman, who was a lovely first boss to have. I was taken each day to my job in the signature blue and white van sported by all the Bryn Tyn children's homes including Westbrook.

I was of an age where this embarrassed me and I did not want people to know I was in a children's home now. In addition, this big van with Westbrook Children's Home sprawled across it did not help matters one single iota.

My first day at Kiss Kiss was fantastic; I was to start from the bottom and work my way up and was taken to the cutting room. However, I was reminded by the chief cutter, that this was actually one of the most important jobs of all. I watched him draw lines with his white chalk on the beautiful cloth set out on a great huge cutting table. I watched closely as he cut the cloth with a cutting machine and the more delicate edges with special cutting scissors. During my first week, I noticed they were making these beautiful white dresses for a department store and I fell in love with them, not able to stop myself from staring at them hanging up on the rails once they were finished.

One day I took one off the rails and held it up against me. I looked in the tall mirror in front of the mannequins, swishing and twirling around totally oblivious to the fact that I was being observed by the company owner. He looked at me and said, it's a very pretty dress. I had to agree and apologised for taking liberties. He turned to me with an endearing smile on his face and asked me if I would like one. I nearly fell to the floor in shock. He said I think you're at least a size 8, picked a dress off the rail, and handed it to me. Then off he went back into his office and wished me a good evening.

I could not believe it, this was the most amazing piece of clothing I had ever owned and I loved it. I stood outside waiting for the van to collect me, swaying from side to side holding my beautiful dress.

While I was waiting a young boy about my age rode past on his bike, and as he passed me by, he slowed down and smiled. He was so handsome I couldn't help but smile back and I felt my heart skip several beats. He then slowly back peddled towards me and asked me my name.

"My name is Amelia," I replied shyly.

He smiled at me and introduced himself as Damian. He was adorable and I liked him immediately – I had never much thought about boys before really, so this feeling I had was a surprise to me! I had noticed boys of course, but had never paid much attention to them. This time was so different, I was just hoping he would ride away now before the blue and white van turned up to take me back to Westbrook Hall.

I was not granted such good luck and no sooner had the thought passed through my mind than the blue and white van turned up on cue as always. Why it could not have been just a few minutes later on this one occasion? Surprisingly, Damian seemed undeterred and waited until I had climbed into the van and disappeared off into the distance. I stared out of the back window until he was gone from my sight. On my return to Westbrook Hall, I ran straight into the cottage and gushed about Damian to my friend, and she reminded me that I would probably never see him again.

The weekend had arrived and I was to go on my first visit to the Norwegian's house. I was very excited and spent ages getting ready and doing my hair. I had recently started to apply full-face makeup bought using my first weekly wages from Kiss Kiss. My bag was packed and I was all ready to spend the weekend with my new family. I was dropped off by a member of staff, who informed me that I would be picked up at 5:00 p.m. on Sunday evening.

Mrs. Price was waiting for me at the end of the path, put her arms around me, and gave me a very tight hug – this I was not used to at all, but it felt so warm and lovely.

She walked me into the house and everyone was there to greet me. Mrs. Price had baked a Norwegian cake especially for me as she remembered how much I loved them all those years ago. I was shown to my room, which had been decorated, for my arrival the week before. It was lovely, with brand new floral bedding with matching curtains, sliding wardrobes for my clothes – not that I had many, and an old wooden dressing table with a mirror. It was perfect, the most beautiful room I had ever seen and it was all mine.

The weekend was pretty perfect. I felt as though things were finally changing for the better. Mr. Price was very pleasant; he sat in front of the TV, mostly, drinking one or two beers to relax. On the Saturday morning, Mrs. Price took me into town to buy some new clothes for me. I told her I had no money and she smiled at me, and then went on to say that I did not need any money as she was treating me. I was so happy and did not want the weekend to end. On the Saturday night, we all sat together watching "Rocky" the movie. The following morning Mr. Price headed off to his engineering company to do some paperwork while Mrs. Price prepared and cooked a sumptuous Sunday lunch. I helped peel all the vegetables, while her boys were at football training. So this was what having a proper family was like. Although I was very happy, I was also overcome with sadness at the life I never had. All the things I had missed; shopping with your parents, cooking with your mother, everyone gathering around the table at meal times discussing the events of their day.

Such simple normal every day things, but to me they had been so far out of my reach all of my life, and now my childhood was gone I would never have it back.

Mr. Price returned at lunchtime all covered in oil, cursing about one of his workers. He went upstairs to clean up, and then the two boys came in through the back door, teasing each other as they ran up the stairs. Eventually, we all sat down to dinner and Mrs. Price always said grace before anyone could eat. We all tucked into the delightful feast set out before us and no one spoke until we had all finished. Mrs. Price looked up and asked for everyone's attention. "Amelia is now one of the family and I want her to be treated as such," she announces, and everyone clapped their hands, followed by hugs and kisses.

To say this was surreal to me would be an understatement; I was so overwhelmed by love and kindness I was not sure how to deal with it. I felt in very unfamiliar territory, as nice as it was, however, it was too much too soon. I never imagined I would feel this way after so much genuine love was given to me; I simply was not used to it. I needed to be sure that my new family was here to stay, that they were for keeps before I could give over to my emotions, as I knew I could not handle any more rejection. I was picked up and returned to Westbrook that very Sunday evening. I lay quietly in my room trying to imagine what my life would be like once I left Westbrook and the care-system once and for all. My destiny would be in my hands for the first time in my life. I had so many plans buzzing around in my head; I wanted to go to night school and complete all of my O-Levels, and I wanted to go to Business College following receipt of my exam results.

College following receipt of my exam results. This all seemed like a pipe dream, but it was my dream nevertheless – I needed to take those exams so I could take myself forward in the right direction. I will not be a statistic; I will not slip under the radar. I want to be somebody, to prove to everyone no matter how hard your life can be you can still be somebody. This was my dream, all I thought about most of the time, I will be somebody one day – when my destiny is in my own hands, that is when my life will really start.

My friend came into the bedroom to ask about my weekend with the Norwegian's, and I didn't stop talking for at least 30 minutes! Once I came up for air, she smiled and gave me a big hug before suddenly offering some advice; "Be careful Amelia, don't allow yourself to get hurt any more." My friend's words stayed with me; they were powerful words, and she was absolutely right - I would not allow myself to be hurt anymore.

The following morning over breakfast, we were all gathered together in the main house, all the girls and boys sat around in a circle. We were informed that Westbrook Hall was going to have a football match with Telford United Football Club reserves, for the 16 years and under.

It would be a fun day, and there would also be lots of other activities for the girls to get involved with. The football team had kindly volunteered their time following a request from Westbrook Hall. We were all very excited about this and could not wait for the following Saturday. All the girls talked about was what they would wear on the big day, and all the boys talked about for a week was how they were going to kick ass on the football field in Westbrook Hall, where the match would take place. Before the football match took place, I had a visit from my Social Worker. She wanted to update me on my visit with the Norwegian's.

She went on to say that, she had had a meeting with Mr. and Mrs. Price and the weekend was a success. They had totally fallen in love with me and Mrs. Price had gone as far as to say I was like the daughter she'd never had, even her sons were happy about me becoming a new addition to the family. I was so happy, I felt reborn. I felt like this was all a dream, that I would wake up any minute and it would not be real, but it was real and this was happening to me. I felt unworthy of all this happiness that had been bestowed upon me. Remembering my friend's honest words, I was also very wary and all too aware of how good things could be torn away from you in an instant. I was also informed, that by the summer of that year I would be officially released from the state-care-system and handed over to the caring hands of Mr. and Mrs. Price. This all seemed too good to be true and I would not allow myself to believe it until it finally happened. I was asked again if I was happy with the decision to go and live with the Prices in the summer, and I advised my Social Worker that I was extremely happy about it and could not wait for the summer to arrive.

My life was seemingly on the up and I was floating on cloud nine...

Westbrook Hall (Football Event)

The day of the big football match had arrived. All of us girls had made a big effort with ourselves, searching through our clothes to find the best outfit we could and ensuring our make up was applied to perfection. I of course, decided to wear the new white cotton dress I had been given by Kiss Kiss fashion house. I looked at myself in the mirror once I was ready and took a deep breath, this was actually the first time I really saw myself as a young woman, very slim with long dark hair and flawless skin. I liked what I saw and felt very grown up.

The grounds in Westbrook Hall had been transformed into a fete-like affair. There were banners and balloons everywhere, an ice cream van was situated on the drive, and there were long benches laid out side by side for everyone to sit on and observe the game. It looked quite amazing and a lot of people had been very busy earlier that morning to transform the grounds. We all looked out of the window as the coach arrived carrying all the footballers. I actually felt nervous but had no reason to.

The coach parked up and all the boys climbed out. They were a very handsome bunch indeed, and as the last ones stepped out of the coach I instantly recognised one of them; it was Damian, as handsome as I had remembered, looking all athletic and strong in his football kit.

I could feel the butterflies circling inside me. I joined everyone else and started walking to the benches. We all sat down in a line and watched all the footballers while they were doing their pre-match warm-ups. Damian glanced over towards me and winked at me, he then smiled not taking his eyes off me for what felt like an eternity. Even as the match started he kept glancing my way, and throughout the match, we caught each other's eyes frequently. It felt as if he was playing the game for me personally, I could not take my eyes off him. I knew right there and then that he was the one for me, I had never felt like this before and I liked the way I was feeling, a lot!

Once the match had finished (Westbrook Hall had lost), everyone was free to mingle for a short while. Damian made his way straight over to me and smiled, displaying his perfect white teeth. He said he thought I was beautiful and could he see me again - I agreed of course, and we arranged to meet during my lunch break at Kiss Kiss, which was the only time we could meet. My insides felt like they were on a treadmill!

I could not wait for Monday morning to arrive; I made an extra special effort to look nice for work, ready for my lunch-date with Damian. The hours passed by slowly at work that morning and I was willing the clock to speed up. I had never felt so anxious in my life; I kept popping into the ladies to check my face and give myself the once over.

Then it was lunchtime, and I practically ran out of the door! I stood outside of the building staring up the road waiting for Damian to arrive. As promised, he was on time and raced down the road on his pushbike. He had that great big smile on his face again, and he climbed off his bike and for a while, we were both a bit awkward. I could not believe he was giving me the time of day, especially as I was in a children's home. What on earth did he see in me? I thought, surely he could have any girl he wanted.

He asked me how long I had been in Westbrook. I gave him a brief overview of my past and all the time I was talking, he just looked deep into my eyes. I had fallen hook, line, and sinker; he was still interested even knowing I came from nothing, knowing I was still tied to the state-care-system. In fact, he was totally undeterred by it all, and this just made me want him even more.

He told me he was a semi-professional footballer and his dreams were to make it big one day so everyone knew his name. He came from a good solid family and had several brothers and a sister. He told me he had to go as he was football training and asked if we could meet at the same time the next day. He never tried to kiss me or assume he could, he just smiled that great big beautiful smile and pedaled off down the road. My stomach was doing summersaults, and I almost felt dizzy with excitement. I could not stop thinking about this beautiful boy that had noticed me and wanted to get to know me, I was in seventh heaven. I met Damian most lunchtimes. We got closer and closer as we talked about our lives, hopes, and dreams; strangely enough, our dreams were not too different.

He was obsessed with his dream of becoming a premier league football player and was already making it happen. He told me that he had been scouted already and I was so proud of him. I was adamant I was going to be somebody one day too! Our relationship was a very innocent one to start with, he was such a gentleman and I was falling in love with him.

The summer appeared very quickly. I had spent the last few months totally consumed by Damian; I lived for the next time I would see him again, spending endless hours after work lying on my bed thinking about him. I had just one week left in Westbrook Hall; it felt so surreal that my release date was finally here; I had spent years and years dreaming of this moment, it always seemed so far away, so far out of my reach, but here I was preparing to leave once and for all.

When the day finally arrived, my Social Worker came to pick me up and sign me out of Westbrook Children's Home for the very last time. My small bag was packed and I hugged and kissed the girls goodbye. The head of Westbrook Hall sat me down to impart some pearls of wisdom before I departed. He told me to be careful, that I was a very pretty young woman and there were people out there that will try to take advantage of me. "You will be very vulnerable out there in the big world, so please, take care, Amelia." I listened and nodded, but to be honest I could not wait to go through the gates for the last time. I hopped into my Social Worker's car ready for the short drive to Mr. and Mrs. Price's house to start the beginning of my new life. I felt like I was dreaming – it was one of those "pinch myself to be sure it was all real" moments. I had informed Damian of my release date and we had agreed to meet the following weekend in the town centre;

my first date as a completely free woman. Amelia now owned Amelia and not the state, not Bryn Tyn, not Westbook Hall, not Colton Hall, and not Breeton House. Amelia owned Amelia; I said it over and over again in my head to make myself believe it.

Broken Trust

As we approached, Mr. and Mrs. Price were standing at the end of their road, waiting eagerly for my arrival; I took a deep breath and now believed it was all real: this was actually happening to me. I climbed out of the car and was greeted by the biggest hug I had ever received from Mrs. Price, she held me so tight I thought I might break!

Mr. Price greeted me with a big smile and said welcome home. We all went into the house where the two boys, Trond, and Segour, were waiting and they welcomed me with open arms and referred to me as sister. Everything was just perfect, almost too perfect, really. After my Social Worker said goodbye for the very last time, I knew I had entered the world finally without the restrictions placed up on me under the care-system. This felt great – no, more than great - it felt amazing; it was a surreal moment in my life. I was asked to go upstairs and look in my room as a house gift had been placed there for me from the whole family. I entered my bedroom and closed the door.

I looked towards my bed and there was a lovely large box with a pink ribbon in the centre set out in a bow. I pulled the ribbon loose and opened the box. I gasped in amazement at my new beautiful red coat. It was the most beautiful coat in the whole world; there was also a pair of jeans, a red sweater, and some socks and knickers. There was also a smaller box and on opening it I almost stopped breathing for a split second, as displayed in a beautiful black velvet box sat a silver Saint Christopher pendant, the patron saint of travelers, a good luck charm to guide you on your travels through your life. I sat down on my bed and finally was overcome with emotion. I broke down in tears and once I started, I could not stop.

Mrs. Price, who I was to call Torwen going forward, opened the door and came to sit down beside me. She held my hands so tight with tears in her eyes and told me I had nothing to fear anymore, that she would always be there for me. I loved her already, she was like the mother I never really had and always wanted. She wiped my eyes and informed me we were all going out to dinner to celebrate my arrival.

Over the next week, I settled in very well. Torwen worked nights for a local company down the road, which was within walking distance. I still worked at Kiss Kiss Fashion House but my apprenticeship was coming to an end, sadly. They informed me I had been a great apprentice and learned very quickly; however, there was not a permanent position available as they were already over-staffed. I was informed if one came up in the future I would be the first on the list. Torwen and Jason were very sympathetic and told me not to worry.

I was fretting over not being able to pay Torwen the £20.00 a week house keeping I had agreed to. She advised me it was one of those things and something else would come along.

I enrolled myself into night school, as it was so important to me to complete my exams. I wanted my O-Level certificates to take me forward and to prove to myself I could do them. I applied for a job in a local office as a junior, and was to start the following Monday - this had been a stroke of luck which I was very grateful for.

I was not to see Torwen very often from there on as she worked nights and I worked days. Jason was always home in the evenings; he would sit down after a hard day running his engineering company with a couple of beers and the remote control in hand.

One particular night I was sat down on the sofa watching a history documentary on the holocaust. I had not noticed Jason sidling up to me on the sofa until he placed his hand on my knee. He startled me and I jumped nervously. He was tipsy, his eyes were bloodshot, and he was breathing all over me, and he kept saying he just wanted a cuddle. I felt sick to my stomach, I ran out of the room and straight upstairs. I stayed in my room until morning and could not wait to get out of the house. Why me? Why Jason, a man I respected and looked up to? This just cannot be happening. I would not allow myself to believe it. At dinner time, this was the only time we were all together, I slowly made my way to the kitchen and then Jason pulled me into the living room and went on to warn me not to say a word to Torwen. He had made a mistake and did not know what he was doing, and finally, his last words reverberated right through me, "Torwen would never believe you anyway, a girl who spent her whole life in care, against her husband, no she would not believe you Amelia, so I am warning you, if you like it here and want to stay, then just pretend like it never happened."

Torwen was calling us all into the dining room for dinner. It was just after 6:00 p.m. and she had to get ready for work soon. We all sat in silence and I was holding back the tears. Torwen could see there was something wrong with me, but I just said I was very tired and needed to sleep.

I lay in bed wide-awake that night, watching the door handle; I was afraid he may try to come into my room, but thankfully, he didn't. I weighed up my options and there was none. The only option left open to me was going back to my mother's and that was a place I did not want to revisit. I had no money and only earned £55.00 per week at my new job as an office junior, and £20.00 per week went to Torwen for house keeping. I was left with the grand total of £35.00 per week for travel expenses, toiletries, as I had to buy my own, and anything else a young woman might need. My options were limited to nothing. My fate for the time being was sealed.

This was supposed to have been my new beginning, my new life, I was so happy. Torwen was the most wonderful woman, I could never tell her anyway, as it would only break her heart and her marriage, and there was no way I wanted that on my conscience. I decided the best thing for me to do was keep out of his way, not to give him any opportunity to assault me again. I avoided him at all costs. I would not watch television if he was in the living room, and I spent all my time studying in my room for my exams.

The following Saturday I was to meet Damian and I had the whole day to spend with him. We walked around the shopping centre, and then made our way to a café for a cup of coffee. I never told him what happened; I was afraid it would put him off me and he would no longer want to see me, as by now, I was officially his girlfriend. We were both 17 in just a few months. Damian had told me he was being scouted by Ipswich Town Football Club for their reserves team, and if they liked what they saw then he would be moving to Ipswich. My heart just sank. I could not bear the thought of losing him. I started crying and he assured me that I was the only girl for him and that he would write often, and visit when he wasn't playing or training.

That night Damian came back to the Prices house with me as they were away for the night on a business trip. Damian and I lay together on the floor kissing and cuddling, and that very night we took our relationship to another level. For both of us this was a special moment and a meaningful one. Eventually he had to leave and we agreed to meet the following Saturday. Damian never judged me, never made me feel worthless because I had nothing, he never reminded me of where I came from, and he always said you can be any one you want to be Amelia, just follow your dreams. I loved him so much, he saw me, he understood me, and he still wanted me even though I was carrying enough emotional baggage to be stopped at customs! One day I decided to try and contact Jake as I was now free to do so and no one could stop me. I called the children's home where Jake was still residing but I was met by a barrage of excuses.

It would unsettle him at this time, they told me. Still we were being kept apart. I would have to wait until he was released from the care-system and then we were both free to be a brother and sister once more. After work one Tuesday, I decided to take a long hot bath while Jason was working late. I lay there swamped in bubbles thinking about Damian and his possible transfer to Ipswich Football Club, when I heard the back door slam hard down stairs. I heard someone stumbling up the stairs, and that's when it dawned on me, it was Jason and he was drunk again.

    I hurried out of the bath, put my shoes against the door, and wrapped myself in a towel as quickly as I could. Before I knew what was happening Jason had barged into the bathroom and made a beeline for me. He grabbed my head tightly in his hands slobbering all over my face. I could smell the strong stench of beer on his breath, and it was disgusting. I tried to struggle free but he was far too strong for me. Then he ripped my towel off, threw it to the floor, and he pushed me against the wall. I was screaming at him begging him to get out and not to do this, but my cries went unheard. He kept saying it's just you and me now Amelia and I always get what I want.

    The tears streamed down my face, and I felt revulsion and disgust as his hands were slithering over my body. I felt like a trapped animal once more. He pushed me to the floor and started to unzip his trousers, and then Torwen came in through the front door calling my name. Her voice sounded like the voice of an angel to me that night, it saved me from a fate that did not bear thinking about. Jason jumped off me and ran from the bathroom into his bedroom; I sat on the floor curled up into a ball crying uncontrollably.

After what felt like an eternity but was only a few minutes, I pulled myself together, got dressed, and went downstairs to see Torwen who was supposed to have been working. She said that she had not been feeling too good so came home early. She made us both a hot drink and we sat talking at the kitchen table, she was telling me how happy she was, that I was like the daughter she never had, she said Jason felt the same way too. I thought if only she knew, this would totally crush her world. She went on to talk to me about love and how one day I would find the love of my life, like she had found hers in Jason. I knew there and then, I could never tell her.

The next day I did not go to work and rang in sick. I was too emotionally distressed to go in. I needed someone to talk to but I had no one. I did not want to worry Damian, the only good thing in my life, with problems; he had far more important things to be worrying about. I once again felt totally alone in the world, I was almost 17-years-old and as much alone as I ever was. So much for my new beginning, this felt like an extension of my past. I started to blame myself - it must be me, it must be my fault. I was at a loss as to where to turn. I decided the only thing I could do was save as much money as possible from my weekly wage, pass my O-Level exams, which were coming up, and then move out. At least then, I would hopefully have enough money for my first couple of months rent to get myself started. As the months running up to Christmas passed by I had saved a few hundred pounds, taken my exams, and managed to keep out of Jason's way. By now, Torwen had noticed the atmosphere between Jason and me and had started questioning it.

She kept asking me if there was anything wrong, had Jason told me off recently or had we fallen out over something. I reassured her that all was well, and that there was nothing to worry herself about.

Christmas day was upon us and a traditional Christmas ensued. I was given a faux fur jacket from the family, which I loved, and we had a traditional Christmas dinner with all the trimmings followed by an afternoon of the "Wizard of Oz." I could not get into the spirit of Christmas at all. Jason kept staring at me through the corner of his eyes every so often, and he would look me up and down as if undressing me whenever I walked into a room. I hated him. I hated what he had done to both Torwen and me - he had broken my trust and reduced my faith in humanity once again.

Over Christmas, I saw Damian and discovered that he had been given a place on the Ipswich Premier League reserves team. I was so pleased for him, but I also felt very sad, I felt like I was losing him forever. He was making it; his dream was actually coming true. What would he want with me now? He would have all the girls throwing themselves at him, I feared once he left I would never hear from him again, we had known each other for 18 months by this time and to me he was my first love. I could not imagine loving anyone else ever. Surely, as if it was written, Damian was transferred to Ipswich Football Club, and it would be a long while before I heard from him. When he did come to visit, we spent our time together but it was soon time for him to leave again. We said our goodbyes at the bus stop, kissing passionately for a long time. We made promises to each other and the one promise I held on to was his promise to write often, once he had settled in at Ipswich Football Club.

I watched the bus carrying the love of my life away and stood there crying for a very long time.

I made my way back up to the house and walked in through the back door as quietly as I could. I knew Torwen was at work and Jason was the only one in the house as the boys were always at ice hockey practice or out with their friends. I started walking up the stairs when Jason appeared as if from nowhere at the top of the landing. I stopped dead in my tracks and turned to go back down. He started walking after me, calling my name. I could tell he had been drinking again, and I made my way into the kitchen and shut the door behind me. Jason burst through the door like a mad man. He grabbed me and pulled me into the hallway out of sight of the kitchen window. He pushed me on to the floor and started kissing my neck and groping my breasts. I felt sick once more, as all I could smell was that putrid stench of beer coming from his breath. He had pulled my leggings down and I could feel his hands sliding up the inside of my legs. I pushed him onto his side and tried to run, but he grabbed my ankle, pulling me back towards him. I started kicking with all the strength I could muster and finally I caught him between the legs.

I ran upstairs as fast as I could, not even thinking about my leggings lying on the floor in the hallway. I put on a pair of jeans and my coat; I packed all my things into my sports bag and sat down to think about my next move. I was heaving and ran into the bathroom to be sick. It was Friday night and I knew Torwen would be back home by 10:30 p.m. I decided to wait for her and do the only decent thing I could think of, for her sake, and that was tell her the truth. She deserved so much better than him;

she was so classy and gracious, a true lady. How she ended up married to this overweight pot-bellied pervert, I had no idea.

I waited and waited for what seemed like hours for Torwen to return. Earlier I had heard Jason slamming the back door and driving off in his old BMW. Eventually, I heard Torwen coming in through the front door; I took a deep breath and walked down the stairs with all my belongings in my bag ready to leave once and for all. Torwen just stared at me. "Amelia, where are you going?" Torwen asked.

I asked her to sit down, and began to tell her everything. She never said a word the whole time I was speaking tears were running down her face as they were mine. I thought she was about to give me a big hug and tell me everything was going to be alright but I was very wrong, nothing could have prepared me for her reaction, not in a million years.

Torwen flew off her chair and slapped me so hard across the face, and then she just carried on hitting me. When she stopped, she looked at me very calm and called me a whore. She told me I was a liar, that Jason is not like that, and that Jason would never assault anybody. I was made to feel dirty. As if I was at fault, she reminded me of everything that she had done for me, giving me a home, welcoming me into the family like one of their own. How could I spout such ugly lies? She shouted at me over and over again. I was in total shock. I just wanted to die right there right then, I could hardly breathe properly for crying so hysterically. I told her I was packed and ready to leave. I made my way towards the back door and Jason walked in,

I could tell by the look on his face that he knew I had told his wife what he had done to me. He looked towards Torwen and she asked him right there and then was it true what Amelia claims you did to her. He looked at me, his face bright red through anger. He consoled his wife with just the right words, telling her he would never do such a thing and that he had no idea what she was talking about. Torwen shouted at me to get out of her house, she never wanted to see me ever again. As I was walking down the path she just kept shouting, "Liar, liar, liar." I could not bear the thought that Torwen did not believe me. This hurt me so much, however, there was nothing I could say to make her believe me.

    I had a few hundred pounds in my pocket, a sports bag which housed everything I owned, and nowhere to go. I had just one thought in my head, your destiny is in your own hands now, Amelia. Do you go home to mother for a while or find a hostel temporarily? Both options did not appeal to me in the slightest.

    I knew there was only one place I wanted to be right now and that was the old ruin. I started on the two-mile walk to Jake and Amelia's special place. I knew I would be safe there; I quite liked the thought of sleeping under the stars in my secret garden. I would anticipate my next move going forward the following morning. For the first time, my destiny truly was in my own hands.

Amelia's Destiny (Book #2)

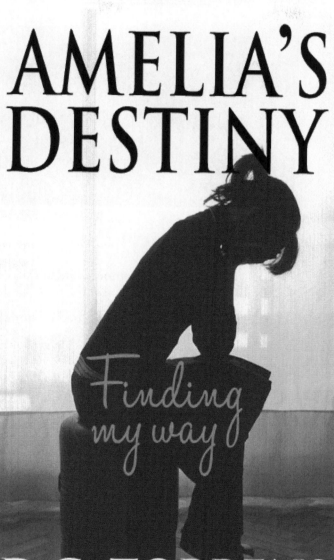

A Hard Decision

The old ruin was just how I remembered it, still very much a ruin, standing tall in all its majestic glory! Untouched by human hands. The beautiful orchard remained as effervescent as always with its sumptuous fruit trees overflowing with a plethora of pears, apples, and damsons! I awakened very early with the feel of the warm sun caressing my face like a gentle comforting hand; I stretched my arms and walked over to the aged-stone birdbath, still half-full of water from the recent late summer rain. I splashed some water over my face before walking over to the apple trees, which were already bearing fruit; I plucked an apple from a low hanging branch and took a big bite. I sat down against the sundial while I gathered my thoughts for a moment. I had made my decision, the only one I felt I could make. I would gather my things and walk the three miles to my mother's home. This was not a decision I made at all lightly.

I just knew the only other option left to me was to book into one of those awful hostels. However, by going to my mother's, at least I was now too big for her to lock into a room. I was hoping against all hopes that maybe she was sorry, and that she would open the door with her arms outstretched. I needed somewhere to live, I had nowhere to go, and not enough money to support the amount of rent required of me. I just hoped that she would at least afford me a bed for a short while so I could gather enough money from my day job to move on and rent my first home. After all, that was the least she could do, surely.

A part of me needed my mother to be sorry. I wanted to hear those words so much; I was just 17-years-old, all alone in the world, and without guidance. I wanted a parent. My feelings were very mixed up and confused where my mother was concerned. I hated her for what she had put me through; however, she was still my mother, and I needed at least to try and forgive her. Maybe, just maybe, time had changed her, and she would be very sorry. Well, there was only one way to find out. I set out on my walk; it was such a beautiful morning. The birds were singing and the sun was shining; the sky was bluer than I had ever seen it. I was feeling very nervous and wondered several times on my walk to mother's house what on earth I was thinking of. I tried to push all negative thoughts to the back of my mind. As I came closer to the estate where my mother was now living, all of a sudden I felt quite sick. All at once, flashes of my childhood came streaming back. I stopped for a break and sat down on a bench near a park. I watched the early morning joggers fly past, breathing heavily, and the dog owners walking their beloved pooches. I took a deep breath and stood up. There was a saying, "Just put one foot in front of the other." So, that's what I did until I reached my mother's house.

I turned the corner and I could see my mother's new house. Well, it was new to me, as I had never lived here. I stood at the end of the driveway; I looked up at the tall red-bricked house. This was definitely a better house than the ones I remembered. This one was quite new, built within recent years, I thought. For some reason I was having trouble moving my feet forward! I stood there just staring for what seemed like an age. Then I took a deep breath and walked up the drive. I knocked on the door with my heart in my hands. It seemed like a lifetime before anyone came to the door. My mother stood there in shock at my unannounced appearance at her front door. She looked so tiny – fragile almost. I knew I had grown, but I did not think I had grown *that* much. My mother, looking tiny, stood there in a pair of shorts and a top; she was about 5ft tall, if that. I was towering over her at 5ft, 5 inches.

I thought to myself, can this really be the woman I was so terrified of as a child? The small woman that stood before me was my childhood nightmare, my torturer, the person who had caused me so much pain and heartache, my mother. I wondered for a moment what on earth was I doing there. There had to be a better option. However, I knew there was no other place left for me to go. She gave me a surprise smile and opened the door wider to let me in. I sat down in the large kitchen silently for a while. I looked around the very dated fittings. The first thought that ran through my mind was that she had carried on with her life very well without her children.

The garden was well tended; it seemed to me that she had not been affected at all. She asked me what had happened at the Norwegians' home, and so I told her what had happened to me.

My mother's only response was, "Did you encourage him to do what he did Amelia?" I could not believe what I was hearing.

I replied, "Of course I didn't, why would I?"

She looked me up and down as if I was dirty or tainted in some way.

I looked down towards the floor and then I asked her if I could stay for a while, and she reluctantly agreed. Once again, within two minutes of being in her company, my mother had the ability to make me feel as if I was nothing, after years of not seeing me. The fact that she agreed to let me stay at all was a huge surprise to me, as I truly thought she would turn me away. But she didn't. A long list of rules was put before me that I had to agree to if I wanted to stay. I had to pay my mother £25 a week out of my £55 a week wage; I also had to ask permission to use the telephone as it was locked at all times, and I had to pay for my call usage. This was the '80s, and portable phones for ordinary households were only just coming into the shops. The phone was a big green one with a large round dial on the front, and it had a little stainless steel lock on it. I glanced at the lock and shuddered. I had to do my own washing and ironing, which was nothing new to me as I had been doing this since I was 13-years-old, and would not have it any other way. I was not allowed to use the toothpaste or toiletries in the bathroom. These were my mother's things, and I had to buy my own. Again, I was used to buying all my own toiletries. Since I was 13, I had been using my pocket money from Bryn Tyn to buy my own toiletries. I was not looking for financial handouts; I just needed a roof and a bed temporarily until I could find my way again.

I was also asked to pay some money towards the electricity. As the list grew, I knew I would have hardly any money left over to save for my future. However, if I did not agree to her demands, I would be out on my ear and heading straight to the hostel. I didn't know which was worse.

Mother never mentioned my time in care, or why we were sent there. These were subjects she refused to talk about. If those times were mentioned, this was on her say so only; and then it was rather incredible what she had concocted and made herself believe over the years. As far as my mother was concerned, nothing was her fault; she had never done anything to harm her children, and she had only ever done right by them. She went on to say how the Social Services were in the wrong, that they had lied about everything, and that everything that happened was all down to some conspiracy against her. Of course, I knew otherwise. How could I ever forget? I was the eldest of all my siblings. I would never forget my horrendous childhood, not ever. It seemed to me that mother was in denial and trying to convince me that she was a wronged woman, misunderstood by the powers that be. The thing was that she had actually convinced herself of this ludicrous story. It was right there and then, that I realised my mother was truly mentally ill; everything just seemed to fall into place. I did not argue with her; I did not agree or disagree with her, as I knew all too well that the woman I knew as a child was still alive and kicking in the same woman sitting before me.

I tried to raise the subject of my father and my grandparents, but I was met by a brick wall. A raging woman stood before me, shouting, screaming and treating me as if I had committed a heinous crime. Her reactions to my enquiries were those of a crazy woman. I knew I would never get any information out of my mother about my father and his side of the family. Well, at least not the information I wanted, that was becoming very clear.

Through her screams she shouted, "Your father was evil. He tried to kill you when you were two-years-old, Amelia. He held your head under the water while he was bathing you. He hated both you and Jake. You were both a nuisance to him, an anchor in his life, and he never wanted you. His mother was a nasty woman; in fact, his whole family was evil." For whatever reason I was beginning to realise that my mother was hell bent on making sure I never found my father or his family. She would not part with their last-known address, or my grandparents' first names, knowing this would make it almost impossible for me to locate them, especially as there was no internet then. You could not just log on to a computer and type a name into Google search. There was no Google, no internet, and no email. Computers were only just replacing word processors and electric typewriters in the work place. If you wanted to find anyone, your only hope was to search the Yellow Pages, or if you could afford to, hire a private detective. There were one or two organisations that could possibly help; however, they required a lot more information than I had to give. Therefore, I put that wish aside for the time being.

My bedroom was on the top floor of this three-storey house. I walked to the top with my holdall thrown over my shoulders, staring in complete disbelief as I passed each bedroom. Each door was fitted with one of those large industrial bolts, just like they always had been in our previous houses, just as I remembered as a child. It made no sense though. *Why?* After all, there was only mother and Harry, her fourth husband, 16-years her senior. Jake had been home only a few months. When I was a child, nothing my mother ever did made sense, and I was finding out that nothing she had done since made any sense either. I was a young adult now, and just as confused by my mother as I had always been. The sad thing was I really wanted her to love me, to look me in the eyes sincerely and say sorry, offer me an explanation. Anything to cushion the emptiness I was feeling.

I instinctively knew I had made a bad decision. I reminded myself that my destiny was in my own hands now, and that each step forward was of my own making. I had to think that way; I had to keep reminding myself of that daily. I did not want to lose sight of my dreams, or I just might lose my own mind. There was absolutely no need whatsoever for those bolts to be on the bedroom doors. They were even on the kitchen and living room doors too. Mother had also convinced herself that I was too young to remember most of the things that had happened, and that a child's memory can be distorted. I had no interest in what she had to say, or what she believed, I knew the truth, I knew where I had spent the last God knows how many years, being moved from one awful establishment to the next. I remembered all too well the nightmares I had because of being locked in complete darkness in my bedroom as a child by my mother. I also knew she could not face the truth of what she had done. Maybe deep down she did feel ashamed.

I had no interest in rubbing her nose in the awful past that was my reality. I just wanted to make my immediate dream possible: owning my own house. This was at the top of my "To do" list, along with travelling the whole width and breadth of our great country. When you have been pretty much locked away all your life in one form or another, you crave freedom. I had never traveled outside of the large grey walls within which I lived. In fact, the only real travelling I had ever done was when I ran away from the children's homes. I had no idea what my country looked like, but I was going to find out.

I decided I needed to find a new job, one that would involve travel of some sort. I would get the Shropshire Star newspaper and start looking straight away. I knew I would not last long at mother's house. The way she looked me up and down told me that. I also knew that to move forward with my life in the way I had always dreamed of, meant moving as far away from Shropshire and my controlling mother as possible, and as soon as possible. I don't know why, but I felt sorry for my mother. I hated her; I loved her; I needed her to love me back, because she was my mother. Every once in a while I could see something in her eyes, a sadness, something that told me that somewhere deep inside of her there was a real human being, with feelings and compassion.

However, I also knew that I would have to dig very deep to find that person. Sometimes I would catch her looking at me in a strange way, a way that was painful to her. Nevertheless, it was a fleeting moment, soon replaced by the mother I had always known. It had saddened me so much, as a young teenager. There were so many things I could not understand, things I needed to understand. I wanted and needed guidance, but there was no one, it was a hard fact, as I felt so alone and scared in this vast, busy world.

My road ahead suddenly seemed daunting. My dreams seemed further away than ever. At times, I wondered if I would ever complete my journey. Would I ever come face to face with my true destiny? Why was I here at all?

It seemed to me at times as if I was a test subject for God, "Let's see what happens if I put this obstacle in Amelia's path. Let's see how much pain Amelia can withstand. And let's see how much it would take to break a human spirit."

That is how I truly felt for the longest time. Because it seemed that no matter what I did, I would find the toughest obstacles in my way, doing their upmost from preventing me from moving forward.

The Reunion

I was finally going to get to hug my brother, after being separated for so very long. The tears cascaded down my cheeks at the thought of all the lost time between us. The pain of that was still strong within me.

Once I reached the top of the stairs, I could hear a rustling sound coming from one of the bedrooms. I peeked through the door, and there sitting on the bed was Jake. I squealed with happiness. The feeling was overwhelming. I had had no news of Jake while living at the Norwegians. I had no idea whatsoever that Jake had recently been released from the state-care-system.

A thought ran through my head. "It's in your best interest," the authorities were always telling me.

"It would unsettle you both to be in contact," they would say each time I requested a phone call to my bother.

"Sorry Amelia, it has been decided to restrict all contact between you and your siblings," I would often be told.

I cried at the recollection of those words. The hurt they caused was irremovable from my memory bank, where I knew they would remain forever.

Jake and I hugged each other very tightly. He was much taller than I had remembered. He had grown into a handsome young man. It was very strange to see him like that at first, because in my head I still had the image of him as a child. His hair was now dark. It used to be so much lighter; now it was jet black. Jake was very quiet, nervous almost.

We spent the next couple of days getting to know each other again. Neither of us talked in detail about our time in care; the memories were still raw, still painful. We never mentioned our pain, the loneliness, the despair, or the longing. We had both suffered greatly. The one thing Jake and I did talk about was the old ruin! A few days after our reunion, we decided to spend the day at our secret garden. We sat against the sundial, reminiscing about past adventures. Oh, how I had missed my brother, and he had missed me too! Although we were young adults now, we were as close as ever. We ate our sandwiches, skimmed stones like we once did as children, peered through the old ruin, and then slowly made our way home.

Our walk home was a quiet but not uncomfortable one. There was a peaceful silence between us, one of contemplation. I could not shake off the sadness that enveloped me. So much time had passed between us; so much of our childhood had been stolen from us. Tears fell from my water-filled eyes as I looked at my very vulnerable brother. It was clear to me right there, right then, that we were both dealing with our inner pain in silence.

The one thing I had noticed was how quiet Jake was now; he had a very distant look in his eyes. He always looked as if he was somewhere else in his mind. He seemed so fragile, there was a look permanently displayed in his eyes, one like that of a frightened kitten. I just wanted to protect him forever. Jake and I had suffered in ways most people only read about in books, and I was determined not to let that pain, that suffering, ruin the rest of my life. Sometimes it was very hard, though, as I would wake up some days shrouded in a dark blackened cloud. This would appear so unexpectedly, without any warning whatsoever. No matter how positive I had felt the previous day, once I was encased in this darkness it was almost impossible for me to function normally, until it had taken flight and left me temporarily once again. Only then could I continue with my quest for a greater life.

At that time, I had no idea that the black cloud was my depression. I had a different name for those dark days. My "abyss" I felt as if I had been swallowed up, and all my will power and strength had been swallowed up with it. I found it impossible to lift my spirit, to climb out of my chasm. However, I did not give in to it. I continued to struggle with it, until eventually; I learned to live with it. I hated those dark days with a vengeance, because they held me back, preventing me from moving forward. However, I had learned to recognise the signs within myself, and I would prepare myself mentally for the appearance of my nemesis. I realised I had not come through my tragic childhood unscathed or unaffected after all. I had been affected greatly. It was now up to me to deal with this affliction of sorts, and work with it rather than against it. I did not believe in therapy; I did not want to talk about my childhood to anyone; I was ashamed of my past; I did not want my life going forward to be affected by the past. I had made a conscious decision to tell everyone going forward that I had spent my childhood in a boarding school. This prevented awkward questions from new friends that came into my life, and future employers going forward.

    I battled with this decision for a very long time; I thought long and hard about whether I was doing the right thing. I came to understand a need in me, a need to fit in, to be the same as all the other teenagers out there. This need was so great, I felt like I had everything to prove to the world, more so than anyone else. I needed to show the world and myself that I could make a great life for myself in spite of my past. So many children once they left the care-system ended up on the streets with prostitution being their only means of income. Or they would journey down another darkened road, with no hope of ever returning. This was the sad reality, a frightening reality, and one that I promised would never be mine.

    I remained at my mother's house for a few more months. Life was not easy at all, and I knew this had been a mistake. I made the decision to look for a new job, one that would take me away from Shropshire. I scoured the newspaper each week, looking for the right opening. In the meantime, I was still working at my office job. I was modeling whenever I could, and I was going out quite a lot with new friends I had made.

    For a while, Jake would remain at mothers also, as he had nowhere else to go. He seemed desperately to want our mother's love;

he fought hard for it. He was a people pleaser; this had become apparent to me over time. He was also shy and needed to be loved. I could not bear the thought of leaving him now; however, it was something I had to do. So many lost years between us, so preventable, time lost forever. Now I was going to leave him behind, I had to leave him behind; but I would come back for him one day. I knew if there was any chance of making it in the big world then that would involve me leaving Shropshire for good, and once again, being separated from Jake.

I wanted to make life better for the two of us. Nevertheless, I knew deep down that I would have to go away for quite some time before I could make that happen. I had no idea how life had treated Jake since we had been separated all those years ago. I prayed that Jake would be okay. I prayed he was strong enough to cope without me, though I knew he was not as strong as me. He was damaged in a way I was not. He was vulnerable, and lacked confidence in himself and in life. He found the future frightening, as he had become institutionalised after many years of being in care. I was the stronger one. I had to be. I had not seen my sisters either. They were sent to Shrewsbury to live with foster parents. I had not seen them for many years, and I knew I would never see them again. I still had my job as an office junior so I decided I would work every hour God sent to make as much money as possible and to keep me out of the house for as long as possible. I joined a gym and went every other night after work.

I started to make more new friends at work now. I was more settled and more sociable too.

I joined as many social activities as I possibly could, and through my hard work and dedication, I was soon promoted. With all my new responsibilities and extra money, roughly £30 per week taking me up to around £85 per week, I actually felt like I was making some progress towards my dream of owning my own home. I saved the extra money that I was earning and put it straight into my savings account.

One day I came home from work and mother was in a foul mood, much like the ones I remember her having as a child. She was waving a phone bill at me, and demanding money from me; I had only used the phone twice, and had agreed at the time I would pay for the calls. Mother demanded £20 off me there and then, which was an awful lot of money then for just two phone calls; in fact, it would be an awful lot of money now. I asked to see the phone bill and reminded her I had only made a couple of calls.

And she said, "If you do not give me the money Amelia then you can no longer use the phone."

I gave her the £20 she had demanded. She never showed me the phone bill. She also discovered I had been promoted and upped my rent to £125 a month, again if I refused she would kick me out there and then. I could not win and realised why she had agreed to let me stay in the first place, money. Not because she wanted to make up for the past, not because she was sorry; she still hated me as she always had done. How foolish I was to think she had maybe changed! How foolish was I to think she harboured some genuine feelings for me deep inside of her somewhere!

Modeling

While at work one day a couple of the women suggested I applied for some modeling jobs. They told me I was very beautiful and could make lots of extra money at weekends! This sounded great. I was so desperate for money; however, I did not feel as beautiful as the two kind women had mentioned. I most certainly did not have the confidence in myself. For a while I forgot about their suggestion, until one day, during my lunch break, the same two ladies came up to me with a newspaper clipping for a modeling competition. I gladly took the clipping and read each and every word carefully, as there was no way I was going to take my clothes off or do any sort of topless modeling work, that was for sure!

Everything seemed to be above board. There was a contact number for a local professional photographer and a time to call him, which was after 5 o'clock in the evenings. The requirements were, you had to be of slim build, size 8 or 10, no mention of age requirements at all. Being only 17-years-old, I thought I would be okay. After all, he was advertising in the job section of the Shropshire Star newspaper.

That evening on my return home, I sat in my bedroom wondering how I was going to call Mr. Harris the photographer. There was no way I was going to call him on my mother's phone. Back then, there were no such things as personal mobile phones. My mind was set. I took a walk to the local phone box just down the road, armed with a stack of ten pence pieces. I had to wait ages for the old lady to finish her phone call. I practically fell into the phone box once it was free! I dialed the number hand written on a piece of paper and waited for the dialing tone. I nearly jumped when I heard a voice at the other end.

"Hello, Mr. Harris speaking."

I took a deep breath and then replied, "Hi, my name is Amelia. I am calling regards your advertisement in the local newspaper this week." The line went quite for a while, and then Mr. Harris said,

"Are you a model?"

"No, I am not a model Mr. Harris; however, I am looking for a modeling job."

Mr. Harris went on to ask me my weight, size, height, bust size, and any previous experience. I told him I was new to this industry and was looking to model part-time for extra money. A meeting was set up for the following Saturday morning at 11 a.m. at my mother's house.

To say I was nervous is an understatement; he advised me that he would go into more detail about the competition when he saw me. Mr. Harris also added that there had been a lot of interest in his advert and many local girls had entered.

Over the next couple of days, I went jogging twice a day, in the morning before work and in the evening. I was drinking plenty of water, and eating like a bird, as I wanted to look perfect for my interview. At that age, I did not drink alcohol at all, and was already a healthy eater.

I tried to quiz my mother as to what time she would be going out on Saturday, as I could not bear for her to be around when the photographer arrived. I could just imagine the reaction I would receive from her. As it happened, she was not going out until much later in the day. I was going to have to tell her about my interview after all.

Why was I here? I had thought to myself. After everything I had been through, I had ended up right back here! I was so desperate to get away once and for all, yet there was a part of me that still very much needed my mother's love. I wanted her to be proud of me. I needed her to say sorry for my childhood. I wanted her to offer an explanation then hug me and tell me she would make it up to me. That going forward we would have a close relationship, go shopping together, watch movies together, all the things that mother's do with their daughters. I knew deep down it would never happen. She was incapable of feeling any kind of emotion. I still dreamed of it, though. However, I was like a deep-filled bramley apple pie where emotions were concerned, steeped through to my very core with emotion of every kind! I seemed to feel for the hurt and pain of others tenfold.

My heart was heavy, my mind confused. Somewhere deep inside I hoped upon hope that my mother may have changed with age, but I was not witnessing any such change as yet.

Mother was still filled with hate; regular daily snipes were quite normal. If I said "black" she would say "white." Whatever I was wearing, she would tell me I looked dumpy. She often looked me up and down with a look of disdain on her face and then she would shout at me,

"What do you think you're looking at?" when she was the one looking at me in a disapproving manner.

I knew I was not dumpy. I was only a size 8 or 10, but it seemed she could not bear to pay me a compliment of any kind. The only pleasure she seemed to get out of me was making me feel as insecure as possible, and she was doing a fantastic job of that. I let it go most of the time, as you cannot reason with the *un*reasonable.

Outside of the household, I had made a few new friends who I went out with after work on Fridays. They knew nothing of my past. Because of our age, the topic of schools came up frequently. This was a subject that at that time, I had no intention of talking about. I had made a pact with myself when I left the state-care-system that I would just tell everyone going forward I had been away at boarding school in Wales. It was easier that way: no awkward questions to answer, no awkward silences from people who just don't know what to say to you. This also gave me a far better chance socially as far as fitting in was concerned. I had a rather posh accent really. I had been moved around so much as a child I was never anywhere long enough to pick up the dialect, and this stood me in good stead going forward.

Finally, I plucked up the courage to tell my mother I had a modeling interview with a photographer and that he would be arriving at eleven o'clock on Saturday morning. She could not have laughed any louder, asking why I thought I was good enough to be a model. I could not muster a response to that and just asked her if she would allow me some privacy for half an hour. Mother grunted, not saying yes or no. I thought it went a lot better than expected. I had been expecting a far worse reaction than the one I received.

On the Saturday morning, I spent two hours getting ready for my interview. I washed and curled my hair, took my time applying my make-up, and already had my outfit laid out on the bed. By 10.45 am, I was all ready and dressed. I popped my lovely new black high-heeled sling backs on to complete the look. I took one last long look at myself in the mirror and smiled to myself. I could not believe the reflection looking back at me was my own, a beautiful young woman. At that moment my mother came out of the kitchen, stood, and stared at me in her usual way, she looked me up and down then said,

"Amelia, are you really going to wear that?" I was flabbergasted, speechless. She could not even find it within herself to tell me, her first-born daughter that I looked nice. I simply replied yes and that I was happy with my choice. My mother then told me she thought it made me look a little dumpy, and maybe I should consider changing my outfit. I knew she was just being unkind; she could not help herself. She knew she could no longer use her physical power to hurt me as she once did: I towered over her by 5.5 feet.

However, I was still afraid of her, she knew how to hurt me emotionally, she knew just how to get inside my head, she was shameless, un-relenting, and it hurt.

Harry, my mother's fourth husband, was a skinny white-haired man who worked in a factory. He had been loyal to his company for over 20 years. His job was a secure one and he never missed a day, a far cry from the men my mother had been used to over the years. Harry was a lovely pleasant man. You could not find a kinder and gentler natured person, and this puzzled me immensely. How on earth had he managed to handle my mother? As the days and months passed by, I was beginning to find out, Harry was petrified of my mother; he did what she said, when she demanded. He would never argue back with her, not ever.

One day Harry came home from work, took off his boots outside of the front door before entering the house, walked into the kitchen, where I was making a drink and mother was cooking. Harry walked over to her and went to plant a kiss on her cheek; mother spun around and punched him square in the face, with no warning at all. I dropped my tea, Harry just looked at my mother with puppy dog eyes and she punched him again and again. I shouted at her to stop, but she then turned on me and slapped me around the face. All this happened with no warning signs whatsoever. Just before Harry came home from work, mother was discussing what to cook for dinner; the radio was on, and there was definitely no sign of a bad mood. I was in complete shock, not because she slapped me too, but because of Harry's reaction or rather lack of it.

He said, and did nothing. Mother told him to sit down and take off his coat, which he did like an obedient dog. I walked out of the kitchen, my mother started after me, screaming at me that I was no better than she was, and that I would never amount to anything. So that was the day I saw my real mother once again, as she re-surfaced in a blaze of unexpected anger. I knew I could not stay there for much longer. Anything was better than living there. I just needed the right job first, and to start a new life, a positive life, as far away as possible from my mother.

My modeling interview went well with Mr. Harris. Over the next few weeks, he helped me prepare my portfolio at a great cost to myself of course! This was standard practice back then it was like an equity card for actors. Without one you would not be seen by the modeling agencies, well at least that's what Mr. Harris had told me. I hung on his every word, believing I was heading towards great things. Mr. Harris took me to Ryder Falls in North Wales. He advised me this was a beautiful backdrop for my new photos; my portfolio would benefit greatly. I packed all sorts of wonderful outfits, swimwear, lingerie, evening dresses, day dresses, and casual wear! I wanted to ensure my portfolio reflected many different looks, and that it would show the modeling companies that I had a very versatile look. On our arrival at Ryder Falls, I was blown away by the sheer beauty of the area.

The famous waterfalls were amazing. Mr. Harris was right: it made an incredible backdrop for the many photos that were taken that day. Mr. Harris was a trusted photographer, and he had worked with many local models that had gone on to do great things. He was also well known locally as a landscape photographer.

The day was perfect; the sun was shining. Mr. Harris made me feel like a princess. I remember one particular photograph he took: I was wearing a simple day dress, sitting on a floating log in the river, with the waterfall directly behind me. It was a very calm and peaceful day. I was leaning back on the log and kicking my feet in the water playfully. It was a very natural photograph. I loved it and still have it to this day. Many films were used that day. Mr. Harris was a perfect gentleman. He always turned around when I needed an outfit change, and he would hold the towel for me when I stepped out of the water. I felt completely safe in his hands. The truth be told, I felt like a true star that day!

Mr. Harris had a lot of faith in me as a future model. He built up my confidence. He started acting as my agent for a while and would get me modeling jobs locally. I remember one was for a local foundry, not the most glamorous of contracts, but a modeling job nonetheless. As far as I was concerned, this was one more step towards my dreams. I had to wear a very tight fitting T-shirt with the company's logo written across my chest, holding onto a fence near a railway line and leaning back playfully. It was harmless. I got paid and was treated very well. That was my very first job. I did one or two jobs like that over the following months. What they did for my confidence was incredible.

Mr. Harris took me on location to the most amazing places for photo shoots; I was always in awe at the beautiful places he managed to find. They were always so peaceful, so beautiful, and so far removed from my own surroundings. I was full of optimism, full of plans, and full of hope. No amount of verbal abuse received from my mother on a regular basis could dampen my spirit. Not any more.

I was saving what money I could, working hard in the daytime, modeling the occasional evening, and every other weekend I was being advised and polished by Mr. Harris. He helped me to think differently; he encouraged me to believe in myself; he was a genuinely nice man. Much older than I was, Mr. Harris was then in his 40s, a man who could be trusted. He never took advantage of me, not ever; he was very fatherly in how he treated me.

My mother hated the fact I had started putting together a portfolio and doing the odd job here and there. She would tell me almost daily that I was not good enough. Who did I think I was? No one would want to hire me as a model. At just size 8 to 10, I was a nice slim build, However, my mother continually told me how fat I was, that I had my head in the clouds and that modeling was not for the likes of me. I was not pretty enough, and I would never amount to anything. This daily taunting hurt me, not because of what she said, but because she was actually saying it to me, her own daughter. She would spout out ugly words about Mr. Harris too, saying he was a pervert, and only interested in one thing. This was not the case at all.

Why I was still surprised by her abhorrent attitude and outrageous behaviour, I have no idea. Looking back now, I realise how innocent and naïve I was. Anyone in her sphere was like a trapped fly in a web. I truly believed at that time, that I had no other alternative place to go. The only other option was a hostel for waifs and strays. Had I taken that option I feared I might have been forced down a road I would never return from, like so many children who leave the care-system. And that was just not an option for me.

I spent as much time away from the house as possible. I had already achieved my O-levels from night school whilst I was living with the Norwegian family, which I had funded myself, from my day job. That was one item crossed off my list. A small door had opened into the modeling world, which was inspiring me further with each passing week. I continued to go the gym and the sauna.

When I needed to escape from reality, I would bury myself in a book. The one I was reading at that time was *Flowers in the attic* by Virginia Andrews. Such a tragically sad story, much of which I could relate too. I often went running into the town park, which was a vast space and great for runners. I had also joined a local cheerleaders group, which were supporting the Wrekin Giants. Each Sunday morning I would head out with my pom poms for cheerleading practice. A big game was just around the corner and all the local press would be there. It was very exciting for us.

Then one Sunday morning, our team leader informed us that a reporter from the local newspaper was here to take our photos in advance of the game. I will never forget that feeling the first time I saw myself in the local paper, the whole group smiling, perfectly posed with our black and white pom poms. I felt so proud of myself. I had a zest for life that could not be contained by anyone. I knew I was on the right path and heading towards a great future.

Trying to be a Teenager

A new nightclub had opened in Shropshire called *Cascades*.

You had to be 21-years-old or over to gain entry into this long-awaited club that was the talk of the town. On the day of the grand opening, my friend Stacy and I spent two hours getting dressed up at her house, and using every trick in the book, we could to make ourselves look much older than our 17-years suggested! We both had permed hair, which had been backcombed to within an inch of its life! We stepped into a pair of brightly colored stiletto heels and then we both stood in front of Stacy's bedroom mirror. We were smiling, quite contented that we had achieved our aim, and thought how grownup we both looked. I was excited. I could not believe I was going to my first nightclub. Stacy was my new best friend. She had been brought up by a loving family, and she was doted on by her parents and wanted for nothing. Stacy was an only child, very pretty, and quite spoilt really. I wanted to be her. She had everything I had ever dreamed of: a loving family, a great education, and lots of friends, as well as her fair share of admirers.

Once we were both satisfied that we were ready, we made our way downstairs, said goodbye to Stacy's parents and made our way to the bus stop. We were offered a lift by Stacy's father; however, we wanted to make our own way to the nightclub. We wanted to catch the bus into the town centre like independent teenagers. We each had the total some of £5.00. This was all the money we needed, as neither of us drank alcohol, and we were being picked up at the end of the night by Stacy's father. It cost £3.00 entry fee to get in and then we would need just the £2.00 remaining for our soft drinks, which cost around 50 pence. It's unbelievable what you could do with a fiver back then. This was the very late '80s and 1990 was almost upon us!

As we got off the bus outside the nightclub, the queues were phenomenal; the line of people waiting to go in went on forever. We walked up nervously and joined the ever-growing queue. As we got closer and closer to the bouncers on the doors we became more and more nervous, convinced we would be turned away. However, much to our delight this was not the case. The bouncers looked us both up and down and then waved us through. We could barely contain our excitement. On entering the club, we were both blown away by the sheer enormity of the place. There were disco balls everywhere; the walls were mirrored, which reflected everything, and made the club look twice the size it actually was. We were in complete awe of the place, and we felt so grown up. There were two dance floors, a burger bar, a cocktail bar, and the main bar opposite the main dance floor. We purchased our soft drinks and stood back against the wall, taking it all in.

The club was filling up fast, and I was watching all the older girls coming down the spiral staircase, looking amazing in their flamboyant outfits. Then I recognised someone, tall, dark, and exceptionally handsome. It was Damian. My heart skipped a thousand beats. I didn't mention him to my friend. I don't really know why; I stepped out from against the wall and positioned myself opposite Stacy, putting myself directly in his line of vision! I prayed so hard that he would notice me. He did. He looked straight into my eyes. I held my breath a very long time. Stacy was saying something to me, but I could not hear her words. In fact, I could hear nothing in the club at this point only the sound of my own breathing! When Damian reached the bottom of the stairs with his best friend, I froze for the longest time. Then he smiled at me and beckoned me over. I had not seen him for months. Oh, how I had missed him! On the sight of him, once again, it just confirmed to me how much I truly loved him, my first and only love!

    I made my way over to Damian; he hugged me, kissed me on the cheek, and then took me to the bar. We talked for the longest time. Damian was now a local hero, he had made it. He had been promoted from the Ipswich Reserves, to Ipswich United Football Club. His name was already known all over the country. He talked about another possible transfer, about his life in Ipswich and how he wanted to be one of the best football players in the country. He was well on his way. My heart just melted. I told him about my modeling, and how I hoped I would get bigger contracts. Damian stopped me in mid-flow.

    "Amelia, you don't have to impress me. This is Damian, and I haven't changed. It does not matter to me whether you are a model or working in a factory."

Oh how I wanted to be alone with him right at that moment. He really was unchanged; he was still the same Damian. I felt so proud to be standing there with him at the bar, everyone was looking at us. I felt like I was floating on air once again, much like the first time we had met.

Damian asked me what I was doing afterwards. I told him I had no plans but to head off home. That was when he asked me if I would go to his friend's house. He advised me that he would make sure I got home all right. My heart was thumping so hard. I went in search for Stacy to tell her I would not be coming home with her, she was not too happy.

"You are leaving me here?" she asked sternly.

"No, of course not. When we leave I'll see you to your dad's car, and then I will head off with Damian."

"Oh, okay Amelia, you seem to know Damian pretty well. How come you never mentioned him before?"

"Because I never thought I would see him again, Stacey. I thought it was over between us, truly."

"I believe you Amelia. Thousands wouldn't," she smiled. For the rest of the night Damian mingled with people he had not seen for a while, and I danced with Stacey on the dance floor. "Soul II Soul" was playing one of my favourite songs, "Weekend Girl" followed by a "Freddie Jackson" number. Great soul tunes that had everyone up on the floor and dancing.

I looked over in Damian's direction. He was smiling at me, watching me dance, and I felt like a million dollars. Of all the girls in *Cascades,* he was watching me. I was truly in love with Damian, ever since that first day I saw him riding past on his bike, when I was standing outside *Kiss Kiss Fashions*!

At the end of the night, I walked Stacey to her father's car, hugged and kissed her goodnight, then made my way over to Damian, who was waiting for me. I could not wait to be alone with him. He was just perfect. And he still wanted me. How things would be between us going forward, I had no idea, I just knew I wanted to be with him any way I could. When I was 17-years-old, he was everything to me.

I was worried now, though. He would have every local girl imaginable throwing themselves at him: beautiful girls, and rich ones. They all had so much more to offer him than I did. How long I would keep his interest was anyone's guess; though he seemed genuinely to like me still. Nevertheless, I was sure before too long he would be tempted away. I did not have the confidence in myself to believe otherwise. We headed off to his friend's house in a taxi. On arrival, we climbed out of the car and headed up the path to an empty house that was on loan to us for the evening! I was suddenly nervous. I suddenly felt body conscious. I had never really thought about my body in this way before, how it would look to a man, but I was feeling it now. It made me feel conscious, as I knew in less than ten minutes, I would be naked in bed with Damian, like I was once before.

However, this time it was different. I was more aware of myself. As we walked through the door, I started mumbling away with nerves! Damian remained quiet. He took my hand and led me over to the sofa situated in the middle of the living room. We lay down together, and then our lips met, before I knew what was happening, we were naked, and making love, in this stranger's house.

It was just as amazing as the first time, if not better; he was kind and considerate, telling me I was beautiful, and that I was Damian's Amelia. I felt like the luckiest woman alive.

We lay together for a long time. We talked and we caught up with each other. I told him I was now living at my mother's house. I talked to him about my dreams of escaping this small town just as he did. I asked him why he had not written to me. Why he had not called me. He said, he was not very good at writing letters, and that the phone was a communal one where he lived, and it was hardly ever free. I accepted this explanation, and never mentioned it again. I asked him if there was anyone else in his life, and he assured me there was no one. I felt relieved. That night passed by so quickly, he never promised me anything; he never lied to me; he just said, "Let's see what happens."

A part of me felt disappointed, I wanted him to promise me the world. I felt selfish for wanting so much. I felt insecure inside. I just knew I would lose him eventually; he was heading towards a world that was so far removed from mine.

At first light, Damian called a taxi, he opened the door and I climbed in, he kissed me goodbye and said he would call me soon. I was no longer sure of his feelings for me, like I once had been.

Sure, he liked me, and he liked me a lot; but something had changed between us. I just could not figure out what exactly.

I felt tearful on the way home. It was around 5 am in the morning, and I climbed out of the car and made my way around the back of my mother's house. She had double locked the door from the inside, which meant I would not be able to unlock the front door. So obsessed she was with locks and bolts. I found that she had doubled locked the back door from the inside too. I sat down in my mother's back garden, too afraid to wake her up. She knew I would not be home until very late. How did she expect me to get into the house? After about an hour I decided to throw stones up to Jake's bedroom window, he slept like a log and could not be wakened. So, I plucked up the courage and threw a large stone at my mother's bedroom window. She was a very light sleeper indeed. She opened her bedroom window, and shouted down that I would have to stay there until she got up a bit later. Then slammed her window shut. I was stunned, and tearful, I tried Jake's window again, throwing stone after stone. Eventually, he surfaced and opened his window. He smiled down at me.

"Oh, Amelia, are you locked out again?"

"Yes Jake, mother has double locked both doors from the inside. I can't get in."

"I will be right down. Just wait there a minute," he advised, shaking his head mockingly. I could hear Jake opening the door. I walked into the kitchen and then popped the kettle on. I was not tired in the least. I was feeling very chatty. I talked to Jake for over an hour about Damian.

Jake was in awe of him and respected him a great deal. He had recently watched Damian on the TV. I took Jake into my confidence, and told him how I felt I was losing him, and that I was convinced I would not hear from him for a while. Jake tried his best to make me feel better, saying that Damian would be a fool to let me go, and that I was more than good enough for him.

Finally, tiredness caught up with me and I crept up to bed very quietly, mindful not to disturb my mother. I slept for hours, finally resurfacing around two o'clock in the afternoon. I took a shower, and then made my way downstairs. On entering the kitchen, I heard the phone ringing. Mother beat me to the phone; she looked at me with a mocking expression on her face.

"Yes, Amelia's here, who is this? she asked.

"Damian, okay. And are you Amelia's boyfriend?" she enquired.

Mother took forever to hand the phone over, she said I had five minutes and then she wanted to use the phone. She always did this on the rare occasion I had a phone call. She hovered in the kitchen, refusing to give me any privacy whatsoever.

"Hey Amelia, I thought I would come over and see you today. Give me your mother's address, please."

To say I was stunned is an understatement. I was not expecting to hear from Damian so soon. I gave him my address and then put down the phone. I was feeling very nervous about him coming to my mother's house. I had no idea how she would react towards him, or what kind of embarrassment she would put me through. She really was that unpredictable.

I ran upstairs as fast as I could. I put some makeup on and my new jeans with a baby blue T-shirt. I smothered my hair with Silvikrin hairspray, flicking it backwards and forwards a few times for maximum volume! This was the '80s and it was all about big hair and shoulder pads!

Damian turned up an hour later. My mother was unbelievable, flirting with my boyfriend, saying he was far too good for me. Eventually, she got bored of trying to humiliate me and went upstairs. Jake was in the garage, doing up an old motor bike. Damian and I headed outside, so I could introduce my brother to him. Jake was in awe of Damian, and they both hit it off straight away. They tinkered around with this old motor bike for the longest time. I sat on the edge of the grass watching them both. Jake was very shy, a very naïve young man, and Damian was very confident and quite a worldly young man, they were so different. Damian was very good with Jake, and gave him so much time that afternoon. That was the only time Damian had ever come to my mother's house. They rode around the front of the house on this old motorbike for the rest of the day. We were all laughing and having the best time. Eventually, Damian had to go; I walked with him to the bus stop and waited patiently for the bus to arrive. I prayed with all that I had that the bus would be late. We stood in the corner wrapped in each other's arms and kissing passionately.

It was then that he told me he was heading back to Ipswich the following day. My heart stopped. I could not stem the flow of tears falling down my cheeks. He brought his hand up to my face and wiped away my tears.

"Amelia, it's only a few months. I'll be back before you know it," he promised.

"Why do I feel like I will never see you again, Damian? You will meet someone else and forget all about me," I cried.

"You know that's not true, Amelia. When I am in Ipswich I don't have the time for anything but training and sleeping. Trust me, I won't meet anyone else."

Before I knew it, the bus was in sight. Damian said he would call me in a few days.

"Be good, Amelia," he said. Then he kissed me once more and jumped on the bus. He walked to the back and waved through the window. I waited until the bus was out of sight. Then I cried all the way home. My heart was so heavy. All I wanted to do was lie down on my bed alone and cry.

Over the next few weeks, I did not hear from Damian. I could not stop thinking about him. The weeks turned into months, and I had all but given up on him. One day while I was out shopping for a new dress in the town centre, I bumped into his friend, Dexter. I asked him if he had heard from Damian. I was not prepared for what he told me. Apparently, Damian had been home recently for a weekend, and he had been seen out with another girl, who he believed to be his new girlfriend. I was devastated. Dexter was so kind, he hugged me and gave me a shoulder to cry on. I spent the rest of that afternoon drinking coffee in a café, pouring my heart out to Dexter. Shortly after that day, I started dating Dexter and we had become very close.

We would often meet up and go to *Cascades* together. He would always see me home afterwards. I really liked him a lot, but not in the same way as I had liked Damian. It was not until many years later that I realised I had started dating Dexter on the rebound. And it was not until I was in my 30s that I found out that I had been deceived by Damian's friend. He had lied to me, thinking I would never find out, as Damian was always away now, and did not come back home very often. Damian had not met anyone else at all. Who knows what may have happened between Damian and me, if his friend had not intervened. I discovered also that Damian believed I had simply just gone off with his friend.

I dated Dexter for a few months, until I discovered that he was also seeing my best friend behind my back. Back then mobile phones did not exist, if you wanted to make a private call to anyone out of earshot, you had to use a phone box. This particular night, I made my way to the phone box down the road, a typical red one, of the likes you don't see very often these days, as nearly all have been replaced. I phoned my friend Stacey; however, her phone was engaged, so I dialed Dexter's number, and his phone was engaged too. I thought *I am not walking all the way back, just to come out again later*, so I continued trying both their numbers until one became free. That was when I discovered their secret; I dialed Stacey's number once again. It started ringing. Then an awful thought formed in my mind. I tried to tell myself I was being ridiculous; however, I could not shake off this uneasy feeling. I placed the receiver back on the hook, and then redialed Dexter's number almost immediately after dialing Stacey's and his too was now free – their numbers had become free at the same time. I felt sick. The thought of being duped yet again did not bear thinking about. With tears streaming down my face, and a lump in my throat, I dialed Dexter's number again.

"Hello, Dexter speaking," he said quite jauntily.

"Hey, Dexter it's Amelia. I have just got off the phone to Stacey," I lied.

"Mmm, oh, yes well, urm, so you know then," he offered, assuming Stacey had told me everything and that this was why I was calling.

"No Dexter, I did not know, I just suspected. Thanks for confirming my suspicions. Oh, and by the way, I no longer want to see either of you again. You and Stacy are welcome to each other.

In a matter of minutes I had lost both my best friend and yet another boyfriend. I was so unhappy. I could not believe Stacey could do that to me. We had been so very close, we went everywhere together: clubbing, shopping, ice-skating, and to the gym. What was I going to do now? I was not very good at dealing with loss; I discovered this seemed to affect me greatly. Once I placed my trust in someone, I expected their trust in return. It just did not occur to me in any way shape or form that they could possibly break that trust. Was it me? I asked myself over and over again. I had just about had enough of people; I started to believe that the only real person who could be trusted was yourself. I decided the sooner I found a job that would take me away from this Godforsaken town, the better.

There had to be more to life than this small town. After all, there was a whole world out there for me to discover.

A Road Less Travelled

Over the next few months, I found a new job, working away from home. For me, it had been a scary move to enter the unknown, once again, putting my safety into the hands of others, something I was never comfortable with. However, it was also something I had to do if I was to find my destiny. This was a job I had chosen to take for two reasons: it took me far away from my mother, and I got to see the whole of my country, from one end to the other. I was to be a sales rep for a company called Fire Guard UK. This seemed the perfect answer to me. I was to be picked up the following Saturday and taken to Burnham-On-Sea. I was so excited, I couldn't wait.

Within less than two weeks, I had joined 20 other young teenage sales reps. We were all put up in a caravan park. We were given a brief training session and then the following Monday morning we were all taken out in the two red Fire Guard UK vans, and dropped off on well-chosen estates, two-by-two. The van drivers were also the owners of the company. We were armed with a folder, a poor sales pitch, and advised that we had to get at least six sales per day each. I had no idea that this company I had joined naively in my desperation to leave my small town was already the subject of investigation by the TV programme, "Watch Dog".

I spent 18 months working for this company. The days were long, the pay was poor, and the expectations were very high. I was very friendly, and spent more time drinking cups of tea, and having conversations with most of my potential customers than I did trying to sell them something they simply did not want. I certainly was not going to force people to buy anything, and I chose to ignore the advice given to me each Sunday evening when we had our sales meeting. This would always be about "Pressure." "Don't accept no for an answer," we would be told. I did not like this doorstep selling. Moreover, I needed to move on. This was not for me. I did not like the tactics they were using. The fact that they would make us feel so guilty if we did not make our daily quota of sales just confirmed to me this was not a very moral company. The staff turnover was quite considerable. The salespeople were never older than 21. Most teens lasted a month, maybe two at most. The reason I lasted so long was because I really did not want to go back to that small depressing town I had left 18 months previously. We pitched up in a different town or city every two weeks; we would stay there for a couple of weeks and then moved on. Our accommodation was always in caravan parks, or very cheap bed and breakfasts. This would initially be paid for by the owners of the company and then taken directly out of our wages each week. For the most part we would be lucky to receive anything more than £35 a week. However, our food, and accommodation were paid for. And I got to travel around the width and breadth of the country. I discovered a great love for Devon, Cornwall, Somerset, and the Lake District, to name but a few. I was seeing the whole of my country, and the weekends were ours to do as we pleased. A few of us would go walking, or swimming, or just visit local museums and libraries.

I did not care about the low pay we received. In my view, it was a great trade off, as I got to travel and see my country. I could not have afforded to visit so many beautiful parts of England at that age otherwise.

One day a young man called Dean, from North Warwickshire, joined the company. He was a year or so younger than me. We became great friends. He was genuine and kind. We had such a laugh together for the duration of my time at Fire Guard UK. He was from a little suburban village called "Wotton." He had told me so much about his beautiful little village and all his friends. He had many, and they had all grown up in the same village and gone to school together there. He spoke affectionately about his best friend, Peter, saying he would love for me to meet him one day, and that I must come and visit him and his friends. He would take me to all the local pubs, and I could stay at his mother's house in the village. This sounded wonderful to me. As far as I was concerned, he had the picture perfect upbringing: a great family, lots of friends that he had grown up with – all the things I had missed out on.

One day I decided it was my time to leave the company. I confided in Dean, and told him that I would be catching the train home the following day.

I was surprised to discover that Dean was also contemplating moving on. Although I was not keen on the job, I had enjoyed meeting lots of people from all walks of life. I had seen much during my travels, and I had also grown up some more. I had now seen all four corners of my country, and what a beautiful country England was. I favoured the Lake District, for its untouchable beauty and vast space. I felt so free there; I opened my wings and breathed in the natural air, unpolluted, and so fresh.

 I had ticked a box on my ever-growing wish list; I had travelled the width and breadth of my country. Now I needed to travel the world. However, that would be sometime away just yet, as this wish of mine required lots of money, I simply did not yet have.

 I left Fire Guard UK. I had just £35.00 in my pocket, and a bundle of enthusiasm. I made the journey back to Shropshire with a heavy heart. This would be just for a short time, I convinced myself. As a teenager struggling to carve a decent life for myself, I was beginning to realise that my destiny was further away than I had imagined. A lot of hard work was needed to realise my most important dream of one day becoming a homeowner and an author. I had a head full of amazing stories. I was already well read for my age, as reading was always my saviour, my escape from reality.

 I was back at my mother's house; we pretty much kept out of each other's way. However, there were times when I saw a different woman, one that had not visited me often in my life. Some days she seemed to make an effort;

she would be pleasant, and quite nice to be around. I actually found myself liking this woman; however, it never lasted long; that rarely seen nice woman would very soon be replaced by the she-devil. Once again my hopes of having a real mother would be dashed. I hated the feeling that it gave me. It was like giving your utmost trust once again in desperation that things would change for the better; wanting things to change for the better, and the possibility of having a proper mother and daughter relationship. Oh, how I needed a parent! A real parent. One that could advise me, help me on my way, point me in the right direction. However, this would never be the case. Leopards never change their spots; they just get older, and less intimidating. This was my road I was destined to travel alone. There was no tour guide, no leaflet, just my own intuition. I just prayed for my intuition. My 0-Levels, of which I was very proud, and had paid for myself at night school, would get me to where I needed to go. I was very clear about one important fact: I needed to go back to night school at some point. I needed to do some sort of business course or accounts course, and then I could apply for a job that paid a decent salary. One that would elevate me to the next level of my plan. First, I needed to decide on my very immediate step. This proved difficult, with very little money and just my enthusiasm and energy to help me along. I had very limited opportunities. Why was life so hard? Life was also very unfair, and it made no sense to me at all. Some people were bad all their lives and yet they were rewarded with good fortune and good luck. Then there were others, who spent their lives trying to do the right thing, having nothing but bad luck, and bad fortune. Why is this? This made no logical sense to me. Surely, it should be the other way around, I would often tell myself.

One Step Forward Two Steps Back

I decided to get in touch with Mr. Harris once more, in the hope that he could find me a modeling job or two. In the meantime, I would look for a day job that would pay enough money to cover all my mother's demands and save enough money to finally leave once and for all. Thankfully, Mr. Harris was more than glad to take me on again; he had a couple of jobs for me. The first was a one-off for an independent period costume boutique. I was delighted; I got to dress up for the day in period costumes. I felt like Juliette, from the unrequited love story "Romeo and Juliette" it was an amazing day. I got paid £50, which was a huge amount of money for me then. I stashed it away towards my future. The next job had not been so easy to obtain. I had to go to a casting and just hope that I was chosen. There was a new hotel in the town where the castings were going to take place. We had to walk up and down in front of a panel of judges, who just looked you up and down, with very straight faces, giving nothing away at all. Then all the girls had to wait for a few days for that dream phone call. I know it wasn't for supermodel of the year or anything like that, but it was for a fashion house and one that would bring repeat work.

I waited for days for that call, which did eventually come. I was ecstatic to say the least. I had been chosen above 200 hundred other girls to model swimwear. In addition, this brought with it a nice financial package for the duration of the job. It would be for one season only. And the shoots would take place all over the country. Over the next few months, I went along to do five shoots. In addition, each time, I was also able to keep the swimwear I modeled, which was an added bonus. I loved modeling; I was taken good care of, and treated with great respect. I was sensible enough to know that at just 5.5 feet tall I could never be a catwalk model, I was far too small. I was a photographic model, which at that time had a much shorter life span. Also, thoughts on the size of models were much different then. You had to be a certain size, and maintain that size for continued work. Plus-sized women developed as an area for consideration much further in the future. Not that I was a plus-sized model. At size 8 to 10, I was an acceptable size for photographic modeling. However, I feared if I put weight on, I would not be hired any more. The pressure of that alone was intense. I didn't tell my mother about this job, as I knew she would expect a cut from the money earned. Therefore, I was able to save it.

I started eating like a bird to ensure I maintained my weight. This was torture for me, as I loved my food. I had to be very careful as I also discovered I put weight on easily if I took my eye off the ball. Therefore, my days were filled with eating very little, running like an athlete, and putting myself under incredible pressure. To me this was about my journey, my destiny. This was not to become a great model; on the contrary, it was a route towards fulfilling my wish list.

After that summer, the job came to an end. I was paid handsomely and had an updated portfolio to be proud of. I had a day job working in a music production factory, producing and packaging cassette tapes. In the very late '80s, computers were just making their way into manufacturing, and I seemed to take to them naturally. I was placed in the back office, on the Sinclair computers, testing all the cassette tapes! It was fun, and seen as a very good job within the factory. I was paid £95.00 a week plus over-time. I was always working over-time. Saturday and Sunday mornings were the norm for me. There would only be a handful of us working on these days.

I would take any odd modeling job that I could get. With both jobs, I earned a fair wage for my age. I was saving quite well. However, since I had started modeling I had developed a love for fashion. I went through a spending phase, one that saw my wardrobe triple over the months. I discovered that when I looked good, I felt good. Like all teenagers, I wanted to fit in, but not at the cost of my soul. I would not lose myself again. I would no longer hide in a corner praying I would go unnoticed, as I had done for many years while I had been in care. No, I was now free, and it felt good to be myself, in the way I wanted to be, not the way others wanted me to be.

The Call That Changed My Life

One day on my arrival home from work, I received a phone call. It was Dean, my friend from Fire Guard UK.

"Hey Amelia, it's me Dean, how are you? he enquired.

"Oh my goodness, Dean! I can't believe you actually called me," I cried.

"I promised I would do you silly girl. Look, I am back in Birmingham now and was wondering if you fancied coming up to stay one of the weekends. You can meet all my friends I told you about."

"I would love to, Dean. In fact, there is nothing I would love more," I told him. I was so happy, not at receiving the call, but that he had kept his promise and had actually called me. I was not accustomed to this. It was agreed that I would travel up to Birmingham the following Saturday, to join Dean and his friends on a night out in Coleshill Town to celebrate his friend's birthday. I was to stay at his mother's house and would have my own room. I was so excited; I spent the rest of that night tearing through my wardrobe, deciding on the right clothes to take to Birmingham.

I wondered what his village was like, he had talked about it so often, how it was a real community, where everyone knew each other and where all the kids had grown up together and went to the same school. I could only wonder at a life such as Dean's.

The following Saturday, I was packed, and sitting on the platform, eagerly awaiting my train. The journey would take approximately 45-minutes. I was to be met at New Street Station by Dean and Peter, his best friend. I was looking forward to meeting Peter, as I had heard so much about him. The train arrived on time and was soon pulling into Birmingham Station. When it stopped, I waited for the doors to open and stepped off the train. I was so nervous, as I frantically looked around for my friend. As if by magic, he appeared out of the blue. He ran up to me and gave me the tightest hug. Pulling away, Dean introduced me to Peter.

Wow! I thought, Dean had failed to mention how incredibly handsome Peter was! He shook my hand, and our eyes locked. It was right there that fate intervened. I suddenly felt very self-conscious, nervous almost; I had butterflies in my tummy. This was a sensation I had felt with Damian. And I was not expecting to feel like that ever again. We walked through Birmingham City and did some shopping, and then caught the 590c bus to Wotton village, which was at least a 50-minute bus ride away. Wotton was a beautiful little village sitting on the border of Warwickshire; it was in the country, quite away from the bustling city of Birmingham. As we passed by all the houses, I looked on in amazement. They were all privately owned and so big too. The gardens for the most part, beautifully cultivated.

I was in suburbia! Instantly, I felt out of place. My heart was racing, as I looked around at the other girls my age passing us by as we stepped off the bus. They all seemed so perfect, dressed to perfection, manicured to within an inch of their lives. I remember looking down at my own not so perfect nails, and made a ball with my hands, so they could not be seen.

Dean said goodbye to Peter, and advised me we would be meeting up with him later in the local pub. I looked back as Peter walked away, and to my astonishment, he too was looking over his shoulder, smiling in my direction, and then he gave me a wink before turning on his heels.

That weekend was one of the best of my teenage life, I fell in love for the second time, I made lots of new friends, and the best part of it all was, at that time they knew nothing of my past. They accepted me into their tight, neat world, and I felt truly happy. I loved it in Birmingham. I felt instantly at home. This was where I wanted to live. That weekend, there were around 15 of us that went out on Saturday evening; we all went on a pub crawl in the next town called Coleshill, a beautiful old coaching town, steeped in history.

We started at the top of the town and worked our way down, one pub at a time. That night, Peter took it upon himself to be my protector from the guys who were all vying for my attention, he said to me.

"Amelia, if you get nervous at anytime, just kick me under the table, okay?" he suggested.

"Okay, Peter," I agreed.

The rest of the evening Peter and I exchanged many kicks under the table, followed by sweeping touches of our hands. I had fallen hook, line, and sinker, for this amazingly kind and sweet guy. I felt like the luckiest girl in the world, and totally unworthy of him. At the end of the night, once we had all reached Wotton village, Peter and I briefly broke away from the crowd. We ran behind the back of the library. There against the wall, was our first kiss, I was totally blown away. We could barely prise ourselves apart. If it were not for a set of headlights beaming directly toward us, we quite possibly would have stayed like that all evening!

Dean stepped out of the car, with a scrunched up look on his face. I could not understand why he was so upset.

"Amelia, I have been looking for you just about everywhere! I was worried about you!" he shouted.

"I am so sorry, Dean. We have only been gone a few minutes," I replied.

I said goodbye to Peter, and climbed into the car with Dean and his other friend. Dean just threw Peter a scornful look and drove off. I sat in the back of the car, trying to understand what had just happened. It made no sense at all. We were dropped off outside Dean's house, and then his friend drove off home. We walked in silence up the front path to Dean's parents' house.

"So, Amelia, do you like Peter?" he asked rather sullenly.

"I think I do, Dean. But if you would rather I didn't, then I won't go near him again," I replied, the reality of the situation suddenly dawning on me.

"I was just surprised, that's all, Amelia. I was not expecting to see the two of you together like that. You see, I was kind of hoping that you and me would become more than friends in time," he confessed.

To say I was utterly shocked does not even begin to explain how I felt. In all the time I had known Dean, he had never once given me the slightest indication that he liked me in that way. He had always treated me like a friend. He had never tried to kiss me, and had never looked at me in a way that would have betrayed his feelings. I was now finding myself in a very difficult situation. I got the feeling I was about to lose a good friend. That was something I did not want to happen at all. We walked into the house, and Dean showed me to my room and then said goodnight. I could barely sleep that night. I felt awful that Dean was so hurt. Yet I couldn't stop thinking about Peter. The following day was the last one of my stay. I was catching the afternoon train back home. I was sad, as I felt this was the last time I would be visiting this pretty little village. I packed my bags and made my way downstairs. Dean had gone to football training as he did every Sunday morning with all his friends. I sat down in the kitchen with his mum, who was profoundly deaf. She was a lovely lady, and it was not long before she was teaching me the alphabet, and then the vowels on my fingers. Before I knew it I was communicating in sign language with Dean's mother, albeit quite badly! I was in awe of this wonderful woman who had raised two grown-up children, who were both of the hearing world. They were a credit to her and her husband. She was totally independent and caught the bus everywhere. In fact, she lived her life as every other mother of a family did.

The only difference was, there was a light that went off in the house when the phone was ringing; to alert her when there was an incoming call. The same went for the doorbell.

I held her in such high regard. It made me realise that everyone has their own personal obstacles to overcome. It was how you dealt with them and then overcame them that mattered. I suddenly felt more normal than I had ever done in my entire life. I was not a freak, with a hidden disability; I had just been born into the wrong family, and that had resulted in many obstacles being placed in my path, for me to overcome. I was not a freak. People could not tell just by looking at me that I was brought up in the state-care-system. I was beginning to learn that I needed to overcome my own inner fears.

After spending a lovely morning with Dean's mum, I waited for Dean to return so we could catch the bus to New Street Station. Dean arrived home, smiled and then ran upstairs to take a shower. Within 20 minutes, I was saying my goodbyes to his parents and heading out the door. Dean and I walked towards the bus stop, then, unexpectedly Dean grabbed my arm and guided me towards Peter's house. My heart was doing ten-to-the-dozen by now.

"I thought you might want to say goodbye to Peter," he smiled.

"Oh Dean! Thank you so much, I don't know what to say!"

"You don't have to say anything, Amelia." Dean knocked the door. We waited patiently for what seemed like an age. Then Peter opened the door. He had the widest smile on his face; I noticed his hands were shaking too, as he was not expecting to see me again. Dean went on to explain that it would be cruel of him to stand in the way of true love.

He knew his friend felt the same way as I did and apologised for his behaviour the night before. He added, he had been naïve in thinking that I had feelings for him, and that it was not my fault at all. I wrapped my arms around him and gave him the tightest hug.

Dean smiled at Peter and said, "I thought you would like to take Amelia to meet her train."

"Dean, mate, thank you!" was all Peter could say.

We both said goodbye to Dean and then I followed Peter into his house to meet his parents.

Peter escorted me into the back room, which was rarely used. I sat down nervously crossing my legs. I was so surprised that Peter was just as nervous as I was. I knew I had fallen in love with him, and I equally knew Peter had also fallen in love with me too. There is no greater feeling than that of reciprocated love. Over the coming months, I spent almost every weekend in Birmingham. I completely adored Peter's parents. They were down to earth, loyal, and adorable. Most of all they accepted me into the family with welcoming arms. I became very close to Peter's mother; she was like a mother to me as well as a friend. She was honest and open, and all Peter's friends liked her too. I remember thinking how lucky Peter was. However, I now felt lucky too, as I was blessed with their acceptance of me. This meant more than anything in the whole world to me.

Moving to Birmingham

After a fair few months, an opportunity was put before Peter and me. One of his friends had been offered a job on a cruise ship, which meant he needed to rent out his flat. He knew Peter and I were thinking of moving in together, so he gave us first refusal. We jumped at the chance; Peter informed his parents that we were moving into his friend's flat together. They were truly amazing about this revelation, which took them by complete surprise. I am not saying they were happy about it. Of course, they would rather Peter stayed at home a while longer. However, they just gave us both lots of parental advice about money and bills, and how expensive we would find it. In addition, they said that they would be there for us if we needed anything. I left Shropshire for the very last time, without a backward glance, just a feeling of sadness at leaving Jake behind, with promises of one day when it was within my power I would come back for him. We hugged and cried that day like we had done once before.

My first couple of weeks in Birmingham was spent living at Peter's parents home in Wotton village. I was now working for the Royal Life Insurance Group. I had been sent on a month's intensive training course, during the weeks before I left Shropshire

The training was held at the Cavern Walk in Liverpool. We had an all expenses paid hotel, a five-star hotel no less, called The Adelphi: one of the most impressive hotels in Liverpool at the time. It had two bars, a nightclub, a beauty salon, and a spa. It had just about everything you could imagine. All meals, all drinks, entry into the nightclub and just about everything was covered by the company. We could even have free use of the beauty salon. We were very well looked after and treated like royalty by the hotel staff too. This was because Royal Life brought a lot of business to the hotel.

The training was from 9-to-5 each day from Monday to Friday. It was very intensive, and I was not sure I would pass all my modules. The homework we received at the end of each day was just incredible. We would all work in teams of four, and sit in the large tearoom and do our homework together and help each other out with each of our difficult areas of understanding, as the modules were really hard. We all desperately wanted to pass. Once we passed, we would become qualified financial advisors, with certificates of qualification to take away with us. Without these, we could not work for the company. We had to be F.S.A registered. I had the most amazing time on this course. Most of the other students were from London. I became very close to a girl the same age as me called Portia.

She was very clever, and very elegant. We hit it off straight away because of our love of reading. We were both reading the same book on arrival at the hotel, which sparked an immediate conversation. And from there our friendship was born. The one part of the course that was particularly easy to me was the case studies;

I loved reading about all these and equally enjoyed the homework on this section of the modules. The part I disliked the most was having to learn all the legal side of things. It seemed so monotonous, but was a very important part of the course.

At the end of the four weeks, we all sat our exams. It was a very intense two days. Once we had all completed our papers we headed straight for the hotel bar. That night there was a party to end all parties. I danced until 4 am with Portia and a few of the girls. Around 4.30 am, we all fell into our rooms and did not surface until lunchtime the following day.

I awakened with a throbbing headache; Portia had slept where she had fallen. We needed to find our way to the vast tearoom for two o'clock that afternoon to receive our exam results. It was already nudging one, o'clock. I shook Portia awake, until she started moaning in pain!

"Come on, Portia. We have just under an hour to wake up, grab a coffee, shower, dress, and meet the director in the tearoom for our results," I shouted excitedly.

"Ugh! What time is it Amelia?" groaned Portia. "It's just after one in the afternoon, come on! Get up! We don't want to be late, Portia. It wouldn't look good, would it?" I shoved a coffee in her hand and made my way to the bathroom.

At 1.50 pm, we both headed downstairs towards the tearoom. This was one of the most impressive rooms I had ever seen, I just loved it. It was like those incredibly vast rooms, filled with beautifully upholstered furniture, chaise lounges, chestnut tables, high back chairs on delicately carved legs.

The ceiling was so high and impressive, with a beautiful giant chandelier in the centre. The ceiling was painted beautifully; a mural adorned the vast space. A period painting, lovingly painted by some incredible artist. I thought that was awe-inspiring.

We waited for what seemed like a lifetime for the Director to arrive with our results. I was so nervous I could hardly bear it. The anticipation was almost too much. Then he walked in, cool, confident, and very serious. I was just 20-years-old, the youngest on the course. Most of the students ranged from 27-to-40-years-old. We all sat in complete silence while he gave us all a pre-talk. A waiter came to each one of us offering us all a glass of wine. The sight of alcohol made me want to throw up, as I was still suffering the effects of the night before.

Finally, the speech was over and we were each handed a large white envelope, this envelope was holding our future in it. As we took our envelopes, some paused, some walked to the back of the room, and some of us stayed seated where we were. I opened mine, took a deep breath and read the contents. I really had to contain myself; I was screaming inside, I had the biggest grin on my face. I had passed with a Distinction. I could not believe it: me! Amelia! A girl from nowhere, with a very poor education had passed the very stringent financial advisors' course. I had passed each and every module. I just could not believe it! I was a qualified financial advisor at the grand old age of 20-

years-old. I had never felt so proud of myself in my entire life. I held onto my certificate as if my whole life depended on it. It might not have seemed like much to some, but it was everything to me. This piece of paper would open so many more doors for me that would have otherwise been slammed in my face.

I was now fully equipped to advise people on mortgages, financial advice, pensions, savings, investments in the stock market, and so much more. Whatever happened in the future, this certificate gave me wings. I was on the right path towards my destiny. However, I still had a long journey ahead.

I spent that last weekend in Liverpool, shopping, celebrating with my newfound friends and generally touring that great city, before I left.

So here I was, living in Birmingham, a fully qualified financial advisor a few months into my job, occasional model, armed with a whole stack of new friends! I was happy, in love, and had a great job. Peter was training to be an accountant studying his AATs. The day came for us to move out of Peter's parents' home and into our rented apartment. It was a studio; it was small, but it was all ours for 12 months. We felt like we were on the top of the world, I went shopping to Wellsbourne Market with Peter's mother for all the immediate things that we would need: bed linen, quilts, pillows, a kettle, crockery, an iron and ironing board and a fair few other bits and pieces. Peter's mum was so kind and bought those first items for us both as a moving-in present to save us some money. I felt like I had won the jackpot. I felt richer than a millionaire. I had everything I wanted. We made our rented apartment look like a home, rather than the bachelor's pad it was before. We were just two miles up the road from all of our friends and Peter's parents. Once we were settled in, we took regular walks to the village for Sunday lunch at his parents',

and to meet our friends in the local pub on a Saturday night. Sunday mornings was football training for Peter, and aerobics for me. I would head off to the sports centre with Peter's friends' girlfriends. Afterwards, we would all jog the two-miles back to the village. We were all so super fit. We became good friends and soon we were going to aerobics four times a week. Peter and his friends were football training at least two or three times a week. Our lives were full and busy for the right reasons.

There were about six couples; we were all pretty close. We often went out for dinner together, or we would go clubbing together. On long summer days, we would all head over to the water parks for lazy afternoon picnics. It was quite perfect for a long time. Before I knew where the time had gone, I had been living in Birmingham over 18 months. My relationship with Peter was an intense one; we were both so deeply in love. I thought he was just perfect, he was so fit, and gorgeous, and I noticed many other girls thought so too. However, at that time I was confident enough in my relationship for it not to bother me. Peter's parents always remained supportive; they were incredible parents. I admired Peter's parents. I thought he was very lucky. However, I felt very blessed that they had accepted me into their family unit whole-heartedly. I could see why he was so confident in all that he did. He had a brother called Kyle who was completely different. Peter and I did everything together; it was as if we were one person at times. We had a great social life; we went out most weekends, whether it was an evening in the local pub or a visit in the city for a night of clubbing.

One lazy Sunday afternoon we decided it was high time we took a trip abroad together. After much deliberation, we chose Greece. I was so excited: my first trip abroad with a boyfriend! We went to the travel agents and booked a ten-day self-catering holiday. We were to fly out in early September, and staying in some lovely apartments with a south-facing balcony, just a stone's throw from the beach. Peter and I went on a few shopping trips to stock up on bikinis and shorts as well as all the usual stuff one needed for the perfect holiday. I was in seventh heaven: the perfect boyfriend, a holiday to Greece, and our own little rented apartment.

All was going so well, until we received word from Peter's friend who had been away working on the cruise ships. He stated that he was coming home to stay, and that he would need his apartment back. This was the last thing we needed to hear the week before we were heading off on our holidays. I was really upset. Where were we going to live? How would we find somewhere so soon? I had got so used to living in our little studio apartment, I never really thought about what we would do on his friend's return. Peter was not worried at all. He was very laid back, and nothing fazed him at all. A couple of days after the call, I received news from my employer that my services, along with those of five other temporary staff, were no longer required. So, within less than five days I was going to be homeless and without a job. I could feel my old friend tapping on my shoulder: the darkness, my nemesis. To me this meant everything; but to Peter it was just a blip. We always had his parents' home to return to, he advised me. This was not what I wanted; although at the time, I loved them as if they were my own parents.

I preferred for us to live on our own, independently from anyone else. This was so important to me, and something I could never quite make Peter understand. I had noticed a shift in our relationship before we headed off on our holidays, but I chose to ignore it. I did not want to face the reality that maybe; just maybe, we were not quite as close as we had once been.

I was starting to feel insecure. I had noticed his eyes wandering when we were out socialising. This had never happened before. At first, I thought I was just being paranoid, but it soon became apparent that I was not. I prayed that our holiday would bring us closer together once again. We would revert to the way we used to be, impenetrable. Over the coming days, I carefully and lovingly packed both our suitcases, sorted out the traveler's cheques, and made sure we had an ample supply of sun cream. I did everything possible to put all negative thoughts to the back of my mind. After having a talk with Peter, he convinced me I was being silly and that I was his princess and always would be.

It was easier to accept Peter's word, than contemplate life without him. I knew that if we were to split up, I would lose not only a boyfriend, I would also lose my friends, as they were the friends he had grown up with. I would lose his family, who I had taken on board as my own. And I would have nowhere to live. Peter could always go home; but me, well, I couldn't. I would lose everything that I had in my life at that time. I just knew I was not ready for that or strong enough to deal with yet another loss in my life, as this usually resulted in me losing everything I had.

Our holiday to Greece came and went in a flash; we had the most amazing time. It was both romantic and adventurous. We made love just about everywhere we could on that holiday. We hired a moped to take us around the island; we happened upon small private coves with cut-off private beaches to which we had to climb down. The only alternative would have been to reach those coves by boat. We headed down the side of the cliffs with a picnic basket in hand. The moped was parked at the top and we just hoped that no one decided to take off with it!

We laid out the picnic, and stripped off naked, it really was that private, no one could just walk by, and we could soon dress if we heard a boat coming! We lay sunbathing, catching a tan, reading books for hours and occasionally getting up for a lengthy swim to cool down. Eventually, we fell asleep on the beautiful white sand beach for what seemed like an age, and then I was woken up by a man talking.

I sat bolt upright, feeling very conscious that I was stark naked. Coming out of the water before me was a much older man, totally naked, walking towards me with all the confidence in the world. I nudged Peter awake. He sat up and struggled to hold back a laughing fit which was proving very difficult for him. I then had to look away, while struggling to pop on my kaftan! I could not look the man in the face. However, after a few minutes of talking it soon became apparent that he was harmless, and that he had a boat anchored around the corner, he said we could join him on the boat for a drink if we liked. We declined, and wished him a good day after sharing our sandwiches with him.

Greece was a lovely holiday, we went skinny dipping late at night; we rode all around the peninsula from one end to the other on that little moped. We frequented a few bars and met some wonderful people. We were even offered holiday jobs by one bar owner we had come to know quite well. He had said that if ever we wanted a working holiday then we should just let him know. He gave us his phone number in case we'd ever take him up on his offer. The time soon arrived for us to head off back to England. I felt so sad. This had been the most amazing time of my life. I loved Greece. This just further increased my need to travel and see the world.

I felt free in Greece. There we didn't live by the clock at all; we rose when we rose; and slept when we were tired! Life was so laid back in Europe. The locals would sit outside the tavern's playing chess and drinking coffee. Groups of teenagers on a package holiday would gather on the beaches to play volleyball, or hop in a pedalo out to sea! Peter and I favoured the private coves and zooming around on our hired moped. I was going to miss Greece a lot, and made a mental note to visit more of the Greek Islands. We were picked up from the airport by Peter's brother, tanned, broke, and in need of a new place to live. We had literally a couple of days to pack up and leave the apartment. I spent the majority of those two days crying and packing. Peter had popped to the pub to catch up with his friends the one night, and on his return advised me he had some good news. He had found us somewhere to stay, but it was very short term until we could find and rent a place of our own. One of the local businessmen in the village had offered us a room to rent in his house.

So, for the next month or so we lived in this house; but we were not happy. We were craving our own space once more.

It soon became apparent that our newfound living arrangements just weren't working for us. Therefore, Peter went cap in hand to his parents asking them if we could move in with them until we found somewhere else to rent of our own. Thankfully, they were not at all hesitant. They were lovely about it, and within a few days, we were moving once again to a more familiar and comfortable home. Living with Peter's parents was not so bad. They were very accommodating and all they asked was that we respect the rules of the house, which was perfectly understandable. It was not until many years later when I became a mother that I truly understood how remarkable his parents were. Not only did they accept us living together at such a young age, they never discouraged us or told us we were too young. They were there for us; they stood by us no matter what.

In my opinion, Peter's parents made a huge sacrifice, as it's not easy having your child's partner living with you. I see that now, I understand what great lengths they went to for us. They treated me as if I was one of their own. I will always be grateful to them for that. I will always respect them for what they did for me. They were truly one in a million. They looked out for me, listened to me when I was sad and in need of someone to talk to. I eventually confided in Peter's mum about my past, my demons, and my occasional visitor, "My nemesis." She was so understanding. We bonded further, and a great friendship was formed. Olivia was a remarkable woman, friend and confident.

Drifting Apart

Amelia age-22-years. Photograph taken in London photographic studios.

I had noticed a shift in my relationship with Peter; we had been living with his parents for almost six months. Peter was going out more with his friends, and we were doing a great deal more separately. My confidence was weakening and his was increasing. It was not long before we were often arguing and falling out with each other. By then, we had been together for almost two years, and our relationship was in desperate need of TLC. My heart was feeling the pain at the loss of the closeness I once shared with Peter. I could almost feel him slipping away and I felt there was nothing I could do to prevent it. We had been so young when we got together. Peter was just 17-years-old and I was 20. So young for such a serious relationship, neither of us had realised that we would eventually grow out of each other. When you are that young and in love you think you will be together forever, and no one can tell you any differently. All you know is what you feel at the time; logic came into nothing. It was all about your feelings. Sometimes I felt as if my heart was far too big for me to cope with.

Peter had reached 19, and I was 22. I was totally reliant on him for everything, I had moved to Birmingham to live with him; I had gained a wonderful new family – his. One of my closest friends was his lovely cousin, Petra, who conveniently lived just around the corner. All my new friends were his friend's girlfriends. I was very aware that if we were to end our relationship I would lose not just a boyfriend, I would lose my friends, my newly found family, my home, and my social life. This was a very small village. I would have to move away and start again, with practically nothing but a broken heart. I could not bear the thought of that knowledge. It visited me often.

I felt desperate and alone with my thoughts. I was facing a reality I could not change, I knew it was coming; it was just a matter of when. I did my best to push negative thoughts to the back of my mind, in the hope that I was just being a touch paranoid. One weekend a group of us, mostly couples, decided to head to the Belfry Golf Course in Warwickshire. The country club had a very popular nightclub often attended by the rich and wealthy of the region. Many teenagers could be seen being dropped off in limos. This was a place we frequented often, as it was not too far away from the village.

As we entered the nightclub I heard Peter scream out, "Look who's over there, it's only Damian Atkins! Did you see that amazing goal he scored in Aston Villa's last game?"

My heart stopped for a brief moment, I could not believe it. While Peter and his friends were cooing over Aston Villa's football players, I just looked straight ahead to see if I could catch a glimpse of Damian. I had never felt so nervous in my entire life. As I glanced in Damian's direction, I could see him looking directly at me. We both smiled and we walked towards each other.

"Hey there you, long time no see, you look great," said Damian.

"Hiya, you. Wow what were the chances of us bumping into one another here?" I replied nervously.

At that moment, Peter and his friends surrounded us! They were all very excited, and Peter's friends could not believe I knew Damian, as I had never mentioned it before.

I introduced Peter to Damian and they shook hands like gentlemen. Damian turned around to Peter and said,

"Make sure you look after Amelia. She is one in a million, Peter."

Peter nodded and promised he would take care of me. Damian and I just looked at each other for a very long time. At the time, I didn't really understand what had happened to us previously. I smiled at Damian as he turned and headed towards the dance floor with his footballer friends. Our eyes met several times that night, and I felt sadness in my heart. I could not explain why at the time. I had missed Damian more than I had realised. However, our lives had moved on, and I was with Peter now. I was in love with Peter, but I just did not feel secure with him.

That night amongst Peter's friends I was a bit of a legend, as Damian was an Aston Villa star and the hero of the moment for the team and big news in the press nationally! All Peter's friends were Villa fans. That chance meeting with Damian at the Belfry Country Club seemed to strengthen my relationship with Peter. I believe it knocked his confidence a little. However, I will be honest. For me it kept Damian in my thoughts for a long time afterwards, as I always felt as if our time together had been interrupted. I always felt as if we had unfinished business. However, I was a complete romantic who believed in happy endings, even though I had not found mine yet. I wanted to ask him that night, why he had just gone off and met someone else. Why he just didn't tell me himself. Instead, I had to hear it from his friend. However, it was a long time ago, and I thought better of it. We had both moved on with our lives.

For a while, I felt confident again in my relationship. Peter was once again attentive and thoughtful, like he had always been before we stumbled into a rut. Our relationship cruised along at full throttle for another 18 months. We both had lots of fun, many weekends away and many unforgettable nights out with our friends. However, it was not to last. I found a beautiful two-bedroom flat for rent in the village with immediate effect. I was so excited I agreed to take on the flat at just £50 pounds per week – an absolute bargain. I could not get home fast enough from work that day. I ran into the house with my news, fully expecting Peter to be just as happy as I was. Alas, this was not the case at all; his response was of surprise and reluctance. I could see immediately that he was not taken with the idea at all.

My heart sank, the tears welled up in my eyes, I feared the worst, and then a delayed smiled appeared across his face.

"Great Amelia, really, just great," he replied.

I was not very convinced, but I didn't question Peter's reluctance. I was far too afraid of the outcome of such a conversation. I certainly would not have been able to deal with it.

Over the next few days, we moved into our new very spacious flat. I was so excited, I truly believed it would reignite our failing relationship, and for a while, it did. We settled in well, had many friends over for dinner and the occasional party. However, I noticed Peter was not as attentive as he had once been, he was spending longer at work, and he started popping in on his days off, which he had never done before. He was going out more often with work colleagues, and not coming home until the next day. I knew in my heart of hearts something was wrong. I knew I had to face the reality of what was going on. I could no longer close my eyes to it. I confronted Peter about his feelings and I was met with indifference. I was made to feel ridiculous and paranoid. He did nothing to convince me otherwise. Following our heart to heart, I grew very suspicious. One day while Peter was out playing football, I decided to go through his briefcase. I truly wished I hadn't. I found an A4 note pad; there was a long handwritten poem in it. As I read the beautiful poem to myself, it soon became apparent that it was not meant for me. My heart was instantly broken, shattered into a million pieces. The poem referred to a beautiful girl at his office. This explained so many things to me, but most of all that we were over.

I felt sick. I held the poem in my hand and read it repeatedly, hoping it would say something different to me, but it didn't. I could not ignore what I had found, as devastated as I was. As heartbroken as I was. I could not stay with someone knowing they were no longer in love with me, and knowing they had feelings for someone else.

That same day I confronted Peter with my findings. He couldn't deny it. He looked away. Then told me he was leaving me and that he was no longer in love with me. He confessed that he had fallen in love with someone else. There are not any words to describe my devastation at that moment. I watched as he gathered his things silently and walk out of the door, just like that. I sat with my arms wrapped around my knees against the wall. Then I found myself begging him not to go, I pleaded with him to give us one last chance, but my pleas fell on deaf ears. His mind was made up. After four and a half years, it was over. I also knew I had lost so much more that day. That is what I was having difficulty accepting.

I fell to the floor. It was as if I had been thrust into a bad dream from which I would wake up from at any moment. However, this was not a bad dream at all; this was my reality. I cried for hours, I lay on the floor clutching a batch of love letters I had received from Peter many years before. The saddest discovery for me was that Peter had chosen to leave all his love letters and cards from me behind. I remember thinking, why did people find it so easy to erase people they once loved from their lives, as if they had never existed.

Peter may not have loved me any more, but my feelings had not changed at all. Over the next couple of days, it soon became very apparent that everyone else had known. I had been the very last person to find out. I knew I had lost everything. I would have to give up the flat; there was no way I could afford to run it by myself. I immediately lost a family, his family, not to mention my friends, who ultimately were his best friends' girlfriends. Now, Peter would be introducing a new woman into his circle. There was no room for me anymore.

It was especially hard for me at the time, because I did not just lose a boyfriend, I lost the flat, I was pushed out of my social circle, and I had to start all over again. However, not before I had a small breakdown. I was so vulnerable, still finding my way in the world, and I depended on Peter far too much. We were both so young, and our relationship was very intense. We both needed to live a bit before we settled down, but at the time, I did not see this. Peter had just simply moved on; he had changed his mind; he no longer wanted to commit to living with someone. He had met someone else and he just wanted to have fun and go on holiday with his friends and have a good time.

It was just far easier for him, because he only had to give me up. I on the other hand had to lose just about everything I had. It seemed so unfair to me. I couldn't take in the fact that he no longer loved me. After four years of true romance, love letters, and even drawings he had sketched of me, all the dreams we shared. Yet he had simply fallen out of love with me. Once again, I was confused. Was this yet another test by "Him upstairs?" Had I not been through enough? Why was it when someone decided they no longer wanted me in their life, I was the one that had to lose everything.

I was the one that always suffered. That's how it seemed to me at that time, because that was all the experience I could draw on.

My Complete Breakdown

My nemesis had returned almost immediately following my breakup with Peter. I hadn't seen it for a while, and then one morning there it was. It had a strong hold on me, choking me, I could barely breathe. Once again, I had fallen into my abyss. I had no wish to open the curtains, or get out of bed. I had no appetite. My will was weak, and getting weaker by the day. I had no one to help me through it; no one to tell me everything was going to be okay. I had no idea where I was going to live. I did not have the strength even to think about all the practicalities of my life. It was all finally too much. One-step forward and then two large steps back. It was becoming truly exhausting. How much optimism did a person have to have? At that moment, I was not quite sure if I had any fight left in me. I had given up completely. My breakdown resulted in a bottle of Paracetamol. I just had no fight left in me; I couldn't bear to trust anyone ever again. Why? Why? Was it me who had to lose everything, each time someone wanted to walk away from me?

This was the last thing that ran through my mind on that fateful day I was rushed into hospital. All alone in the flat, lying on the floor, it was a young man from the village that called the ambulance.

He even came with me to hospital. He was at university at the time and studying hard; he stayed at the hospital all that first night with me, and studied while I slept. He was so kind to me, and so thoughtful. I was simply heartbroken; I could not imagine ever being happy again.

Peter never came to see me in the hospital; however, he had heard that I had been rushed in. However, Peter's parents were amazing. They looked out for me, and made sure I did not feel alone. In fact, it was their kindness that helped me through the awful mess I had found myself in. Sometimes you really have to hit rock bottom before you can truly appreciate life.

Eventually, I gained a little weight, I was crying less, and it was then decided that I was fit to be discharged. I went to stay with Peter's cousin for a few weeks, until I found somewhere cheaper to live. I was on sick leave from work, and still being paid, so all was not lost. Peter's mum was very kind and worried about me. She watched over me, and even gave me money to help me get back on my feet again. I really don't know what I would have done without her support. She truly was like a guiding light through a very dark time. It was not Peter's fault I had decided to give up on life that particular day. It was the fault of my entire life and the lasting effects it had on me up to that very moment. It was all the bad things I had gone through collectively that had finally brought me to a standstill that day – not just the break up of a relationship.

– not just the break up of a relationship. Peter simply did what most young people do and that was out grow someone, and moved on. He was not to know the devastating effect the breakup of our relationship would have on me.

Starting Over Once Again

A couple of weeks later Olivia came to see me. She had some good news. There was an elderly lady who lived at the other end of the village, who just happened to be looking for a lodger. Her current lodger of three years had recently gone on to pastures new. The lady was called Blanche; she was 64-years-old, single, and a member of the amateur dramatic society in the village. She still worked, part-time these days as a secretary for a firm of solicitors. She was rather posh and liked things just so. I agreed to a meeting with Blanche to see if we would get on. The day I met Blanche was a life-changing day, only I did not see it that way at the time! We were so different, I was 24-years-old, 40-years her junior.

I was afraid at first that she would be too strict, and that in her house I would not be able to breathe without her commenting. Nevertheless, they tell you not to judge a book by its cover. Blanche turned out to be a Godsend. We were good for each other; she understood me, listened to me, and really made me feel as if I could do anything. She was like a guiding angel sent to me at a very low time in my life. Of course, it did take us both a while to adapt to one another. Olivia had brought us together, two single women both in need of companionship for completely different reasons, and it worked.

Blanche had given me a lovely master bedroom. I had a free run of the house, and we soon became friends. She had already been told about my recent action that had landed me in hospital for a few days. She never once mentioned it. She seemed to understand my heartbroken state. When she could hear me crying after work in my room, she would simply knock on the door, she would not enter; she would just knock it twice and then walk back down the stairs, not wanting to enter my private space without an invitation. Once I opened the door there was no Blanche; instead, a beautifully made-up tray would be outside my door, with a hot cup of tea and a slice of cake, or a sandwich complete with a napkin. Blanche knew I was not eating very much and was a bit under weight. Again, she never lectured or advised me. She would simply do the most thoughtful things without saying a word. It was because of these very silent gestures that our unspoken bond was formed, forever. I was in awe of her. I had the utmost respect for her. I warmed to Blanche very quickly, and she wanted only a small rent in return for board and lodgings in her beautiful home.

She took me in not knowing me at all, and gave me a home; she made me feel welcome in a way I never had expected. We had our meals together each evening after work. She would make me breakfast each morning for when I came downstairs. She was truly amazing. I was very depressed when I moved into Blanche's home. My nemesis had insisted on moving to Blanche's with me with no intention of leaving anytime soon. I had lost the man I thought I was going to marry, and I had never considered my life without him. Now here I was single, alone, and having to restart my life once again.

My nemesis would not leave me. Each day I woke shrouded in this dark nothingness.

I felt despair, and discouragement. I decided to apply for a new job in the hope it would make me feel better, and have more prospects for me. There was a huge buzz around about a new project in the West Midlands called "The Channel Tunnel Project." I applied for the job as "Design Scrutiny Assistant" and within a few days, I had totally convinced myself that I had not got the job. Until one day, when I received the all-important call advising me that the job was mine. It was on a two-year sub-contracted basis due to the nature of the project. This was the best news I had received in a long while. I jumped up and down and could not wait to tell Blanche. This was just the lift I needed. I was always lucky with positions I applied for, never remembering a time when I had failed an interview.

That evening over dinner, I told Blanche the news. She was delighted. She was genuinely happy for me. The following Saturday I caught the train into the city to go shopping for some new work clothes. I wanted a new suit, shoes, and a coat. I had a lovely day. I met my friend for lunch. We had a bottle of wine to celebrate; we laughed; we talked and we hugged each other. That was the first day out I had been on since parting with Peter. It was a great day, and I went home with a newfound confidence.

The following Monday I turned up at my new place of work early and eager to please. Dressed in a black pencil skirt and white fitted shirt, finished off with a pair of black high-heeled sling back shoes, and my long hair knotted at the nape of my neck. I looked like the ultimate professional woman and I felt confident and very proud of myself for landing such a great role. The job itself was very intense; I occasionally went into work on the weekends to keep on top of my workload. I made new friends from the Derby office and once again, my social life picked up. It was not long before my weekends were filled with invitations to wedding receptions, parties and dinners.

I was asked by my friend Sadie, who lived in Derbyshire if I would attend her birthday party the following weekend. She said I could stay at her mother and father's country pub. She also advised me that there would be lots of local single bachelors and maybe one would catch my eye. I assured her I was not in the market for love anytime soon! Too often, I had allowed my heart to get in the way of my head. I was on a journey, and I would not be deterred again. At least not until I had bought my dream house, anyway!

Before I knew it, the following weekend was upon me. My bags were packed and I was on the train to Derby. Sadie met me at the station, and we headed off into the country to her parents' pub. It was an amazing elegant country pub. The food was their specialty, and people travelled for miles to dine there. This particular Saturday evening the pub was closed to the public and instead kitted out with their daughter's birthday balloons and banners just about everywhere. It looked amazing. There were fireworks set up in the garden, ice sculptures strategically placed around the pub. I could not believe the trouble Sadie's parents had gone to for their daughter's 21st birthday party. It was the talk of Derbyshire.

We grabbed a bottle of wine and headed up to Sadie's room to get ready. A-line mini skirts were the fashion at the time, I had a beautiful black one, and a little fitted jacket to change into, topped with black diamante strappy heels. I loved my new outfit and felt excited about the party. Nearly eight months had passed by since I moved in with Blanche, and my whole life had changed, my job, my friends, and my home. Pretty much everything had changed in a short space of time. My nemesis had taken leave a couple of months beforehand, and I was on a roll. I was determined not to encourage a trip into my abyss. After two hours of preening, drinking, laughing, and dancing to the Ministry of Sound in Sadie's bedroom, we eventually made our way downstairs to the party, which was already buzzing. I couldn't believe how many handsome men there were at her party: some with girlfriends and some without.

I was not ready for a new partner, so I mingled from one group to the next, grabbing a glass of wine here and there. I eventually had enough of the loud music and decided to make my way into the garden. It was such a beautiful night. I sat down on the garden chair and just looked out to the vast rape fields in the distance blanketing the scene before me, a beautiful bright yellow. Before I knew it, a man approached me,

"Hey my name's Adrian. May I ask yours?"

"My name is Amelia," I replied shyly.

"Lovely name, Amelia. Can I join you?"

"Sure, take a seat, but I am warning you I am not looking for a boyfriend," I offered just like that!

"Well at least we are clear on that, then. Now, how about I join you and share the view you are admiring so dreamily?" he replied.

I assented with a smile. He was pleasant and unassuming. I felt comfortable with him. It turned out he was a professional "Deep Sea Diver" for a living, with an Engineering degree. He was strawberry blonde; another word for a touch red. He was very pale skinned. We talked for hours. He bought me many drinks, and by the end of the night I pretty much knew all about him and he knew next to nothing about me, and that was how I liked it. I had mastered the art of having a conversation with someone and revealing very little about myself.

That evening I spent the night with Adrian. We had a one-night stand. I was not proud of it, and when I woke up the following morning, I looked to my right to see him still there fast asleep. I could not have jumped out of bed quickly enough. I got dressed and flew downstairs, looking for my friend.

"Ah there you are, you little minx, you," said Sadie.

"Oh my God, Sadie, what have I done?"

"Oh don't beat yourself up about it Amelia. You just had fun that's all. And Adrian is an okay guy. You are both single, so what is the problem?"

"I had one of those mornings after the night before moments, you know, when you look at the person next to you and think, oh God!"

"Well, look, it's happened. He will be fine about it if you don't want to see him again. It was probably good for you to let your hair down and have some mindless raunchy sex," she laughed.

I had to agree with her, so I stopped thinking about it and made my way into the dining room for breakfast, where everyone else was already eating.

"Morning Amelia, come sit over here," suggested Sadie's best friend.

At that moment, Adrian walked into the room. He made his way straight over to me and took the vacant chair next to me.

"Do you mind, Amelia?"

"No, no, please sit down," I replied, a little embarrassed.

Adrian

We sat in silence over breakfast, neither of us knowing what to say. I knew I didn't want to date Adrian. I had simply had a drunken one-night stand and was not looking for a boyfriend. Adrian, on the other hand, was in the market for a girlfriend and he made it very clear that he fancied me. I had put myself in this situation so I had to get myself out of it.

I told him I could be friends but nothing else. He seemed fine with this, and said he could do with a new friend. I thought *how sweet*! I really liked him. I just did not fancy him. The following day he offered to take me back to Birmingham and drop me off home. We talked and laughed along the way, and over the weeks became great friends. I believed that he had accepted our friendship and no longer saw me as a girlfriend but more of a best friend. He was a great friend. He would take me all over the country visiting castles and stately homes… We both loved walking and hiking, so we often went to the Malvern Hills hiking on summer days. We had the perfect friendship. I had a great deal of respect for him.

However, I never developed any feelings for him other than those of friendship. Adrian spent months at a time out of the country, in Abudabi, Dubai, Russia, Norway and many other faraway places. During these times, he often asked me to board a plane and meet him at his expense. However, I refused for a very long time, as I did not want to take advantage of his good nature. But eventually he wore me down and I agreed to meet him in Amsterdam for the weekend. He had sorted out my plane tickets, which would be waiting for me at the desk in the airport. I boarded the plane, and within 45-minutes I was walking through Schiphol Airport, nervous, and praying that Adrian would be there waiting for me at Arrivals. That was the first time I had ever flown in an airplane by myself.

Thankfully, as agreed, he was waiting for me as promised. The airport was so huge that I could hardly believe it, considering Amsterdam was quite small. Amsterdam was on my Places-to-visit list, so I smiled and made a mental tick in my head off my list. We spent the weekend like real tourists, visiting the sites of Amsterdam, including both sides of the canal. The last special place before I departed Amsterdam to visit was "Ann Franks" house. We walked around the city and we ate in many little Bistros. I even tried a space-cake, which had me giggling all day. No wonder everyone in this city seemed so chilled out, I thought, they were so friendly. Of course, they would be with space-cakes and weed on the menus! Nevertheless, you could not go to Amsterdam and not try one of those famous cakes! The truth was I had eaten three of those cakes, they tasted so good, and the more I ate the more I wanted.

We had a simple hotel, with separate rooms, Adrian never assumed anything, and made it clear we were best friends now. So I felt totally comfortable with him. The following day he waited with me until my flight arrived, and then waved me off.

I didn't know until I reached England that Adrian had slipped a credit card into my pocket, a kind gesture that I couldn't accept. I was in the taxi on the way home from the airport, sitting back for the ten-minute journey home, when I discovered the Visa card in my pocket with a note stuck to it:

"Amelia, I know what you're thinking, but please, I have more money than I know what to do with. Please accept this, even if you don't use it. Keep it for emergencies; at least you know you will always have that security should you need it. Love, Adrian."

A tear fell from my eyes. Why could I not fall in love with him? He would be perfect. However, I just did not have those sorts of feelings for him. I started to wonder if he had hopes of us getting together in the future. I needed to know, as I didn't want to lead him on, and I needed to make sure he understood we could only ever be friends. He was a great friend, sometimes too perfect. I wrote him a letter subtly asking him about our friendship, to make sure he was happy with everything the way it was. I waited two weeks for a reply. A long letter arrived, saying I was being silly, and that of course he understood that we were just best friends, which was better than marriage really, as friends often last longer! I laughed at his letter and once again was assured we were singing from the same hymn sheet.

On his arrival back in Britain three months later, he called me and we arranged to go out for dinner. I could not believe the gifts he had brought me back from his trip. There was a large box. On opening it, I saw that it was filled with Chanel perfume, Chanel body lotion, Dior sunglasses, and a D&G watch.

….."Please don't refuse them, Amelia. I would be really insulted. After all, I have no one else to spend my money on. So who better than my best friend?" he assured me.

I accepted the gifts, and it was that day I developed a great love for Chanel perfume. It is still a favourite to this day.

I said goodbye to Blanche and off we went to dinner. He had booked us a table at none other than the beautiful Walton Hall, a converted stately home which was now a five-star hotel and restaurant. I was very impressed indeed. He ordered Bollinger Champagne and poured me a glass very elegantly. It was that night I caught him looking at me in a way not used for looking at a friend. He really looked at me with deep and thoughtful eyes. In just an instant, I felt his eyes glide all over my body in a dark way. Then before I knew it, he was smiling once again, and my best friend Adrian was back with me.

I convinced myself I was over-reacting, even a little paranoid perhaps. Adrian only had one glass of champagne, so I polished off the lot slowly during the three courses and over four hours. Adrian said he had a surprise and I was to close my eyes, so I closed my eyes. When I was prompted to open them there were two waiters holding the most amazing pure chocolate cake, which said, "For my wonderful best friend."

I was truly blown away. I could not believe he had gone to all this trouble. He took my hand and said that my friendship meant the world to him, and that he did not know how he ever managed before without me in his life. I guess right there and then alarm bells should have rung in my ears. However, they didn't – not for a long time afterwards.

Adrian advised me that he would be heading out to Dubai on a six-month diving contract the following week. Laying pipes at the bottom of the seabed. I congratulated him on yet another fabulous contract, and told him we could go to dinner before he left the country. Over the next couple of days, I worked long hours, and literally came home from work, showered, ate my dinner and fell into bed. Therefore, I did not take any calls on Blanche's landline or at work.

On the third day, I was walking out of the office at the end of a long hard day, and there was Adrian, standing at the gates waiting for me, not looking at all happy.

"Where have you been?" he shouted furiously.

"What are you talking about Adrian? I have been either here or at home sleeping. I told you I would be working long hours this week. Anyway, what are you doing here? I thought we were going to meet up tomorrow night."

"Well, I just had to come Amelia. I hadn't heard from you. I was worried," he explained. I looked at him; his eyes were full of confusion and silent anger. I explained to him that I had been busy, and that I was just on my way home. He told me to hop into his car and he would take me home. He drove slowly, I asked him to put his foot down, and he said he didn't want to, as this way he got to spend longer with me.

Then I felt uncomfortable. I wanted to talk to him about his behaviour that day, but I didn't, I chose to ignore it and hoped it would blow over.

Once we reached Blanche's house, I climbed out of the car and told him I wanted an early night as I had an early start the following morning. He was not happy at all and begged me to let him come in for a while. I stuck to my guns and said no. He drove off in a stroppy mood leaving tire marks on the road behind him. Blanche opened the door and gave me a hug,

"We have chicken tonight, Amelia."

Oh how I loved Blanche's dinners! She was a great cook, and always prepared meals with fresh produce, never frozen or tinned. Blanche could always tell when there was something on my mind.

"Come on, Amelia. Out with it, what's troubling you?"

"Well it's Adrian. He's just being a bit full on. I mean, he knows we are friends, and I think he wants more than that, but I don't see him in that way at all."

"So, have you explained this to him, Amelia?"

"Yes, I have, but I don't think he is taking what I said on board at all." As always, Blanche was a great listener. I felt much better having spoken to her about it.

Over the following weeks, I withdrew from Adrian slightly. He had left the country for Dubai on a six-month contract. He would be based out at sea, which would be his home for the immediate future, diving, and sleeping for the most part. I did not see him before he left and I felt really bad about this, as I knew how upset he was. I thought about him a lot and, of course, I missed my friend.

Life was not as exciting when he was away. However, I didn't know how to solve my problem, as I dearly loved him as a friend and didn't want to lose what we had. At the same time, I did not want to give him false hope of there ever being anything more between us than as friends.

After a few weeks, I received a letter from Dubai. I was very excited and tore open the signature blue envelope indicating that it was an airmail letter. As I read the words, my jaw dropped to the floor. Adrian had proposed to me. He stated he knew I was not in love with him. However, that did not matter. What are marriages based on anyway, he said, friendship and trust. We have that, Amelia. Please consider my offer. I will take care of you always. Give you the life of your dreams. You will never want for anything. I will always be there for you, no matter what. I will never leave you, hurt you, or abandon you when you need me the most.

As I continued to read the words, the tears fell from my eyes. They were the words I had so desperately wanted to hear from Peter at the end of our relationship. Why oh why could I not fall in love with Adrian? Why did I keep pushing him away, not allowing myself to give us a try? My mind was running wild with thoughts from every direction and from every possible scenario. Then the craziest thought came into my head: would it really be such a bad idea? I love his company. I love our friendship, and we had the same love of the great outdoors, hiking, swimming, climbing and much more. He knew all about my dream to be a published writer one day and fully supported it, rather than making me feel silly for even imagining I could be an author one day.

So what was the problem? Why could I not love him? I didn't have the answer to this question, which kept me awake at nights for weeks. This friendship confused me. We were very close, yet there was something about him I could not put my finger on. I knew he could be controlling at times. I really did not like that side of him, and he assured me he was just being protective of me.

I did think about his offer very seriously. Then I did the only thing I felt I could, I said no. I replied with a long heart-felt letter, explaining that his friendship meant far too much to me for it to be ruined by marriage, a true friendship lasts forever I advised him. How many marriages can you say that about? I said I would understand if he no longer wanted to be friends with me and I would await his reply.

Due to the slowness of air mail to and from Dubai, I didn't receive a word for two weeks. I could tell from his words that he was saddened by my response. However, he said he understood and totally respected my decision. Adrian advised me not another word would be spoken about his proposal. Our friendship remained as was, and he would see me in a few months. At the end of the letter, he asked me to take myself shopping with his credit card. Please buy yourself something nice, a gift from a friend. I was sad, and yet relieved, that finally; he knew where he stood with me. I felt in my heart of hearts I had made the right decision. I could never marry anybody for anything less than true love my heart would not allow it. I was a hopeless romantic and believed that love was the answer to everything. That when two people fell in love with each other there was truly no better feeling in the world, and everything just fell into place.

I knew this from experience, and I missed it immensely. I longed to be in love again one day, but not just yet.

During the time Adrian was away, I worked hard, went jogging, and did one or two modeling jobs. I had my portfolio updated, and went for a few castings. The Channel Tunnel project was the talk of the country. This was to bridge the gap between England and Europe; this was history in the making, and to be able to travel under the sea by train to Europe was an incredible thought… I was privy to lots of information about the overnight sleeper trains, which were being built at Met Cam just outside Birmingham City Centre. One day our office was taken on a tour to see the "Mock up trains" which had been built in the large hanger. They were really amazing! The engineers talked us through the technical problems confronting them at the time, saying that much work still needed to be done. I was fascinated, and could not wait to go on a trip to Europe via the sleeper trains. A couple of months later a meeting had taken place with the directors. They had decided to hire a female model for the night trains. They needed a model to take a shower in the mock-up trains, to wash her hair, and dry herself off to test the mock-up shower that had been erected.

This was to take place in front of at least 20 engineers from all over the country. The idea behind this was to see if the size of the shower cubicles on the overnight trains would work efficiently, not just technically, but also practically. They needed to ensure there was enough space for one person to comfortably take a shower and wash their hair, and also that water flowed out as it was supposed to and did not over flow. The model would not be naked of course; they were to wear a swimming costume.

My director knew I did the odd bit of modeling here and there, so he decided to approach me first before going to a modeling agency. Of course, I snapped up the job! I was prepped fully as to what would be expected of me. I was to wear a red swimming costume, to shower in, and wash my hair. A few weeks later I turned up for work as usual, with my swimming gear, and waited to be escorted to the mock-up trains. It was very daunting – more so than I had anticipated as there was a room full of engineers all holding cameras. The shower cubical was all transparent for the purposes of the experiment. It was also open, not enclosed behind walls, I dropped my dressing gown and stepped into the shower as instructed, and then spent the next hour, being asked to stretch my arms up, then down, and then sideways, then I had to wash my hair as I would do normally at home in the shower! Flashlights were going off ten to the dozen, and it was all a bit crazy really! Nevertheless, fun, to say the least.

That day I got paid £150 for one hour's work. I also received copies of the photographs taken for my portfolio, plus a free spa day at a local health farm.

I felt so proud of myself, and I was the talk of the company for a while! I had three requests for dinner that week, all of which I turned down.

A few weeks following the photo shoot, Adrian arrived back in England. He surprised me and met me from work. He had a large bouquet of white and yellow roses which were my favourite and also a black velvet box that on opening revealed a large bottle of Dior perfume and body lotion. He kissed me on the cheek and said, "Please accept this gift, and it's just to say sorry for putting you in an awkward position." I did accept the gifts, and then he took me for dinner to an Italian restaurant in Birmingham. I told him all about my surprise-modeling job for my company and he was so proud of me. I told him I wanted to buy my own house, which I was saving hard for with the hope that in the next couple of years I could buy my first home. My dream house was a Grade II Listed property, olde and worlde with large rooms, a typical old English country house, or at least as close to one as I could afford! I advised him that I had enquired about doing a sociology course through the Open University too. The course also covered menology and phenomenology … I had always been fascinated with the mind, and thought this would be a great course to take. It would open more doors for me in the future, not to mention increasing my earning potential, which was very important to make my dream of owning my own perfect house a reality. The benefit of this course was that I could do it from home in my spare time, with a two-week summer camp at a university to take my exams the following summer.

He did not seem as excited about my plans as I was. He was quiet, displaying very little reaction.

"That is great, Amelia," he grumbled.

"You don't seem very happy for me, Adrian?"

"I am happy for you. It's just that you are making plans, that don't seem to include me, Amelia." "Look, Adrian. I have had nothing but dreams all my life. They were just dreams, ones that encouraged me out of bed on days when I felt like there was nothing to live for. How many times have I told you, I want to own my own house, one that will be my home and no one else's to take away from me when things are not going their way? It will be my home and security for me that I have provided for myself, something for me to be proud of. My plans do not affect our friendship. They never will. But please don't hold me back. Don't make me feel bad for wanting to move forward. All I want is to be financially independent, to own my own home, to write that book I've always talked about and some day to have a family of my own, one that I belong too; one that is truly mine because I have made it. They are my dreams, Adrian, and one day they will be a reality."

Adrian was very quiet. He quickly changed the subject, and talked about his next contract in a few weeks. He would be heading to Norway. I was so pleased for him. He was an amazing diver. The work was flowing in from all directions and he was having to turn some down. "Look Adrian, you are living your dream. You had a lot of help along the way, you had great parents, a great education and you have been supported in all that you do. So I'm asking you to be happy for me as your friend.

Nothing has changed between us. I will just be studying and saving as hard as possible, not to mention working in the week and doing the odd modeling job that comes my way.

"I am just trying to move one foot in front of the other one step at a time. I am trying to make the right decisions to elevate me forward Adrian."

New York

Eventually, Adrian came around to my way of thinking; I convinced him that our friendship was not going to suffer while I worked towards my future. For a while, all seemed well. I was busy working all the time and Adrian had flown out to Norway. My friend Sally approached me at work one day and asked me if I fancied a four-day holiday to New York. She had a friend who worked for a travel agent and could get us a good deal. I jumped at the offer, and before I knew it, I was on a plane to The Big Apple. We flew with British Airways; I had bought all new luggage and clothes for the trip and was full of wonder at what lay ahead.

Sally and I had become rather close since working for the Channel Tunnel Project. She was 38-years-old, had never married and was without children. I was only 26, but it made no difference to our friendship. We had clicked. We were both dealing secretly with our own demons. She had been in a ten-year relationship with a married man, who had been equally in love with her. He had been a doctor in the private sector, and he was married with two children. He had bought Sally a two-bedroom flat in a nice part of town and visited her whenever he could. Then one day she had not heard from him. One day turned into two, then three, and so on, until what she had always feared the most had happened.

Sally was contacted by a solicitor and advised of the death of her lover. She had a complete breakdown; she did not leave her flat for almost 12 months. In his will, he had provided for her; of this, she had no knowledge of at all. He had left her financially secure and the flat was paid for. She had been totally loyal to him all those years. He was waiting for his children to finish school and then he was going to divorce his wife. That's what Sally had believed, anyway. Sally had all her shopping delivered to the house so she never had to leave. It was not until almost a year later when she decided to pull herself together and start working again. She got herself a PA job working directly for the Director on the Channel Tunnel Project at Met Cam in Birmingham. That's how we met and became friends. She was still heartbroken and mourning her loss when she started working for the company.

We clicked immediately, and it was over a year before either of us confided in the other about our losses. Then one day we went to a wine bar for lunch, and I told her all about my break down after the end of my relationship with Peter. Then she told me her tragic story. We cried and hugged and then cried some more. We truly bonded that day.

On arrival at JFK Airport, a dingy scruffy one, I thought, we had to wait forever to get through customs. However, once we did we were soon boarding our Greyhound coach and on our way to the hotel. I will never forget the millions of yellow battered taxis that were bumper-to-bumper and frantically beeping their horns. It was just like in the movies, I thought: chaotic and mesmerising! The hotel was a basic one, nothing fancy; it was on Fifth Avenue, not far from the Empire State Building. Our room was large and pleasantly furnished. There was no bar and no lounge, just rooms and a reception. We did not like the male receptionist at the hotel; he was a bit creepy and eyed us both up and down as if we were his next meal. I thought to myself, "You are not having me." We dropped off our bags and headed straight back outside, to take in the sights. We walked all the way to the Twin Towers, heading for the World Trade Centre. On the second floor there was a whole designer shopping experience just waiting for us! Gosh, we were excited! It took us ages to walk there as we kept stopping off along the way to take in our surroundings. It is fair to say we were truly fascinated. We stopped off for a coffee along the way at an Irish bar.

The coffee was flowing and the clientele friendly. We were having the time of our life in one of the most famous cities in the world.

Before we knew it another hour had passed, and so we made our way out the door to continue towards the Trade Centre. I was blown away by the Twin Towers. They were an incredible sight. We made our way up to the second floor and into the vast shopping area. Wow, it truly was amazing! We stayed there until closing time, going through rail after rail of discounted designer clothes, belts, gloves, bags, and jewellery, before we were practically forced to leave the building! I had bought the most amazing black patent leather bag. The leather was so soft, it cost me $150. It was worth it, one of the best bags I have ever purchased. I still have it to this day! I also bought a Versace belt for $50 – another fabulous bargain! We had heard so much about the World Trade Centre before entering the USA, and we were not disappointed. We left armed with bags full of goodies. That night we decided to go for a meal on Fifth Avenue to a beautiful new Japanese restaurant. It was a truly delightful place, so clean, and they cooked the food fresh right in front of you. We enjoyed a five-course dinner and left the restaurant fit to burst. As it was near midnight, we walked back to the hotel. The following day would be busy. On arrival at the hotel, there was a different male receptionist on the desk, another creepy guy, who gave us both the strangest look as we headed for the lift. Just five minutes after we had entered our bedroom, the phone in our room started ringing. We looked at each other, and then Sally answered it. She slammed down the phone and said, "That was a creepy call Amelia.

A man on the phone asked, 'Is this the room of the two English ladies?' I said yes, and then he said, 'We want you. We are coming for you right now,' and then he put the phone down." My heart skipped several beats as I tried to digest exactly what had just happened.

Then all of a sudden we heard the lift doors open, we both froze on the spot, we could hear footsteps outside of our room, getting closer and closer. Then all of a sudden, there was a bang on the door. We both screamed. Then we just sat there in silence for the longest time. We were too scared to leave the room and go down to reception, so we called reception instead. We told the man what had happened and he laughed, saying that it was just not possible. We were so confused, we demanded to speak with the hotel manager and again the man on reception laughed and said he was not often at the hotel, so we told him to call him or we would call the police. The call was then made to the manager of the hotel who lived in Brooklyn somewhere, we were advised that there was no need to call the police and that he would personally come and see us the following morning. We were so scared that night; we had pushed the dressing table up against our bedroom door, to ensure no one could get in. We barely slept a wink all night, both of us convinced something awful might happen to us. By the following morning we were both relieved daylight had arrived. Somehow, everything felt so much safer in daylight. True to his word, the hotel manager arrived at the hotel the following morning, full of apologies. Apparently, this was not the first time that British guests had been spooked by anonymous phone calls in the middle of the night.

He assured us he would look into it and that it would not happen again. He spoke to the new Japanese restaurant owner where we had dined the night before and he arranged for the two of us to dine there for free as and when we wanted to for the term of our stay as a way of apology. We agreed not to call the police and went about our day. We visited the Empire State Building, just before dusk to watch all the lights in New York City switch on. It was a truly amazing sight. We then hopped into a yellow cab to Time Square. All the shops were still open. There was hustle and bustle just about everywhere: people selling designer knock-offs on every street corner, people walking on stilts and attempting to juggle at the same time, this I have to say was quite impressive! It could not have been easy. Just about, everyone everywhere was trying to sell you something. We must have stuck out like a sore thumb: two female tourists in New York. I was surprised we did not get mugged. We were in awe of the place, often standing still to watch someone doing magic tricks, or someone being arrested! New York was truly just like we had seen it on the movies.

That night back at the hotel, we had an undisturbed night. Our room phone did not make a sound, but we still slept with our eye on the door. The next day was our last one. We headed off to Macy's, the world's most famous department store. We shopped, then lunched, and then jumped in a cab and headed to Bloomingdales. Our final destination was Tiffany's, the world famous jewellery store! We had no intention of buying anything; we couldn't afford it for one thing. We just wanted to replicate what Audrey Hepburn had done decades earlier in the famous movie she starred in, "Breakfast at Tiffany's."

We even dressed up for the occasion and grabbed a coffee along the way! On arrival at Tiffany's we took the lids off our coffees and just stood outside Tiffany's admiring the window before us. The glittering jewels looked amazing; we stood in silence until we finished our coffee and then made our way back to the hotel to prepare for our long flight back to the UK.

Another two ticks of my wish list – the list of things to do before I die going to New York, and doing an "Audrey Hepburn" outside Tiffany's. I was so happy. Apart from the incident on the first night of our stay, the short trip had been a wonderful one. Before we knew what was happening we were boarding our BA flight home, bound for England. This trip just further increased my need to travel; there was so many more places I wanted to visit, so many things I wanted to do.

We arrived back in England, weary from a long flight. It was very early in the morning, so I had a quick catch up with Blanche and filled her in on my trip and then went to bed as she headed off to work.

The following day I was due into work, and there was some great news waiting for us. As the Channel Tunnel Contract for Met Cam was coming to an end, as a thank you to everyone who had worked on the project we were each given a free trip on the Euro Star to any one of four destinations: Paris, Holland, Germany or the Netherlands. We did not get to choose, but we would be advised within the month where we were going for the day. We all jumped up and down in disbelief. We would get to journey on the Euro Star to a European destination a month before it opened up to the public.

We were to travel first class, and it would include a champagne breakfast, as we would be travelling early. News soon filtered down the line that we were going to spend the day in Brussels, specifically the Grand Place. It would be on a workday, and the full cost would be met by the company. I was so excited, especially having just returned from New York and already wondering where to go next.

Shocking Revelations

One day I received the news I always knew would arrive.

Blanche was retiring and selling up. She was heading down to the south of England to live; she wanted to be closer to her son and grandchildren. I was devastated, but tried not to show it. This was the best thing for Blanche in her retirement, as she would be living just around the corner from her family. But oh, how I would miss her! She had been the most amazing influence on me. She had been my guiding angel during those first few months when I had arrived on her doorstep, depressed, heartbroken and alone. She had taken me in, given me a home, advised me along the way and listened to me whenever I needed a shoulder to cry on. We had become very close, like family. I had a couple of months to find somewhere else to live. I was not quite ready to purchase my own home yet. I didn't have quite enough saved for the deposit required.

One day I was talking to Olivia, my ex Peter's mum, who I was still in touch with.

Olivia often called me for a chat and checked in on me to see how I was getting on. I had told her that Blanche was selling up and that I needed to find somewhere else to rent. As if by magic, Olivia had something up her sleeve. As always.

"I might have just the solution to your problem Amelia," said Olivia. "Do you remember Josie? An acquaintance of mine, I think you met her a couple of times. Well, she lives in the next village and is looking for a lodger to help pay the rent. Do you want me to have a word with her for you?" she asked eagerly.

"Oh Olivia you are the best! Yes please! That would be fantastic, and most definitely the answer to my predicament."

About a week later Olivia called me, informing me she had spoken with Josie and she was more than happy to rent a room to me. Olivia had set up a meeting so the two of us could get acquainted before I moved in. The following week after a successful meeting, it was decided that I should move in as soon as possible. The rent had been agreed and was the same I was paying Blanche. All I had to do now was tell Blanche. I was so sad. I sat Blanche down and told her that I had found somewhere to live. She was happy, as she had been very worried about where I was going to live. We were both very sad though. A week later, I moved into the next village with Jose, and for a few weeks until Blanche left for Bristol I would pop over and have dinner with her. On our last meeting before she left Birmingham to start her retirement in Somerset, she took me to dinner at a lovely All I had to do now was tell Blanche. I was so sad. I sat Blanche down and told her that I had found somewhere to live. She was happy, as she had been very worried about where I was going to live. We were both very sad though. A week later, I moved into the next village with Jose, and for a few weeks until Blanche left for Bristol I would pop over and have dinner with her. On our last meeting before she left Birmingham to start her retirement in Somerset, she took me to dinner at a lovely posh establishment called the Grimstock Hotel. We shared a bottle of wine over a three-course dinner and reminisced over the last three years. With promises made to each other always to remain in touch. A few tears were shed; we hugged and said our goodbyes. My heart was so heavy that day; I was going to miss her so much. However, I knew Blanche would be a lifelong friend, one that I would visit as often as I could.

Josie

Josie was completely different from Blanche. She was 47-years-old and still looking for her dream man after a long marriage followed by a divorce. With her divorce settlement, she had bought this lovely little two-bedroom house. She had three sons who came to visit her often. Josie and I hit it off immediately. We also became friends. We would go to the cinema together every once and a while. We would eat out or share takeaways on a Friday evening. I had given Adrian my new address. On his next short stay in England, he came to visit me. He seemed different somehow, and then he told me he had met someone. It was not serious but they were dating. I was so pleased for him and no longer had to worry about his feelings for me. He had truly moved on from that. We went out to dinner and he told me all about his trip to Norway. It was fascinating hearing all about his diving experiences around the world.

We saw each other a few times before he headed off again, this time to the Emirates. Before he left, I handed him the credit card that he had given me a long time ago.

I did not feel right with it. It felt wrong to keep it. I had used it several times. At his suggestion, I had been shopping and bought new work suits. I had used it in Brussels, and I had used it to pay a bill. I assured him that I would one day pay him back, but Adrian insisted I kept the card. He said it was a gift, and that he wanted no payment from me whatsoever.

He left once again, this time on his new Suzuki motorbike. Wow! What an incredible machine that was! It really was beautiful. He loved his cars and bikes he had two cars and a motorbike. He liked to give them a good airing when he was home.

A few weeks after Adrian's departure, Josie asked me if I fancied going on a week's holiday to Tenerife, in Gran Canaria. She was going with her friend and said they would really like me to come too. I thought this was a great idea, and agreed. Within a couple of months, the holiday was all paid for, and I found I was shopping a lot in my spare time for holiday clothes!

I was still running daily, a great love of mine. I did not feel complete unless I had run several miles a day. I was so fit and toned. I was truly happy with my physique; I had always worked so hard to stay fit. No matter what was happening in my life, for the most part a good run would always sort my troubles out, help to make me feel better about myself, and keep my nemesis at bay. I found exercise really helped fight my nemesis, unless it was very severe which was not too often. Therefore, I found I could pretty much control it with a healthy diet and lots of exercise. I had learned to live with my nemesis. I was learning to control it, and the visits were becoming less frequent now.

Only around once a year would I be rendered disabled by it. I just allowed it to overwhelm me and wait for it to leave. I was excited about my holiday. This infused happy hormones, and I was so excited about going to Gran Canaria: another tick of my wish list, another country visited. This would be my third trip abroad in just 12 months; I had developed a taste for travelling: from arriving at the airport, to the journey, and the excitement of getting off the plane in a completely different country. I loved it.

Our holiday was soon upon us. The flight was only four hours long. I will never forget stepping off the plane and being hit by the overwhelming heat. It was blistering. We had to take an hour-long coach drive to our apartments, and I remember on arrival how impressed we all were with it. It was beautiful; we had a large three-bed apartment, with a balcony and sea view. It was amazing; the sea looked so blue, so clear, and so clean. We all had the most amazing week's holiday; we toured the island, went on day trips and shopped in the island's beautiful boutiques. I bought a couple of sarongs at a poolside catwalk show featuring none other than beach wear!

I could have stayed there for weeks. The people were friendly; it was so relaxing; and the food was to die for. However, like all good things, it had to end. Before I knew it, the holiday was over and we were heading back to England, all refreshed, relaxed and recharged, and sporting great tans!

Finally, my own home!

(Amelia pictured in her first home)

I did not live with Josie for very long, a year at most. Then I decided I was ready to have my own home. I had saved; I had a good deposit; I had saved money over the previous two years from modeling jobs, some for Marks and Spencer's, some for catalogues, and some independent jobs. I had made good money from these jobs. In addition, I had a fair bit of money put by. I was ready to live on my own. I felt confident that I could support myself financially. I had a good monthly salary. I still did the odd bit of modeling on the occasional weekend and I had savings. I knew it would cost around £1000 pounds per month to run a home of my own, what with the mortgage, bills, and food. I could comfortably afford this now and still be able to save a little, go on holiday once or twice a year, and continue with my at-home studies.

It was not long before I was moving out of Josie's and into a rather derelict Grade II Listed townhouse in the small town of Coleshill in Warwickshire. I instantly fell in love with this house. It was full of original beams all throughout the property. The ceilings were very high and the doors small. There were secret little compartments, and a tunnel, which took you all over the house. It was an incredible house, which needed much work. It was in need of a complete re-wire throughout. The wooden beams needed treating, and then preserving, it needed re-plastering throughout, a complete new floor put in downstairs, and a completely new kitchen fitted, as there was virtually no kitchen at all. Nevertheless, this did not deter me. It was beautiful and very old: part fifteenth and part sixteenth century. It really was a unique property.

I was very lucky to be able to buy it when I did, as house prices were low. This house had been empty for quite a long time. The fact that so much work needed doing to the property had driven the price down very low. I was lucky to purchase it for just £65,000 – a bargain. My dream home: old, listed, and all mine. I will never forget the day I received the keys. I walked through the door of my new home, and ran all over the house laughing and screaming with pure joy.

I was shouting aloud, "It's all mine, it's all mine, and this is my home. No one can take this away from me, not ever." I celebrated by myself that night, and that was by choice. I wanted to take it all in. I needed to let it all sink in properly. I had borrowed a camp bed from Josie; I had a kettle, and an iron, a mirror and a toaster and my amazing collection of books. And, of course, my expansive wardrobe of never-ending clothes and shoes which had become a passion of mine. That was what I moved in with. Over the next few weeks, Josie, her son, and Adrian, helped me put the first lick of paint in the large bedroom, which was to act as my living quarters for the next two years while I renovated the property. The bedroom was painted cream in between the beams. The curtains went up and the thick cream carpet went down. I purchased a brand new double bed and a TV. I had just what I needed to live comfortably while the renovations were taking place. Each day I had to pinch myself. Amelia was a homeowner. Amelia owned all this, and Amelia was on the property ladder. It was all so surreal. At Just 28-years old, I felt I had travelled such a very long road already. Things were finally starting to go my way; things were starting to work out the way I had always dreamt they would.

I had never felt happier in my life. I was single, independent, employed and a homeowner. I was on cloud nine. Over the next 18 months, I went from room to room, with the help of a local handy man that a lot of the locals used and recommended. As and when I could afford his services, I would employ him to, plaster, tile, and treat the beams, put in a new floor and finally a new kitchen. I painted the whole building, which was huge.

I helped lay floors; I helped put in skirting boards, and had the whole place rewired. The roof had been repaired as there were a few missing tiles. The pointing was fixed and the rendering sorted. At the finish, I had the whole place carpeted, all new furniture delivered and new lighting put in every room. The house looked incredible. It was like something out of one of those house and home magazines. It really was beautiful. I had transformed the inside into my dream home.

To this day I remember the pride I felt. I had travelled so far; I was well on my way to accomplishing my wish list. It was when I had completed all the works on my house that I decided to invest in a computer and printer. The internet was a huge phenomenon I wanted to familiarise myself with. This new tool was the latest fascination of the world: the doors it opened, the information you could have access to. I wanted to jump aboard this new speeding train and join the world in this new experience, which was appearing on every computer in every office across the country. I had already had a taste of what it had to offer through work, as the internet had recently been installed onto everyone's computer. It was a truly fascinating thing. You could type in almost any question and there in an instant the answer would appear. I was truly in awe of it as many people were; this was changing everyone's lives in ways they had never imagined before. I bought a second hand computer from my employer, at the bargain price of £100. It was a refurbished one, complete with Word, Excel, and all the packages needed to get me up and running. This was when I started writing again.

One weekend I locked myself away in my house, unplugged my phones, purchased a bottle of rose wine and started writing my very first novel. A thriller-based novel called *Cruel Intentions*. I had had this story in my head for a long time, so once I started writing I could not stop. By the end of that weekend, I had written 16,000 words. I was doing exactly what I had always wanted to do, writing. My next major dream was to complete a novel and try to get it published.

I was approaching 29-years-old now and I was ready for another holiday. I decided I wanted to revisit New York for a short break. I called my friend and before I knew it, we had organised and paid for our trip. I booked the time off from work, and before I knew it, the day had arrived. I met my friend at the airport and then boarded the plane.

We had the most amazing time. We dined, we skated, and we took a horse and carriage around Central Park. We shopped and we toured new places. I loved New York; it was so full of life, so fast, and so exciting. On our return home, we made a pact to visit New York at least once a year. On my return, I had met a young man seven years my junior. He was only 22-years-old, tall, and very handsome. I had met him through a friend of a friend. He was from a wealthy family, and had been rather spoilt. At the age of 17, he had been given a BMW for his birthday, and subsequently ran it into the ground. He was unrepentant, a bit wild and rebelling against his parents. He was living with his best friend in a privately rented apartment. He worked for his uncle, in an engineering works, and basically had never really had to do a great deal for himself. Everything had been handed to him on a plate.

However, on meeting him I discovered he was not happy, that he wanted to prove to his family he could make it on his own. He had a good and loyal heart, when it came to his friends and more especially to his girlfriend – me. I met him at just the right time. I had been on a few dates, but did not take them any further: they were either too arrogant, too selfish, not my type, and basically not what I was looking for.

By the time Patrick came along, I was ready for a relationship. He had been attentive at a party; he was the complete gentleman and I liked him. Within a few short months, he had moved into my house and we were living together. At first, all was well; he applied for a new job head of sales for a large company in the West Midlands. He took to it like a duck to water; he was a natural. He had a basic salary plus commission. The commission he was earning was incredible. We cruised along this way for a while. I was writing my book in my spare time, picking it up from time to time and then leaving it untouched for a few months. By now, though, I was up to 45,000 words. I had also started documenting certain events of my life: the big events, the main parts of my journey. I kept a journal and wrote in it from time to time, worried that I may forget things over time.

Amelia aged 22-years-old

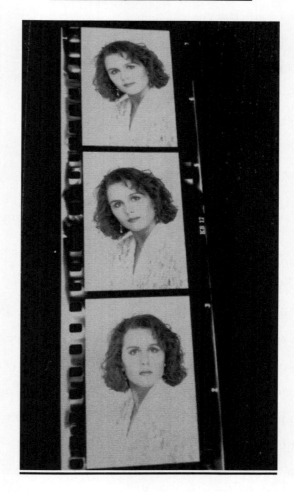

Re-visiting Old Ghosts

One day having spent several hours writing up my journal, I decided I wanted to see all my care records. I wanted to have a complete picture, as so many things did not make sense to me and I was curious about what had been documented about me and my brother Jake over the years. I called the head of Social Services in Shrewsbury and spoke to them about getting access to my records. I already knew that I had a right to them for the next 70 years. I was given a number to call, to arrange a meeting to view all my records. I called the number immediately; a date was fixed for me to visit and I was given an address I recognised. I asked the lady if she was sure she had given me the correct address, she said that she had. Breeton House?

"But that is a children's home" I said.

"Yes it was once Amelia, but now it is a Social Services records department," she replied. I thanked her and put down the phone. I looked at the address in front of me. My heart sank. That was where my siblings and I were separated many years before.

That was the children's home where I last saw my sisters. I recalled once more waving goodbye to them crying hysterically, knowing I would never see them again. I held back the tears and pocketed the piece of paper. I wondered if I was strong enough to go back there, once again to come face to face with Breeton House. Would it still look the same? How would I feel once I was there? I decided to be strong; I needed access to my care records. I needed to know all about my past, even if I came across things that I had no idea about. I wanted to document my own life for me.

The following week I caught the train to Shrewsbury, and then walked the two miles to Breeton House. I had butterflies in my stomach as I turned the corner and the familiar building came into view. I felt strange, I felt nostalgia, and I felt pain. The building looked just the same as I had remembered it. I walked up the long wide drive to the entrance. I pushed open the impressive large oak door, which dated from my earlier recollections, and walked through to the atrium, which was now a reception area. I gave my name and waited for someone to come and collect me.

"Hello, you must be Amelia. I have everything ready for you, my dear. I must say there were an awful lot of boxes to dig out for you. I am guessing it will take you all day and then some to go through that lot." I was escorted to an empty office. There were two tables: one was empty and the other one was full of boxes of my records, case review reports, NSPCC reports, school reports, doctor's reports, and dental records: it was all there.

I was advised that I could not take the original documents, however. I could photocopy what I wanted to take away with me. I spent the whole of that day wading through all the paperwork, making new discoveries about my family and not good ones, discovering even more horrible things my mother had put us through. The NSPCC reports were especially hard to read. Everything had been documented, even things I had had no knowledge of, and things that maybe I had just forgotten, upsetting things.

I spent the whole day photocopying as many documents as possible, and filed them into the large empty folder I had brought along with me. Against the advice given, I also slipped a few original documents into my folder, the ones I thought were the most important, and the documents from the NSPCC. After all, they were of no use to anyone else now. I was an adult, and these records were just shelf-space now. Once I was done, I asked if I could walk around the building. I told them I used to live there as a child. They were very accommodating; they made me a cup of tea and a sandwich and let me walk freely around the building.

I felt so sad; so many memories came flooding back to me, the little girl who was brought in late one night, pregnant and scared. Jake and me running away to Sears Hall, to beg the head of Social Services not to split my brothers and sisters up, to beg them to keep us altogether. Then of course the day I was separated from my only remaining sibling, Jake. I broke down completely; it had all been too much to bear, more than I thought possible. I was not strong enough to deal with all the emotion flooding through me like a whirlwind.

I stepped outside for a short while to get some air and compose myself. Then I continued through the building. I had come this far, so I might as well complete this journey. The kitchen was just the same. Unchanged. It was used for the staff now to prepare their lunch. The bedrooms were now used as offices, and the games room was now a boardroom. One of the office staff came up to me and asked me what was it like to live in a children's home? I told her that you felt like a bird with broken wings, unable to fly. She smiled at me, and with a tear in her eye she said,

"You are a very brave girl Amelia. It was a pleasure to meet you today."

I walked back to the train station and headed home. I knew I wanted all the information I come away with, but I was not sure of the purpose. I just had to have it. It was as if I was trying to complete an impossible jigsaw, with all the pieces scattered all over the country. Little clues here and there would lead me to the next piece in the puzzle. At that point, in my life I had no intention of writing my life story. I was afraid of how it would be received by the people I had lied to about my childhood. I was afraid of being judged negatively by other people, and how they would treat me going forward. So writing my life story was out of the question. I just wanted to document all the facts of my life for myself. My visit to Breeton House encouraged a visit from my nemesis. This was a long and hard visit, one I was not prepared for, and one that for the first time in my life forced me to pay a visit to my doctors.

For the first time in 12 months, I called into work explaining that I had a virus and would not be in for the rest of the week. This dark cloud gripped me like no other. I was lower than I ever imagined. I could not lift myself out of my abyss, and I would not confide in Patrick, I just told him I was ill. He accepted it without question. Thankfully, he was going away for a few days, on a work-training course, which meant I could deal with this alone and without question.

    I sat in front of my doctor, and confessed everything. I briefed him on my life story. I talked to him about my nemesis, and how up until now I had managed my depression with exercise and diet, and I had learned to live with it. That for the most part I was happy these days, and visits from my nemesis were few and far between. Only this visit had been too much for me. I could not cope with it, I was a prisoner of it, and it would not let go of its stronghold. My doctor recommended I try a course of anti-depressants, a fairly new drug called Prozac. I was given a prescription for 40 mg per day. It was immediately effective. He signed me off work for seven days and told me to come back to see him in a month's time. I felt very uncomfortable about taking Prozac. I had read so much about this drug in magazines, and was nervous about its effects on me; but I felt I had no other option. I went to the chemist, and within five minutes had the drug in my hand. I went home and closed the door behind me. I read the instructions including the possible side effects, and then popped my two pills. The first day, I didn't notice much of a difference. However, my goodness, by the second day I was flying; in fact no, I was soaring! I felt amazing.

I was a bit spaced out, to say the least, but it was a nice sensation and one that made me feel as if I did not have a care in the world, like I could cope with anything. Therefore, that is when my relationship with Prozac began.

During the seven days I had off work, I spring cleaned my house, went running for miles each day and caught up with my reading. I loved reading so much and I had not read enough of late. By the time I was due back at work I was happy, confident and ready for anything. The pills had taken hold. My nemesis had gone and I was feeling amazing. By then, I had been at *Auto trader* for three years and I was ready for a complete change. Therefore, I resigned from my job, giving the company a month's notice. They were very sad to see me go, and tried to persuade me to re-consider. However, my mind was made up, I had gone as far as I could within the company and was ready for a change in career.

The break up

During that month I applied for a couple of jobs closer to home, the first one I did not get because of my lack of experience. However, the second one I did get. It was an accounts position working for a local construction company in their head office. It was literally just down the road from where I lived, just perfect. On nice days, I could walk to work. It would take me just 20 minutes. This was great. I had got myself a new job, without the long commute into the city and a far higher salary. I could not be happier.

The weekend before I started my new job I went into town and impulsively had my belly button pierced! My 30th birthday was upon me and I wanted to mark it in a special way. I loved my new belly ring, it was a gold diamond stud and it looked amazing. I needed to mark my 30th birthday as this was a milestone, and I was leaving my 20s. Everything was going so well, work-wise and in my social life. The only thing I was not happy with was my relationship with Patrick. This was new territory for me, as I had always been in a relationship that I never wanted to end. I had been the one who was left heartbroken.

However, this time it was me that did not want to be in the relationship; it was me that was not in love with my partner; and it was me that was faced with the awful task of ending the relationship. This was where I discovered something new about myself, I just could not end it, and I did not want to hurt Patrick's feelings. I attempted to have the conversation several times but I just could not do it. Therefore, I remained in the relationship for a further 12 months. During which time we grew further and further apart. Patrick was socialising with his new work friends more and more; I was throwing myself into my new job and writing a few words in my novel whenever I had a spare moment.

I loved my new job; it was like one happy family. Everyone got on with everyone else. The one exception left eventually. I was socialising with the girls at work; we would all go out once a month into town on a Saturday night. All was perfect. I got the company involved in the charity runs that were being organised all over the country called "The race for life" and managed to persuade the office girls to take part. The company sponsored us and paid for us to have T-shirts printed and hats with the company logo on the front.

After some time I was given the position of social secretary for the company. This was an unpaid position that was totally separate from my current position in accounts. I chaired a committee and once a month we would get together for lunch, paid for by the company and organised the company's social events. This could be going to the races; paintballing or bowling, anything that would be good for all ages and involve everyone. I was good at this:

a good organiser, and very sociable. Therefore, I took to this role perfectly.

Eventually, after many months, I plucked up the courage to end my relationship with Patrick. It was just awful; he did not take it very well at all, which in turn made me feel terrible. I hated doing this to him. Nevertheless, we were not love's young dream. We had stopped socialising together and barely talked any more. I could not pretend any longer.

Patrick packed his bags that weekend and moved back in with his parents. I felt very sad, but also relieved that I had my house back. I spring cleaned the house, washed all the bedding, and bought two baby kittens that weekend. They were just five weeks old and their eyes were barely open. I called them Pepper and Tiger, for very obvious reasons, one was peppered and the other one looked just like a tiger. I loved them instantly and swore to myself that weekend that no one would move into my house again, unless of course I got married, and I did not see that happening for a long time.

I spent my weekends writing in my journal documenting my life. I had put my novel aside for the time being in favour of getting my own story down on paper. It was like a need in me I had to fulfill. I never told anyone about this; my friends had no idea I was documenting my life story, for the simple reason they had no idea about my true past, only the one that I had told them about. I loved spending weekends in my beautiful home. I never really got used to the fact that it was all mine. I would often curl up on my sofa on a Saturday evening with my cats, watching a movie with a glass of wine in hand.

I felt like I was really home. I felt happy, secure, and was right where I wanted to be at that moment in my life.

I was thinking about doing a martial arts course, as I had always loved the martial arts. I had heard about a local Kick Boxing class, which took place twice a week. I thought I would look into it at some point and see about joining. Overall, I could not have been happier at this point in my life. It had been a couple of years now since I had asked my mother about Jake, so I decided to try again. However, once again I was met with a brick wall. I could not get a forwarding address out of her. I was finding this really upsetting and had no idea what to do about it. I continued to send birthday cards for Jake to my mother's house each year for her to pass onto Jake for me. I could only hope that she passed them on to him.

The Affair

As far as I was concerned, going forward it was just the cats and me. Twelve months into my new job Christmas had come round again. We had all received our yearly bonus and we were all talking about the company ball. I had bought the most beautiful full-length black dress from Coast. I loved it, and the dress was so elegant. I had a new pair of strappy diamante shoes and had started kickboxing to aid my running. The ball was in a posh hotel, and everyone was able to bring their partners too. For those of us who did not have partners we would go with each other, and share a room at the hotel.

The ball was a success. A great time was had by all, and it was the talk of the office for a while after. I really loved this company. I really liked my co-workers and some had become very good friends. I was particularly close to one particular girl called Priscilla. We went to each other's houses for dinner, often popped to the pub for a drink after work on a Friday and became really good friends. Priscilla was an older woman, far older than me; she was 46, and married with two children. I had met her family on several occasions and really liked them. I would meet up with her occasionally on a Saturday and we would go shopping and then go for a long lunch.

It's true to say I trusted her implicitly. She kind of mothered me at times, and was quite protective of me too. A true friend.

Life coasted along perfectly for a long time. Before I knew it, almost four years had passed by. I still loved my job and was very happy to remain there for the foreseeable future. I had racked up five belts in kickboxing and passed each one of my kick boxing exams with a distinction. I loved the martial arts, and found that I was a natural.

Then one day it was announced by the company that they had purchased a new building just around the corner. There were some brand new buildings that had been constructed, and our company had purchased one. Our current old listed building was no longer big enough to cater for the ever-growing workforce, so a move was imminent. Many of us were saddened by the move, as it was to bring two of the holding companies under the same roof, doubling the workforce and also changing the dynamics completely. I think many of us felt that it would never be the same company again. It was going to be less personal, more professional, and overall a less enjoyable place to work. However, we all went a long with it, as we had no choice in the matter. Before the move a night out had been arranged locally. A couple of the directors came: the HR manager and the head of the accounts department. We all went to the Coleshill Hotel for a three-course dinner. That night I noticed a spark between my friend Priscilla and one of the directors. I saw they were holding hands under the table, which surprised me immensely. I never knew Priscilla was like that. I thought she was happily married.

What about her family? I never mentioned what I saw that night. However, the next time I went for a drink with her I brought the subject up.

"Priscilla, I hate to ask and if I am on the wrong track then I am sorry, but is there something going on between you and Ben?"

Priscilla went quiet for a long time. Her eyes were red and water-filled; then she nodded.

"Amelia, please don't tell anyone, yes, I'm having an affair with Ben."

I was stunned; Ben was practically 60-years-old. He was the least popular director. He was very sneaky and had got a lot of people into trouble or worse, sacked, often shifting blame on to others, where it was not deserved. I did not see the attraction at all. Priscilla was married to a lovely man who doted on her; it made no sense to me. However, it was her life, her choice; she was a grown woman of 46. This affair went on for some time. Eventually Priscilla told Ben that I knew about them, and that I would tell no one.

One day Priscilla approached me and asked me if she could use my house one lunch time to meet Ben, as it was just up the road from our offices. I reluctantly agreed, but only because he was a director and my job was in his hands. After that secret meeting at my house, it became a weekly occurrence. They would leave separately at lunchtimes and meet in secret at my house. It was never meant to be a regular thing. I no longer wanted them to meet at my house, but I did not know how to tell them. I was afraid that Ben might turn on me or make my life difficult at work. Eventually that is exactly what happened. Twelve months down the line I told them, I no longer wanted them to use my house.

That their secret was safe with me; however, they needed to find somewhere else to meet, as I did not feel comfortable with the arrangements. As I feared, this did not go down to well at all. At work Ben started to ignore me, he started making my life difficult in meetings. I used to chair monthly finance meetings, as I was chief credit controller. It was my responsibility to get in the money owed to the company from other housing organisations. This could be anything up to several million pounds. I was also responsible for the payroll accounts. Each month I had to update the directors, Ben included, of the funds collected and money outstanding, why some companies had not paid and what their issues were. I had to provide reports and graphs and sometimes the meeting could go on forever. It was in these meetings that Ben started to do his best to make me look incompetent. His attitude towards me was unacceptable, and generally, he was succeeding in making my life hell at work.

My friend Priscilla had become less friendly, and kept her distance from me. It soon became apparent that Ben was not comfortable with the fact I knew about him and Priscilla. One night after work, Priscilla stopped me in the car park. She looked very serious and then said,

"Amelia, you do know if you lose your job there is nothing I can do about it, don't you?"

I was stunned; it took me a minute to understand exactly what she was saying.

"What are you saying Priscilla? Do I need to be concerned for my job right now?"

"I am just saying that whatever decisions Ben makes has nothing to do with me. Anyway, I can't drop you home tonight as I am going the other way, goodnight Amelia."

And with that, she climbed into her car and drove off. She had the following week off work. I went home that night and I felt sick. I was panicking, I was going to lose my job all because my friend was having an affair with the director of the company, and it no longer suited him for me to know about it. I knew this had all stemmed from me not allowing them to use my house any more. Nothing had been the same since. I could not lose my job. I had a mortgage to pay, bills to pay, I had no family to run to if things went wrong. I had no one to borrow money from, should I run out of money and no longer be able to pay the mortgage. I loved my house so much I was not going to lose it because of someone else's stupid affair.

I phoned my manager that night. We were also very close. She was very good to me. I confided everything to her and my concerns about my job too. Although she believed me, it was very hard for her to believe what I was telling her because this involved Priscilla. My manager's husband and Priscilla's husband were close friends. I was told not to worry and to say nothing for now. Over the next couple of weeks, Jeanie watched Priscilla and Ben closely; she was not sure what to do either. This was huge; she had noticed how Ben's treatment of me had changed. There was also something happening behind the scenes that I was not aware of, that made my confessions believable.

Priscilla and I worked very closely together, but we were no longer talking. It was so uncomfortable at work. Another colleague confided in me, told me to watch my back, and that my job may well be at risk. No more details were given. That was it. I could no longer deal with the stress of it all, and I was not going to be sacked because of other people's wrongdoing. Therefore, the following day I went to my doctors; I told them I was under immense pressure at work and that I was being forced out of my job. He signed me off for one month with work-related stress. My manager came to visit me; she was so kind and very worried about me. She took my sick note into HR and I waited for their visit to my home.

A couple of days later a lady from HR came to see me at my home. I explained everything from the beginning. Priscilla and Ben were having an affair; I described how I kept their secret and how they used to meet at my house. But most importantly how everything went wrong once I stopped them using my home to meet. HR was not surprised at all, I don't know how they already knew about the affair, but they did. They had been seen before. They said that my story completed a jigsaw for them, and that it made complete sense now why Ben was hell bent on getting rid of me. I felt instantly relieved. I felt believed. I truly thought I would have a battle convincing them of my story; however, that was not the case. However, the whole thing was kept hush, hush from the office workers. Although they were aware something was going on between me, Priscilla and Ben, I don't think they knew any details.

Eventually, HR and the other directors spoke with both Priscilla and Ben separately. They each denied the affair, of course. However, very surprisingly Priscilla handed in her resignation and just left the company. Ben was due for retirement in a year or two, and I was asked to come back. I told them that there was no way I could ever work in the same company as Ben. I was offered another solution to this problem. If I took a redundancy, package of £8,500 plus my salary paid into my account for the next three months. I would have to sign a legal document, which meant I had to keep my lips sealed about what had happened. Basically a gagging order. I accepted the offer, the tax free money of £8.500 was paid to me by cheque the following week and I continued to receive a salary for the following three months.

But now I was without a job, a job I had loved. I also knew that many people within the company had no idea of the truth of the situation, and believed me to be at fault. I do not blame them though. In their situation, I would have thought the same. Whatever rumours went around were most definitely not in my favour, that's for sure. The worst of it was I was unable to talk to anyone about what happened, so I had to let it go. This was an awful time for me, although money was not an issue, as I had some savings as well as the redundancy money, I was once again visited by my nemesis and sunk deep into my darkness once again. I could not believe this had happened to me. I had been a friend; I had kept their dirty secret, and this was how I was repaid. I always knew Ben was a ruthless man. The stories I had heard about him over the years were unbelievable. As soon as I no longer served a purpose to them, I was thrown aside and treated like rubbish that needed to be swept away. This hurt a lot.

After about a month, I decided to pick two countries I wanted to visit and book two separate holidays. I thought this was just what I needed. I would travel alone and find my confidence once again, which was at an all time low at this point. I booked a four-day break to the European city of Prague, a place that was on my "To visit" list. I had once seen a beautiful picture of people standing on the famous Charles Bridge looking up to the sky as it was snowing down on them. This was a magical scene, and one that I wanted to make real for myself. Charles Bridge is a stone Gothic bridge that connects the Old Town, Mala Strana. It was actually called the Stone Bridge during the first several centuries. This was the most visited place in Prague and on my "Must visit" list also. I also booked a luxury all-inclusive seven-day holiday to Fuerteventura, for a week of total relaxation and pampering. The short break to Prague I went on almost immediately, and had an amazing time. It was early February and extremely cold in Prague. Just as luck would have it, snow was also forecast during my stay. On the second day of my visit, I put on my Timberland boots and waterproof jacket as it had been snowing heavily the night before. I had jeans and layers of tops on. I popped on my gloves and hat then headed off towards the famous bridge. On arrival at the Charles Bridge, I was immediately in awe of the place. It was truly an incredible site. The bridge was extremely wide, there were people selling hot mulled wine and roasted chestnuts along its length. I bought some mulled wine and stood in the centre of the bridge looking over the side, when all of a sudden it started snowing; I looked up and smiled from ear to ear!

That was an amazing day for me and another tick of my wish list. I came back feeling revitalised and less depressed.

The second holiday was all paid for but not due until almost ten months later. I thought it would be nice to have a holiday to look forward to and plan for throughout the year. I was beginning to like travelling alone. It was refreshing, and it made me feel adventurous. Therefore, that was two more foreign countries ticked off my "To visit" list.

My Soldier

On my return from Prague, I registered with a temping agency in the hope of getting a new job as soon as possible. As luck would have it, I got the first job that I applied for. This was another accounts position with a great salary, private health care, a yearly profit share and a great company pension. Up to this point, I had chosen to take a couple of months off work. I spent some money on my house, on myself and of course on the holidays. I had a few thousand pounds left in the bank and a new job to start the following week. I had been very fortunate where jobs were concerned. I had never had trouble getting a job, and I had always got the job I applied for, well almost always. I was nervous about this new job, though. Would I fit in? The company was ten times bigger than any I had ever worked for. I would be responsible for bringing in millions of pounds into the company every three months. The expectations were high, and it was a fast-paced environment. The mornings were early mornings and involved a long commute to the city. This I hated, as it would add two hours each day on to my working day. I would leave the house at 7 am and not arrive home until almost 7 pm, during the week it was all work and sleep.

However, it was a good position, and I needed the job. The money in my account would not last forever. I called my last manager with whom I was still in touch and went power walking with at weekends and I told her about my new job. We met for lunch and celebrated. She asked me if I fancied a weekend away to Dublin in Ireland. I jumped at the chance and left her to deal with the arrangements.

The following Monday I started my new job. I was very nervous as I approached the vast building in the city. It was huge. There were hundreds of office workers all sitting at their desks, tapping away on their keyboards. The one thing I noticed about my new open plan office was how quiet it was. So many people and yet so quiet. I hated my first day, I felt uncomfortable. I did not like the open plan environment at all. There was no privacy whatsoever. Nevertheless, over time I got used to it. I made many friends and I was fortunate once again to have a great manager, one that was fair, and looked after her staff. I longed for the weekends just so I could write in my journal and pen a few words of my novel, which kept being neglected, as life kept getting in the way. One Saturday on my way back from the hairdressers, I bumped into Joshua. He was only 19-years-old, and had grown into a handsome young man and exceptionally tall. I had known him since he was 14-year-old, when he used to play football outside the back of my house with his friends. He had always had a soft spot me, and often deliberately kicked his football onto the low roof of my house, which would then serve as an excuse to knock my door and strike up a conversation.

I thought he was so sweet. I had not noticed how much he had grown over the last five years. There he was stood, all grown up and handsome. That day he asked if he could come in to my house just to talk and I said yes. We talked for hours about everything. He told me he had joined the army, and that he was in training. He told me of his love for skiing, and how that he had always fancied me since the first day I moved into the house. I was a woman in my thirties and advised him I was far too old for him. He told me that I was being silly, and that he wanted to see me when he got back from training in a few months. I told him there was no way I could get romantically involved with him. Maybe if he had been older things could have been different.

Another year passed by, one weekend whilst out running, Joshua appeared running along side of me!

"Hey gorgeous long time no see, do you mind if I join you?"

"Of course not. It's great to see you. How are you?"

"I am great, all the better for running into you," he laughed.

That day Joshua came back to my house. I surprised myself and did the unexpected. Joshua and I bathed together and made love for the first time. It was truly amazing. He was so incredibly attentive and strong. He would pick me up and hold me against the wall, then throw me on to the bed it was the most amazing day I had shared with a man for a long time. I knew I could fall for him easily, but I held myself back. He was barely 20-years-old. Although he looked older and acted older, he was still very young. I was so much older than him. Joshua was leaving for a few months with his regiment. He took my mobile number and asked if he could call.

I agreed and kissed him goodbye. I felt so sad at his departure. I wanted to tell him how much I liked him too, how much I would miss him, and how I could not wait to see him again. Nevertheless, I didn't. I had to be strong and hold myself back. The age gap was too big for it to be able to work successfully, I believed. I thought I was doing the right thing by both of us. Even though I did have strong feelings for him too.

    I stayed in touch with Joshua over the months. He sent me the loveliest messages, telling me, how much he missed me and how he could not wait to see me. I reminded him that he had a girlfriend and that he was being unfair to her. He joked with me, saying I was just playing hard to get. Then he would get all-serious and ask me if I was seeing anyone yet. I told him I had not met anyone, but I was ready to now. I wanted to settle down.

    During the next few months, I had become close friends with a man at work, one of the client accountants. He was very popular and single; he was very good looking and was living the single life. We hit it off straight away and started spending all of our time together. We became like the best of friends almost, advising each other on our love lives, going out partying and sharing our lunch hours together at work. I had been on one or two dates that were not too great, and I had no interest in seeing them again nice guys, just not my type. I was beginning to wonder if there was a perfect partner out there for me. I told Lucas all about my young soldier and about our amazing day together all those months before. Lucas, being Lucas, just said, "What difference do a few years make if you like each other? You are both consenting adults.

However, the age gap bothered me. Not to mention the fact he had a girlfriend of two years.

The next time Joshua came home, I saw him again. We made love together, and it was even better than the first time. God he was beautiful! I could so easily have fallen in love with him. That day he told me, he loved me. It really threw me; I was not expecting it at all. After he left, he sent me text messages asking me when he could see me again. I was fighting my feelings here, because my heart wanted him so badly, but my head was saying otherwise. I was in my thirties and he was barely 20-years-old. I was being sensible and boring. I wanted him, but I would not allow myself to have him, and it hurt really badly. I knew after a while he would look for someone his own age, once the novelty had worn off. I could not risk being hurt too. Therefore, within a couple of weeks I told him I could no longer see him. He was devastated. He had genuinely fallen in love with me. I was close to falling for him too. I had to use all the will power I could muster to stop seeing him. Why couldn't he have been a decade older? He was perfect; he made me feel beautiful and sexy, and he made me laugh in the loveliest way. He looked at me in a way all women should be looked at. He was just a beautiful person.

My Husband

Over the next few months, I had agreed to go on holiday with Lucas and several other work friends. We were to go the following May, about seven months away. We were all great friends and both inside and outside work. We would have a great holiday. We had booked to go to Zante in Greece. During the run-up to that holiday, Lucas and I became more than just friends; we became an item. We kept it very quiet because we were not sure how the company would take to our newfound relationship, as relationships between co-workers were not generally encouraged. Therefore, we had a secret relationship to which only a few selected friends were privy.

Lucas was the ultimate romantic; he treated me like a lady; he understood me; and by this time he knew everything about me from the minute, I was born until the present day. None of my story fazed him at all. He was saddened that I been through so much, but also very proud at what I had achieved for myself. He said he would never have guessed if I had not told him that I had lived the life I had led. He said most people here assumed you were posh and from a good upbringing.

When Lucas told me that, I knew I had been successful. I had achieved my main goal in life. I had not become a statistic, and I had turned myself into a successful woman. I felt really proud of myself.

Our love for each other grew and grew. Lucas was now staying at my house at least three times a week and we would drive to work together. It was lovely. It was perfect. For the first time in my life, I felt totally comfortable with myself. I rarely suffered visits from my nemesis anymore and I had stopped taking Prozac. I did not feel that they were working for me anymore. I had discovered a side affect I did not like. They had the ability to prevent you from truly feeling anything, your reactions to things became a little slower and they in themselves had a certain amount of control over your mind. I did not want to spend my life on Prozac, nor did I want to give in to my occasional visit from my nemesis. I was where I wanted to be no drugs, happy, fit and healthy. In complete control of my life in every way. By the time we were holidaying in Zante, we were inseparable. On the second night of our holiday, Lucas had a surprise for me. I had no idea what it was until we all went to a quaint restaurant in Zante. It was empty but for us. We all sat around a long table and then Lucas got down on his knees and proposed to me right there, right then.

All our friends knew about it, and were almost in tears. I said yes immediately and he slipped the beautiful diamond engagement ring on my finger. I was so happy; it really was a complete surprise. It was the most magical night of our holiday. The rest of the holiday was perfect; we took a boat trip out to visit the famous Turtle Island, and the Blue Caves. I had never seen anything so beautiful. It really had to be seen to be believed.

On return from Zante, we announced our engagement and planned a huge party in the Pitcher and Piano wine bar just around the corner from work in Brindley Place. Everyone attended and it was a great success. There had been a collection for us from the office, which was presented to us the same day as the party. We had planned to get married the following year, around nine months later. Finally, everything had fallen into place. I was ready to start my own family, but was unable to conceive naturally. Lucas also wanted a baby, so about six months before the wedding; we went to see my doctor, who suggested we try IVF treatment. After many discussions over a very long weekend, we decided to go for it. It would be a long and painful process, which in the end, might not work. Over the next few months, we went through the process backwards and forwards to hospital, taking daily hormone drugs and a hormone injection into my leg daily for a few weeks. The hormone drugs were awful and very mood altering, but it was a small price to pay for my dream of becoming a mother. The process was long and arduous. However, every time we visited the hospital we received good news, the egg extraction went well, and my eggs received a perfect score.

During the IVF treatment, we were also planning our wedding and discussing the possibility of moving from Coleshill to the other side of Birmingham, to a bigger house, more suitable for a family. Lucas had a house that he rented out; it was this house we were considering moving into. However, nothing was set as yet. So much was happening so fast: an upcoming wedding, IVF treatment, a house move, there was no time to think about anything!

I sent a message to my mum telling her I was getting married and could she please tell Jake. I was met with the most awful message: that she did not believe I was getting married, that no one would ever want to marry me, and if they did, it would not last. The abuse went on and on, I stopped reading the message halfway through.

We had planned a small wedding, in the Malvern's. We were to stay at the beautiful Abbey Hotel and then take a honeymoon to Lake Garda in Italy. I could not wait to get married. My dress was beautiful. It was classy and elegant with a fitted bodice; then it fell straight to the floor. It was also in rose red. It really was a beautiful dress. We had just 14 guests, Lucas' family and my best friend. I had still not found my family. That was one of the main reasons I did not choose a big wedding. Lucas' side of the church would have been full, and mine would have been empty! I had lost touch with Jake over the years. He had left mother's house a year or so after me. He had since been married and had two children; however, when I contacted mother she refused to give me Jake's address always. She said she would pass him my details, but clearly never did. I would have loved my brother at my wedding. I had no idea where he was living, in which city;

I had no idea if he was in Shropshire or whether, like me, he had decided to leave the dreary place.

A couple of weeks before I was due to marry Lucas, I received a call from Joshua. He wanted to see me. He was only home for a few more days and then he was shipping out to Afghanistan. I told him I could not see him that I had met someone now and I was getting married in just a few weeks. He pleaded with me to see him.

"What if I never come back, you will regret it then" he joked.

"Joshua, look it would be a betrayal to Lucas if I see you. I can't."

"Look, I just want to talk, catch up with you. That's all. We can share a bottle of wine. I just want to see you one last time before I go."

I never did see him before he went. A part of me really wanted too. I wanted to wish him good luck out there, as so many young soldiers were coming back in boxes. I wanted to send him away with a tight hug. But I couldn't. I would have felt as if I was betraying Lucas. Not to mention Joshua's girlfriend. I received a few text messages running up to the wedding, telling me how much he loved me. That I was his first love. I cried when I read them, wanting to say goodbye to him, but I didn't. Would seeing him before he was shipped out just to say goodbye of been such a bad thing? A question I have often asked myself. Just to say goodbye would not have been a betrayal, surely.

A few weeks later, I was married. The wedding was perfect, with the Malvern's as the backdrop. A three-course dinner and the cutting of the cake followed the ceremony. It was really a perfect wedding. We were happy and ready to spend the rest of our lives together.

We stayed at the romantic hotel for a few days then returned home, as we had a hospital appointment to determine whether or not the IVF treatment had worked.

The following week we arrived nervously at the hospital as newlyweds. We were both so nervous; we could hardly bear the anticipation of the wait. Then finally, we were called into the consultant's office.

"Well it's good news. You are pregnant."

I let out a scream, I could not believe it, I had always believed I was not able to get pregnant, and here I was four weeks pregnant! It was another dream fulfilled; I was to become a mother. I made a promise to myself that day to be the best mother in the whole world. My child would never know pain, or rejection. My child would receive all the love a parent could give. I never once thought the IVF treatment would work. It seemed like such a long shot to me. It was the last thing I was expecting to hear that day. The very last thing indeed. My husband Lucas was also shocked, he never spoke a word for ages, he simply sported a wide grin on his face. I knew Lucas would make a great father, he was kind and thoughtful and very considerate.

I informed work three months later that I was pregnant. I knew we were having a baby girl, which I was so pleased about. I had wanted a girl, a little princess, but I kept the sex of the baby a secret. I also told them I would be going off on maternity leave the following November. My immediate boss informed me that she was both pleased and sad to be losing her best worker! I worked throughout my pregnancy.

However, the seventh month I was waddling around like a goose. I had grown so huge, all tummy and all frontal.

Amelia - photographs taken in Greece

The Death of a Special Friend

One Friday night in October, I was lying down on the sofa. Lucas was pottering around the house, when something on the Central News Channel caught my eye. They were showing a picture of a fallen soldier on the screen. It took a while for it to register that it was Joshua. I turned up the TV and listened intently to the news bulletin.

Joshua had been killed by a roadside bomb in Afghanistan; he was due to be flown home in the next couple of days. He was just 23-years-old. I burst into tears, crying uncontrollably, our last conversation flashing before me.

"What if I don't make it back Amelia, you will regret it." I climbed up the stairs and fell on to the bed. I curled up into a ball and cried for hours. I briefly explained to Lucas what had happened. He knew to leave me to mourn and cry it out of my system. I barely spoke a word that whole weekend. I was in total shock. As I was pregnant, I was even more emotional and took the news much harder. No one but Lucas had known about Joshua, certainly no one in my town. It took me a while to get over the loss of Joshua. He was so young, and he had the rest of his life in front of him. He was also right: I was regretting not seeing him that one last time.

If I could rewind time, I would have seen him, and sent him away with a tight hug, wished him Godspeed and a safe return. However, it was too late. That moment in time had gone, and so had Joshua. I will always regret not saying goodbye to him face to face. An old saying ran through my mind, "Time once passed can never be retrieved."

However, I was so worried about upsetting Lucas if he had found out. Thinking about it now, I would have done nothing wrong at all. I simply wanted to send Joshua away with a hug and a face-to-face goodbye. How can that have been wrong? Why did I feel it would have been a betrayal? I just know if I could turn back the clock now I would most definitely have seen him before he was shipped out to Afghanistan. However, sadly, once a moment has passed it has gone forever.

That was a significant moment in my life. Because I was carrying my beautiful daughter, Lilliah, a living being growing inside of me. It was a very strange thing to receive news that someone close to me had passed away while I was carrying a life.

A couple of months later in the December, I had put my house up for rent with a local estate agent. Lucas and I were paying two mortgages and it was a lot of money per month to part with when you had a baby on the way. In a very short time, I had received a phone call from my estate agent informing me that they had recently showed some one around and they had fallen in love with my house. They were quite happy to pay the monthly rent and wanted to move in almost immediately. I was so happy as everything was falling into place.

We would be so much better off each month, and this way I managed to keep my house and would not have to sell it. I did not wish to part with my house; it was so much more than just a building to me.

I had enquired about the person who would be renting my house. It was a lady who had recently separated from her husband and needed a place of her own for just six months while she figured out what she wanted to do. I was asked if it would be okay if the new tenant could drop some personal effects off at the house in advance of her moving in on the Monday. Of course, I agreed. I also mentioned that I would make one last visit to the house on the Saturday to leave a welcome basket for the new tenant and a list of contact numbers for her.

On the Saturday morning, Lucas and I arrived at the house. We made our way inside and I carried the welcome basket, which consisted of chocolates, wine and a house-warming card. I dropped them off in the kitchen and started walking towards the bedroom. As I approached the bedroom door, I just froze. Lucas also stood in silence. I don't think he could quite believe what he was seeing either. There were large pictures of Joshua lined up against the bedroom wall. My Joshua, the soldier that never made it back. This was too much. I could feel my heart beating harder and faster, I turned to look at Lucas. He left me alone and walked into the living room. I walked into the bedroom to take a close look at Joshua in his uniform, resting against my bedroom wall. This made no sense to me.

I didn't know Joshua's family at all, and they didn't know me. The town was a little too big to know everyone and their business, unlike the previous village I had lived in. What were the chances of this happening? A million to one, surely! My house had been rented out to Joshua's grieving mother. Was this meant to be, I wondered? This whole situation was so surreal to me. Nevertheless, it was actually happening. It was also purely coincidental.

Joshua's mother lived in my house for six months. She was an amazing tenant. We were in contact via email from time to time about matters purely to do with the house and anything that needed fixing from time to time. However, she had no idea who I was. It was just one of the strangest moments of my life.

The birth of Lilliah

(Amelia pictured above with her daughter Lilliah 2009)

My baby's due date had arrived: New Year's Day 2009. I woke up feeling none too great. I was bleeding and had to be rushed to hospital. They said it was nothing to worry about; however, my baby was ready to be born! So that day the midwife kept me in hospital and induced me. Within a very short space of time I was 8cm dilated and screaming for my life, it seemed. I never knew you could feel such pain. I thought I was dying for a while. Of course I wasn't! I was simply giving birth, like millions of women before me. Lilliah was born within 55 minutes, with a shock of jet-black hair, weighing just 6lb 3oz. I was not prepared for the instant love I was to feel the minute I held my beautiful baby in my arms. It was as if everything I had been through in my entire life had purpose and was leading me to this very moment. If I had lived a different life, I would not be holding my beautiful Lilliah in my arms. I was a completely changed person that day. I was a mother, a devoted mother, who would spend her life protecting her baby. Lucas was there throughout the entire labour. He cut the cord his proudest moment, he advised me. He cried on seeing his daughter for the very first time. Lucas held my hand and told me he loved me. He said he was so proud of me and thanked me for giving him our beautiful baby. We waited all day to be allowed home. Once we were on our way, we could not wait to get home. Lucas's family were waiting to greet us on our arrival. His mother had cleaned our house from top to bottom. They had put flowers everywhere and just could not wait to see the new addition to the family. It was the most incredible day of my life. Lilliah was the first grandchild to be received into Lucas's family. I just knew she would be loved beyond words and doted on for always. Lucas and I were natural parents, I insisted on breast-feeding Lilliah, and so I did for the next 12 months or so. I knew what unconditional love was now. I knew my daughter would come before anything and anyone. I was in awe of my beautiful princess, I had been blessed, I was a mother, and I would never ever let her down not ever. During the first few months of Lilliah's life, I joined Face book, with the intention of finding my father's side of the family. I had no idea if he was interested in seeing me; it was very possible he had a new family. Giving birth to Lilliah only resurfaced my need to find my father and grandparents. I wanted them to know they had a grandchild and great grandchild. I wanted them to meet this amazing little person, my daughter.

Discovering My Family

Amelia's newly found grandparents, picture taken in 1945 on their wedding day.

Once I signed up for Face Book, the first name I typed in was my father's name. A few names popped up on the screen, but there was one face that stood out. It was an old face, of about the same age as my father would be. Therefore, I sent a direct message explaining who I was and that I was looking for my father. As I pressed, "send", I took a deep breath. What if he was not interested? What if he rejects me again? I could only hope that he would at least message me back if he was my father. I needed to complete my life's jigsaw puzzle. I needed his side of the story; I needed the entire story.

The next day I received a long reply back. It was my father. He was living in the Philippines, and married with three children. I was both elated and disappointed. On the one hand, I had found my father, but on the other hand, he was a 24-hour plane ride away. I gave him my email address and we started communicating instantly. I received an email complete with pictures attached; those pictures were of me when I was a toddler. We were in a park, I had on a white cotton dress and I was running. There were more pictures of my father when he was young man in his twenties. I must have looked over those pictures a hundred times. Tears filled my eyes, thoughts of what could have been ran through my mind.

My father told me all about his life: how he had been married three times, and that he had a further three children from his second marriage: Debbie, Rosie, and Justin. My half-sisters and brother from my father's second marriage had had a good life with my father: private schools, travelling the world, and more often than not a five-star life style. My father had become Chief Engineer for the Sultan of Brunei. On securing this incredible position with the Sultan to work on his many private planes, my father had moved his family out to Brunei, where they lived an amazing life. Money was plentiful, and he was on his way to becoming a millionaire. Only he was too fond of spending money: five-star hotels, boats, and expensive restaurants. I was fascinated with the life he had led, and thought how lucky his children from his second marriage were. He told me how every time the Sultan took a flight anywhere in the world, he insisted on having my father aboard the flight. After each flight, the Sultan would hand my father a large brown envelope full of cash.

This could be anything from £10,000, £20,000 to even a £30,000 tax-free lump sum cash as a bonus, which he received on top of his enormous salary. He was living the high life.

By the time Debbie and Rosie were in their teens, my father started having an affair with his maid, right under the nose of his second wife. Eventually he separated from his then wife, who was devastated as she was so in love with my father, and there was no one else for her but him.

Eventually, he packed his second wife back to England with her youngest child, Justin. Debbie and Rosie chose to stay in Brunei with our father; their life was in Brunei, their schools and their friends. Over time he married the maid and had a further three children.

I was shocked at the news that he had a total of eight children, including Jake and me. I was unsure how to feel about my father. My father also advised me that my grandparents were still alive, and that they would love to hear from me. That's when he informed me that he had not spoken to my grandparents for ten years, following a fall out, and that he had no future plans to, either. He gave me their address and left it for me to get in touch with them. As my father and I exchanged emails, I told him all about my tragic life following his departure from it. He was shocked to say the least. He was saddened, and said that Jake and I should have gone to live with him.

This statement confused me really, because I knew he had not bonded with us as babies, and he could not have got away from us fast enough in the end. However, I pushed negative thoughts out of my mind, and continued to get to know my father as well as anyone can by email.

I filled him in as best as I could on my life and Jake's. He had told Debbie and Rosie about me and said that I should meet them. They were in there late twenties now and were living in England. They had returned when they were around 16 to 18 years old, because they hadn't got on well with my father's new wife, Cynthia. Debbie had gone to university in Oxford and Rosie had gone to university in Bournemouth. Over the next couple of months, I met Debbie first. She was adorable, and tiny. Debbie had a gentle heart, and we hit it off straight away; a bond was formed immediately. My first thoughts were that my daughter Lilliah had an aunty, who would also be a good role model, too. Debbie and I became close, exchanging phone numbers and talking often. I felt instantly comfortable and at ease with Debbie. A short while later I met Rosie. She was the older of the two, very beautiful, and completely different to Debbie. She was equally lovely, but in an altogether different way. The first time we met in Birmingham city centre; we had a lovely long lunch and confided our stories. We became friends too. The three of us met up once again in Bicester village, just outside Oxford. My husband and my daughter came along too. It was a lovely day; we shopped; we lunched; and we talked.

It was so lovely finally to have family, and sisters to call my own. We had a lot in common; we all loved food, shopping and running. We had the same views on humanitarian issues and many others.

My dad's emails were beginning to show a theme: one of arrogance, self-importance, one of me, me, and me. Over time, his emails became more about him, and less about me.

He seemed so wrapped up in his own life. It started to annoy me a little. He would take no responsibly for what happened to Jake and me. As far as he was concerned, it was out of his hands, which was true. However, my question to him was, "Did you ever try to find us?" He said he never had; he just assumed that we had our own life and if we had wanted to know our father then he felt it was up to us to find him. It was the way these words sounded when he wrote them to me; they seemed so cold. I had written a letter to my grandparents, leaving my phone number on the bottom. Then one day, a reply came through the post. After reading my grandma's beautiful letter, I just cried for the next few hours. I was finally going to meet them. My husband and I arranged to drive up to Lancashire to see them. It was cold, wet, and winter was upon us. I will never forget that first meeting. As we approached the bungalow, we had to stop the car so I could compose myself. I was emotional and nervous. I really wanted them to like me. I wanted to bond with them and spend as much time as possible visiting them with what little time we had left with them. They were 85 years old, an incredible age. Finally, we climbed out of the car, then walked up the drive and knocked the door.

My grandma opened the door and straight away cupped my face with her tiny hands. It was a very emotional day, a day we all thought would never happen. So many years had passed by, a lifetime almost, over three decades. My grandma had baked a delicious cake and made us salmon and cucumber sandwiches. I completed a jigsaw puzzle for my grandparents that day too. There were so many unanswered questions for them also.

Once I had told them my full life story, my grandma was truly devastated. She told me how grandparents had no rights at all back then. She told me how she had got on her knees and begged my father not to sign his rights as a father away all those years ago. She knew they would never see us again once he did that. She knew in her heart of hearts that my mother would sever all connections with my father's side of the family. It broke my grandmother's heart to discover the tragic life we had led at the hands of our mother.

We talked forever that first day, then we hugged, and we took pictures. Before we left, my grandma had asked my Uncle Nigel, my father's brother, to pop over to meet us. It was truly lovely. He was a very kind and gentle-natured man and very close to my grandparents. He watched over them and was always on hand, should they fall ill and be in need of his help. He was a great son to my grandparents. For many years, my uncle Nigel was also out of touch with my father. Around the same time I had found my father just a couple of months previous, Jake and I were once again reunited. He was now divorced and very unhappy, and wanting a complete change in his life. He was feeling very despondent about his future and hating where he was living. This was where I was finally able to uphold my promise to Jake. My house was currently empty. Joshua's mother had left and it was now free. I had just the perfect idea. Jake could move in. Coleshill was such a beautiful old coaching town in Warwickshire; it was surrounded by beautiful countryside, unlike where he was living then.

This would be perfect for him. Therefore, Lucas and I went to visit him one weekend to put my idea to him. Jake could not have been more happy. I showed him pictures of my house and the old town. He just fell in love with it on sight.

It was a month later when Jake moved in; he loved living in the country. He loved the house, and all the glorious fields and rivers at the back. He said he had never felt happier in his life; accept for when his children had been born. It may have taken many years, but I finally got to fulfill my promise to Jake. I got to meet my beautiful cousin, Chloe, she was bright and beautiful and just 12 years old. I got to see her often, as Jake would bring her over to see us. Lilliah instantly adored Chloe, and Chloe just fell in love with Lilliah. They were so good together. I also had a nephew called Daniel too, a lovely quiet 15-year-old teenager. I was proud of my brother. He had done a great job along with his ex-wife on bringing up two wonderful children. I had learned a great deal about my father: from his emails, from my Grandparents, and from one or two of my newfound siblings. It seemed that my personal judgment of him seemed to be correct. He was not a very nice man. This was confirmed a couple of months later when we were emailing each other. It was Jake's birthday, and I truly thought he would have sent Jake a card as I had emailed him Jake's address in Coleshill. After all, it would have been the first one Jake had ever received from his father. But nothing arrived in the post. Jake was surprised and disappointed. I emailed Dad. I said it would have been a nice gesture to have sent a birthday card to his son after all these years.

If he really was happy to be found, this was not apparent in his efforts. He did not jump on a plane to come and see us; he did not make any suggestion that he would fly out in the future either. I had previously said I would fly out to see him, so he could meet his granddaughter, but I was beginning to think I would be wasting my time.

As the months went by, our emails became fewer. We drifted apart before we had even met. The truth was very apparent to me: he had his own family now, and his last remaining three children at home. He had a life in the Philippines and had no intention of ever flying out to see me. I did not like the person I was getting to know in the emails. I did not like the things I was hearing about him. Eventually my father and I fell out; he sent me a couple of nasty emails, all because in one email I reminded him that he had eight children, not just three, and because I had said it would have been a nice gesture to have sent a birthday card to Jake. His reply to me was vicious: a personal attack on me as a person, a person he did not know at all, and his daughter that he happily signed away all those years ago. His efforts at bonding with me were truly pathetic. I finally deduced that he was not interested at all. That all the things I had heard about him must be true, because I was beginning to see it for myself. After receiving a truly insulting letter through the post from him, I immediately deleted him from my Face book. I deleted his email address from my contact list and have never spoken with him since. He did not give me a chance. If he had been genuinely interested, he would have got on a flight and at least come to meet me face-to-face. If only once.

Nevertheless, he did not. He never suggested it and was never going to. I was devastated at his nasty words in the letters I received from him. It showed his true character; it showed to me that anyone capable of writing such a hurtful letter to a daughter they had abandoned over three decades before was not a person I wanted in my life, anyway.

My dreams of my daughter meeting her grandfather faded instantly. He barely asked about Lilliah. He mentioned her from time to time, but it was more out of courtesy than interest. I had already bonded with Debbie and Rosie and remain in touch with them to this day. They are lovely girls. However, if I am truly honest, I have always felt closer to Debbie. Lovely, sweet Debbie, we bonded effortlessly. We hit it off straight away. I warmed to her instantly. Rosie was also a lovely girl. I really liked her, I just did not feel as close to her as Debbie. I think this was because of her close relationship with our father. One weekend we went to our Uncle Nigel's wedding. I was outside the venue chatting with Rosie, and I started to talk to her about the awful letter I had received from our father a few weeks before. However, I was stopped in my tracks. She already knew about it. She said she did not want to get emotionally involved. So after that I never really felt as if I could talk about my father to Rosie. She had a close relationship with him,

so it made complete sense that she did not want to discuss the letter with me, and I really did not want to put her in an uncomfortable position. It would not have been fair to her. Though, I was hurt by this. However, I didn't let it show that day, and immediately changed the subject.

The discovery of my new family was not the great one I had hoped for. My father once again rejected me. This made me angry with myself for allowing this to happen once again. After all the trouble I had gone to in finding them; I had left myself wide open to be hurt. And hurt I was.

I was developing a very close relationship with my beautiful grandparents. They were amazing; it was as if we had known each other for years. However, they were so fragile, and my grandfather was not in the best of health, which made me so sad. My grandma tells me often that I had just made it when I found them. A few years later and I may have been too late. I love my grandparents, and so does my daughter. We go up to visit them at least three times a year; we book a hotel and stay by the seaside for a few days. Although things did not work out with my father the way I had hoped, I felt blessed that I had my grandparents in my life again. And I would make the most of what time we all have left together. My time with my grandparents is what is important to me. They have been in my life for two years now. We take lots of pictures each time we visit; we talked about everything and anything. I had never felt complete as a person before. I used to feel alone in the world; I always felt as if something was missing. But now I felt totally complete; I have my beautiful princess, my husband, and my grandparents. I have my family, the family I had always wanted so badly. I was no longer alone. I love my grandparents very much. It's as if I was never separated from them. However, as lovely as my newfound sister Debbie is, she recently announced her marriage to a wonderful man called Stephen.

I was so happy for her. I was so pleased she had finally found happiness. She called me up to tell me that she would be having a small wedding over the next 12 months, mainly for our grandparents. There was no mention that myself, Lilliah and Lucas would not be invited.

So the following week, assuming I would be invited I went out and bought a lovely new dress for the occasion – a very classy knee-length dress with matching shoes.

A few weeks later, I received a text message from Debbie informing me that her upcoming wedding would be just a small one and only her sister Rosie and my grandparents had been invited. To say I was shocked is an understatement. We had only been in each other's lives two years. Debbie had stayed with us at our house on a couple of occasions. We had cooked for her and made her feel at home. I thought we had formed a special bond. I was very upset. I cried for quite a long time. I never would have expected that news, not in a million years, especially as she had known of my life, and the rejection by our father and my mother. I thought I was a sister too. I love her dearly; I am so happy for her, but very disappointed that I was not invited to her wedding, which was taking place in London just an hour's drive away from where I live. I could not get my head around this at all. My husband was devastated for me. He could see the hurt etched all over my face. He told me to forget it and not take it to heart, that she meant no ill feeling towards me, "It's your grandparents that truly matter. They love you, Amelia." I thought yes, Lucas, you are right. I had gained two new half-sisters and loved them dearly even though I was feeling rejected, and disappointed.

I had to look at the situation from Debbie's point of view, if she had of invited us, well, she would have to invite all the other people that were not invited too, then it may of got complicated for her. However, I could not help thinking how lovely it would have been to have seen my newfound half-sister getting married and to have been a part of it all.

I was never reunited with my two sisters that I was separated from all those years ago when we were all children. They are grown-up now and living their own lives, I expect. I wish I could tell you that we are altogether once again, that we found each other and became close like we were all those years ago. However, sadly we are all lost to each other now. I have to be forever grateful that Jake and I were reunited and that to this day we remain as close as ever.

Becoming a Writer: My Destiny

When my daughter turned two, I decided I was going to write my life story for her; it was such an incredible one. I often wondered how I would tell her everything. Therefore, I started writing my autobiography. Now I had all the pieces to my jigsaw puzzle. Although I had never intended to write my story, my idea was inspired by my daughter. It is for Lilliah that I am telling my story. I want her to have a complete jigsaw; I want her to have all the answers to any questions about her mother. I did not want her to walk through life with half a puzzle, as I once had. It was so important to me that she felt complete. So by the time Lilliah was two years and 9 months old, I had completed my first book, "Amelia's Story," the first part of my journey. Twelve months later I completed book two Amelia's Destiny the conclusion. I realised my dream and have since written and published several books. I still have to pinch myself often to remind myself I am not dreaming!

I am happy now. My life is a good one; but it did not come at all easy. I still hold on to the thought that a person can lose everything they have in an instant; it's these thoughts that keep me very grounded. My princess is now three and a half years old.

I write full-time now, my perfect job. I am passionate about two things: my daughter and writing. They both complete my life. I know my grandparents are proud of what I have achieved in my life, against all the odds. They have their granddaughter back. I visit them as often as I possibly can; I know our time together is very limited as they are both in their late 80's now and not in the best of health. My grandma often says to me that I found them just in time.

Whilst writing this book I was taken on the most incredible journey through time. I re-visited old ghosts, and came to terms with my past. Finally, I was able to lay it all to rest. I had kept my promise to Jake and moved him closer to me and my family and gave him a lovely home where he too could feel secure for the rest of his life. I had realised my own dream of becoming a homeowner, a writer and a mother. I will never take my life for granted. Now I cherish my life more than anyone could possibly know. I make the most of every single second.

My wish list is still growing; I have ticked many things off along the way, and added many more too. I still have dreams to fulfill and a strong determination to accomplish them.

I have learnt so much along my journey, the most important thing is this: don't allow others to stand in the way of your dreams. Anything is possible if you want it badly enough.

When my daughter smiles at me, my heart melts. When my daughter says, "Mummy I love you," my heart melts. When my daughter gives me the tightest hug and kisses me goodnight, again my heart just melts. My daughter is my whole world. Amelia is happy now.

The child, first and foremost.

THE END

A note for Lilliah:

Lilliah, every decision you make in your life will have a ripple effect on all those around you. Every action you take will have a reaction. If you walk through your life with a kind and thoughtful heart, the ripple effects you create along the way will be memorable for the right reasons. The reactions caused by your actions will be positive ones.

Life is so precious and the time we have to enjoy it fly's by in the blink of an eye. Just be happy darling and be your own person no matter what. Don't follow the crowd if it feels wrong, step forward and take a different turn. Don't ever be afraid to swim against the tide.

I love you with all my heart
God bless you princess xxx

Amelia 2014

Jake 2009 ~ Holding Amelia's Daughter

Amelia with her husband and Daughter 2009

Amelia 2009 ~ With her daughter Lilliah on a weekend break in the Malverns

Amelia with her daughter 2013

Amelia's princess 2014 aged five-years-old

Amelia's princess 2013

Amelia's princess with her newly found great-grandparents

Amelia with her daughter Lilliah 2009

Amelia's princess 2009

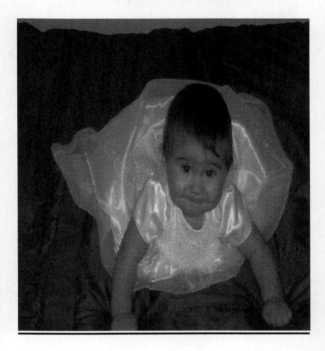

__Amelia 2014__

Amelia with her husband attending Blanche's 80th birthday party ~ 2012

Amelia

Amelia's princess 2012

Also available by D.G. Torrens

BROKEN WINGS - *(Contemporary Romance)*

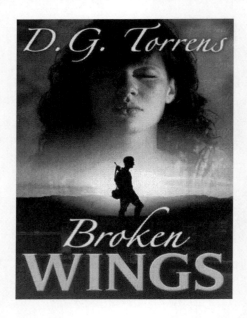

EXCERPT:
Chapter one

They stood naked in the shimmering cool water; the warm March night was calm and still, unusual for the time of year. The moon shone beams of light onto the vast lake, shadowing the curves of their naked bodies. Neither said a word as they looked deep into each other's sad eyes, their united silence saying so much. Angelina did not want to let him go, fearing she would never see him again.

Joshua smiled. "I will come back to you, I promise."

Angelina placed her head on his chest, tears falling down her reddened cheeks. "I could not bear it if I never saw you again, please don't go," she pleaded with all her heart.

"I have no choice. You knew when we met that this would be a possibility, Angelina. I will be back before you know it. This is my duty as a soldier, I have to go, this is what I do."

She felt her heart closing in, the tightness was suffocating her. All those young men who never made it home alive… She did not want her Joshua to be one of them; however, she also understood that he needed to go along with the rest of his regiment. This knowledge did not make it any easier to bear. She had a bad feeling about this posting in a way she didn't have with the other one. She just could not shake it off. Joshua had informed Angelina that he was being posted to Afghanistan for a second tour. He had an urge to share his inner fears with her but he held off, knowing this would make his leaving far harder for Angelina to deal with.

This was their last night together and they had decided to spend it down by the lake, their very special place. This was where they had spent their first official date together. That first date had sealed their rare and irrevocable feelings for one another; feelings that could not be denied. They had never looked back. When they were together, it was as if the rest of the world didn't exist and time stood still, just for them. Joshua fought his undeniable feelings with all that he had, not wanting to get involved with anyone, knowing he was being posted soon. But the draw was too strong and the fight was over before it began. He was mesmerized by her. Angelina was deep and sensitive, the suffer-in-silence type. He liked that about her. She was unlike anyone he had ever known, she understood him in a way no one else ever had before.

Angelina wanted to hold Joshua, never let him go and keep him safe from harm. She held him so tight as if her own life depended on it. "I love you so much, Joshua, please come back to me." She was crying uncontrollably now, her head buried deep in his chest.

He took off his ring that had been passed down to him by his grandfather many years before and placed it on her finger. "I promise you when I return; I will make you my wife." With that, Joshua kissed her gently on the lips. He hated leaving her; he knew this was as hard for her as it was for him.

"Joshua, when you're gone, time stands still until you return to me. I can't move forward or backward. I can't sleep because of worrying about you. There are so many soldiers returning back home in boxes. Every time I turn on the TV, there is a news item about a young soldier not making it back alive, the families left behind tormented by their grief."

"Last week, there were two soldiers from the West Midlands who were killed by a roadside bomb in Afghanistan headlining the news. What if that happens to you, Joshua? I know the loss you suffered on your first tour of Afghanistan; that could so easily have been you. You are my very reason for existing so you better come back to me. Do you hear me?"

Joshua looked into Angelina's beautiful almond eyes. He wrapped his large arms around her and held Angelina tight. "I love you with all my heart. I promise I will return to you and then I will be back for good. I will not be extending, I promise you, and it's only six months. It will fly by. I promise I will write to you all the time." Angelina could not stem the flood of tears falling down her cheeks, she could hardly breathe from the fear that this could be the last time she ever saw him alive. Joshua ran his finger slowly over the small scar etched into her right eyebrow. He held her face in the palms of his large hands and kissed it, brushing the tears from her sodden cheeks. He felt her pain. He was feeling it too. No words could take their pain away; it was something they had to endure together until his return.

They lay on the bank together side by side with nothing but the glistening stars and the glow from the moon as cover. Their silence was a comfortable one, one that could only be shared by two souls that truly understood each other completely. Angelina turned her head towards Joshua and looked at him intently, taking in every inch of him, searching his face as if discovering him for the first time. Her heart was beating so hard she feared it would burst. Joshua sensed her anxiety and pulled her to him, "Angelina, we have to go now. I wish I could stay here like this with you but I have just five hours before I have to report in."

He was hurting now, feeling the pull of his heart; he had to be strong for Angelina, and he did not want to make his departure any harder for her than it was already. "Joshua, I want you to write me whenever you can. I want to know how you're feeling out there, what you are going through, I want to know everything, I need to feel close to you as if I am right there with you. Please promise me you will do that for me?"

Joshua held her face in the palm of his hands, his eyes were glistening and this did not go unnoticed by Angelina, "I promise, darling." He pulled her to him tightly, holding her as if for the last time. They stood up, his hand entwined in hers as they made their way back to his car.

Thoughts of Joshua's last tour in Afghanistan ran amok through his tormented mind. He had something more to fear this time, not making it back to his Angelina. He knew this was a distinct possibility as one in six soldiers were either killed or wounded in action. Bomb disposal experts were in higher demand than ever in Afghanistan, with over one thousand new bombs planted every day. Afghanistan had become an IED war. The large number of bombs was seriously disrupting NATO operations in the country.

He now knew how all the other soldiers felt when they had to leave their loved ones behind for such a long time. This was the very thing he had avoided for years for this very reason. "You okay, Josh?"

"Just thinking, sweetheart. I am fine; don't worry about me, okay? I just need to know you will be strong for me."

Joshua threw her a pleading look, one that needed no answer. This was going to be the longest time they had spent apart. His first tour of Afghanistan had taken place way before he had met Angelina; he had been deployed there for six months. This time was going to be so different; he had found his soul mate, the very person he wanted to spend the rest of his life with. He now had someone to miss, to ache for and this worried him. Being touched by Angelina's love had changed his perception completely. He knew only a few people experienced this kind of rare love, the passion, the whisper of a thrill, the calling in your heart that takes a hold of you and won't let you go. The angst that true soul mates suffer once they are apart. He was totally consumed by her and could not bear the thought of being away from her for so long.

During Joshua's last tour in Afghanistan, he had lost his best friend just two weeks before they were due to return home to England on leave. They had come under enemy attack from insurgents. Four British soldiers were killed after their armoured vehicle was caught in an explosion. Jason was killed instantly and Joshua had never really recovered from the death of his childhood friend. He had watched it all unfold before his eyes like a bad dream. Two further attempts to clear and repair the route had claimed three more casualties. The deep ditch had provided insurgents with the perfect cover to creep along the side of the road and plant the explosives on it. Joshua was in another armoured vehicle a few hundred feet behind. He knew it could just have easily been him and this had been his awakening.

He was devastated and on his return, he visited Jason's grieving wife. That was one of the hardest things he had ever had to do. She was inconsolable, barely able to breathe for crying. Her heart was so clearly broken and vulnerably displayed before him. He had no words to offer her, he knew a part of her had died with Jason; it was in her sad, lifeless eyes. He had kept up his visits to Chloe for many months following the tragic death of his best friend, to comfort and console her until she moved away to the south of England. For a while afterwards, Joshua had been plagued and tormented by nightmares that would have him sitting up all alone in the middle of the night in a cold sweat. He was plagued by the haunting voice of his lifelong friend, calling out for help. Of course, this was a bad dream, a twisted nightmare that would not let go and one that gripped him like a vice to this very day. He knew there was nothing he could have done; none of them could have known what was going to happen on that fateful day.

Jason's memorial service was over-flowing with civilians lining the roads in his home town as a mark of respect. This had become a common sight in towns all across Britain during the ten year war against Afghanistan. Many of the local high street shops had closed for the duration of the memorial service out of respect. This had been Joshua's seventh memorial service for fallen brothers in the last two years. This had completely changed his outlook on life and he had sworn to himself that he would not get involved with anyone romantically until his term in the British Army was completed.

However, he had not figured on Angelina. He had seen too many devastated lovers, wives, mothers and fathers. He hated death, funerals, and more than anything, he hated what the war was doing to the innocents and those that got left behind. The carnage and devastation that war left behind, and for what? This was a question he was asking himself more often these days. Joshua was already a nine-year veteran of the Army at the age of twenty seven; and he had seen far too much of death that his yearning to see more of life was becoming stronger by the day.

He had made up his mind that he would not re-enlist in the army. He had served his country well and now it was his time to live. This was his last posting, and he knew it was going to be his hardest one. Six long months without Angelina was more painful than anything he'd ever had to endure.

Joshua pulled up outside Angelina's house; he turned off the ignition and climbed out of the car. Angelina was already making her way up the path as she turned to him. "I have something I want you to take with you tomorrow. You have to promise me you will not open it until you arrive at your destination." Angelina unlocked the door to her small cottage and turned the lights on as she entered the dark hallway.

"I cannot stay, Angelina; I have not got much time left so please come here." Joshua held out his arms as she slowly walked towards him; he pulled her close and held her tight. He pressed his lips to hers with all that he had and held onto the moment, and then Angelina buried her head in his chest, sobbing.

"I'm sorry; you know how much I hate our goodbyes." She reached for an envelope from the mantelpiece and handed it to him. "Remember, do not open it." Smiling, he kissed her once more and then headed out the door.

END OF EXCERPT

About the author

D. G. Torrens recently released her knew military romance novel, **"BROKEN WINGS"** this is a heart-wrenching and intense romance, one of love, loss and undying hope. Joshua a bomb disposal expert in the British Army and Angelina an editor for a small town newspaper, are unexpectedly brought together when fate intervenes. However, many obstacles are placed in their path; can their love survive Joshua's deployment? The story is set between Lake Windermere in the UK and Afghanistan. Now available on Amazon for kindle.

D. G. Torrens is happily married with a five-year-old daughter. She lives in Birmingham, England, has written, and published ten books since 2011.

The author loves to connect with her readers; you can find her author page on facebook http://www.facebook.com/dgtorrens

Alternatively, pop over to the author's website http://dawnsdaily.com or why not connect with the author on twitter @torrenstp

Printed in Great Britain
by Amazon.co.uk, Ltd.,
Marston Gate.